# Forensic Science

*Forensic Science* provides a comprehensive overview of the sociology of forensic science. Drawing on a wealth of international research and case studies, it explores the intersection of science, technology, law and society and examines the production of forensic knowledge. The book explores a range of key topics such as:

- The integration of science into police work and criminal investigation
- The relationship between law and science
- Ethical and social issues raised by new forensic technology including DNA analysis
- Media portrayals of forensic science
- Forensic policy and the international agenda for forensic science

This new edition has been fully updated, particularly with regard to new technology in relation to the various new forms of DNA technology and facial recognition. Updates and additions include:

- Facial recognition technology
- Digital forensics and its use in policing
- Algorithms (such as probabilistic genotyping)
- Genealogical searching
- Phenotyping

This new edition also reviews and critically appraises recent scholarship in the field, and new international case studies have been introduced, providing readers with an international comparative perspective. Engaging with sociological literature to make arguments about the ways in which forensic science is socially constituted and shapes justice, *Forensic Science* provides an excellent introduction to students about the location of forensic science and the ways it fits within the criminal justice system, as well as systems of professionalisation and ethics. It is important and compelling reading for students taking a range of courses, including criminal investigation, policing, forensic science, and the sociology of science and technology.

**Christopher Lawless** is associate professor in the Department of Sociology at Durham University. He specializes in the application of science studies to legal and regulatory issues, with specific research interests focusing on forensic science, criminal investigation and critical infrastructures. Chris originally trained as an analytical biochemist, gaining a BSc in biochemistry and microbiology (Sheffield) and an MRes in instrumentation systems (UCL) and made the transition to the social sciences via a PhD at Durham University, focusing on the sociology of forensic scientific reasoning.

# Forensic Science
A Sociological Introduction

Second edition

**Christopher Lawless**

LONDON AND NEW YORK

Cover image: © TEK IMAGE/SCIENCE PHOTO LIBRARY
Caption: A fingerprint with a DNA (deoxyribonucleic acid) profile illustrating identity.

Second edition published 2022
by Routledge
4 Park Square, Milton Park, Abingdon, Oxon OX14 4RN

and by Routledge
605 Third Avenue, New York, NY 10158

*Routledge is an imprint of the Taylor & Francis Group, an informa business*

© 2022 Christopher Lawless

The right of Christopher Lawless to be identified as author of this work has been asserted in accordance with sections 77 and 78 of the Copyright, Designs and Patents Act 1988.

All rights reserved. No part of this book may be reprinted or reproduced or utilised in any form or by any electronic, mechanical, or other means, now known or hereafter invented, including photocopying and recording, or in any information storage or retrieval system, without permission in writing from the publishers.

*Trademark notice*: Product or corporate names may be trademarks or registered trademarks and are used only for identification and explanation without intent to infringe.

*British Library Cataloguing in Publication Data*
A catalogue record for this book is available from the British Library

*Library of Congress Cataloging-in-Publication Data*
Names: Lawless, Christopher, author.
Title: Forensic science: a sociological introduction / Christopher Lawless.
Description: Second Edition. | New York, NY: Routledge, 2022. | Revised edition of the author's Forensic science, 2016. | Includes bibliographical references and index.
Identifiers: LCCN 2021043637 (print) | LCCN 2021043638 (ebook) | ISBN 9780367648060 (hardback) | ISBN 9780367647148 (paperback) | ISBN 9781003126379 (ebook)
Subjects: LCSH: Forensic sciences. | Crime--Sociological aspects.
Classification: LCC HV8073 .L3335 2022 (print) | LCC HV8073 (ebook) | DDC 363.25--dc23
LC record available at https://lccn.loc.gov/2021043637
LC ebook record available at https://lccn.loc.gov/2021043638

ISBN: 978-0-367-64806-0 (hbk)
ISBN: 978-0-367-64714-8 (pbk)
ISBN: 978-1-003-12637-9 (ebk)

DOI: 10.4324/9781003126379

Typeset in Bembo
by Taylor & Francis Books

I would like to dedicate this edition to all the students I have worked with on my module Sociology of Forensic Science and Criminal Investigation since it began in 2012. I wish to thank them for the very constructive discussions which have informed the preparation of this edition. I would also like to dedicate this to future students who I hope will find this edition insightful and valuable.

# Contents

1  Introduction: Forensic studies: from crime scene to court and beyond     1

2  Forensics in the media     17

3  Shaping forensic science as discipline and profession     32

4  Forensic and biometric policy in the UK     48

5  Reconstructing a reconstructive science: Probability and performativity in forensic investigation     62

6  Law–science interactions and new technology     79

7  Forensic DNA technology: Social and ethical issues     94

8  Facial recognition     111

9  Digital forensics     125

10 Conclusion: Imagining and re-imagining forensic and biometric technologies     139

*Index*     152

# 1 Introduction

Forensic studies: from crime scene to court and beyond

## A plurality of actors and spaces

Forensic science derives its name from the Latin *forensis*, meaning 'in open court', and is generally taken to refer to the use of science in the service of law. Forensic science encompasses a diversity of actors, including an extensive and highly differentiated population of forensic practitioners, ranging from crime scene examiners and managers to laboratory technicians and specialist scientists. Forensic practitioners may work within a wide variety of subdisciplines and specialisms, such as fingerprint analysis or DNA profiling, through to areas as diverse as entomology, linguistics and computing. In addition, a broad array of actors from the wider domain of the criminal justice system can be considered stakeholders in forensic science. Included here are police officers, members of the judiciary, politicians, civil servants, commercial organizations, government bodies and general publics who may serve on juries or come into contact with the police. The development of forensic science is influenced by a wide range of interests, not necessarily limited to just law and science but which include political, media and commercial interests as well. Attempts to understand how forensic science upholds law and establishes authority and how it shapes understandings need to take into account the interactions among this plurality of actors and influences.

Forensic trace evidence has sometimes been portrayed as 'silent witnesses' (Erlich et al. 2020), passive, inert, recovered material which nonetheless reveals seemingly immutable truths about the identities and activities of suspects. An alternative rendering of forensic evidence, however, views it as a more fluid and emergent social phenomenon. Forms of scientific evidence, such as DNA profiles, have been framed as 'articulate collectives' (M'charek 2008), suggesting that forensic evidence acquires its power only when embedded within specific relationships and orderings between people, objects and institutions. Studies have indicated how the production of credible and convincing evidence involves sequences of practices taking place over time and space, requiring different actors to work together in particular ways (Lynch et al. 2008; M'charek 2008). These interactions may reflect, but also influence, wider political, legal and economic orderings (Williams et al. 2004; Lawless 2013). This alternative rendering depicts forensic evidence as an emergent product of the criminal justice system but one which is provisional and vulnerable to challenge.

Forensic science brings together a variety of actors but also different forms of experience and knowledge. The question of how collective understandings emerge from this plurality is not a trivial one, given that scientists, police, lawyers, judges and juries employ different conventions and norms when assessing claims to knowledge and making decisions. The situation is compounded further if one considers that those working within criminal justice systems often contend with sets of circumstances which may evade straightforward explanation.

DOI: 10.4324/9781003126379-1

The contexts in which forensic science becomes embedded raise several questions. For example, what kind of balance is struck between the procedures and priorities of law and science, and just how stable is that balance? How do law and science cope with the contingency of criminal behaviour or the possibility of esoteric knowledge being used to solve cases? How do scientists communicate with police and lawyers given differences in terms of training, interests and incentive structures? These kinds of questions have attracted concerted sociological interest.

Given the variety of people and practices involved in the criminal justice system, it is difficult for any individual actor (be they forensic practitioners, police, lawyers, publics, etc.) to be well positioned to observe all that goes on. Indeed, these participants may not be aware of the totality of practices and interactions needed to ensure the continuity of processes through which forensic evidence is translated across a range of spaces.

The phrase 'from crime scene to court' is often invoked in discussions about forensic science (see, for example, UK Government 2021). It captures the way in which forensic evidence is the result of processes which engage and embed a variety of stakeholders (Kruse 2016). This starts from the investigation of an incident at a particular location, which may entail the recovery of material, which may in turn be transferred to a laboratory, where it could be turned into information which might inform the pursuit of a police investigation. This could become evidence, scrutinized in court by legal professionals and members of the public who may act as jurors. The criminal justice landscape extends further if one considers how this evidence could lead someone to serve a custodial sentence. To illustrate with a simple example, a cigarette butt found at the scene of a suspected burglary may attract the attention of crime scene examiners. The butt may be collected in a sealed evidence bag and sent to a laboratory where scientists may attempt to extract DNA (saliva is a particularly good source of DNA). A resulting DNA profile could then be compared with a police database. A match might lead to the investigation of a suspect, an arrest and a possible prosecution.

Social studies of forensics have traced the construction of evidence across the criminal justice system. Research has charted how forensic evidence is created and interpreted through the activities of different stakeholders with different levels of scientific understanding, standpoints and interests. In what follows I provide an overview of how social research has addressed a range of inter-linked spaces and actors, from crime scene to court and to sites in which individuals serve custodial sentences. Traversing these spaces enables us to see how evidence is the result of a dynamic and complex series of social practices and interactions. These may challenge ideas of what constitutes scientific knowledge and method. Much research has focused on certain Western jurisdictions, such as England, the Netherlands, and the United States. Researchers have also gone further afield to address international interactions such as the Prüm regime of European forensic data-sharing.

## The crime scene

The crime scene is the starting point of the forensic process. In England and Wales, crime scene work has been analyzed through quantitative methods (Adderley and Bond 2007, 2008; Adderley et al. 2007). Attrition models evaluate crime scene work and evidence recovery in terms of the proportion of cases which lead to detections, chargings and convictions (Fraser and Williams 2009). Some social research has, however, challenged the idea of crime scene work as a simple and instrumental step towards prosecution which can be modelled through quantitative measures to evaluate the performance of examiners. The work of Williams (2003, 2007) cast crime scene work in a different light. Williams' research, which utilized ethnographic methods and participant observation, questioned the notion that crime scene examiners (CSEs) were merely 'forensic dustmen' (Wayment 1982) engaged in the simple collection of material. Williams' research drew attention to the skills required of these practitioners. Crime scenes may yield a potentially high variety of evidential forms, but apprehending and comprehending scenes presents significant challenges. Fingerprints, for example, may be invisible to the naked and untrained eye. Understanding precisely what evidence from a scene may best assist investigators to reconstruct events may be highly contextualized, such as the perceived severity of an incident. CSEs were found to develop reasoning patterns to help them decide what specific forms of evidence were recovered from scenes (Williams 2003, 2007). This work charted how, in the face of time pressures and other constraints, CSEs' acquired experience over time led them to develop reconstructive knowledge of criminal activity which helped them locate potential evidence. Williams also highlighted the significant degree of embodied skill and proficient use of a variety of technical apparatus to recover material such as fingerprints, footprints and toolmarks. Later work identified the avoidance of evidential contamination as another key proficiency (Wyatt 2014). The question of whether CSE work could be regarded as 'scientific' had been the subject of earlier debate within the forensic community (Jamieson 1999; see also Chapter 3). While crime scene work may not appear to entail experimentation or hypothesis testing, CSEs were nonetheless found to develop distinct skills and play key roles in initiating and maintaining the transfer and translation of evidence from crime scenes to the laboratory and ultimately to the courtroom (Wyatt 2014).

Williams also examined how CSE work was perceived by police (Williams 2004). A comparative study found variance in such perceptions. In some force units, police regarded them as mere collectors of evidence. Other police officers elsewhere viewed them differently, regarding them as expert collaborators whose advice and insight were valued. A later study (Ludwig et al. 2012) of Scottish police officers and laboratory forensic scientists found a similar split in perceptions. 62 per cent of Ludwig et al.'s respondents saw crime scene work as complex practice, while 38 per cent saw it in terms of simple collection. Forensic scientists were more likely to take the latter view. Later research based on interview data also highlighted the collaborative nature of much crime scene work in contrast to management regimes which formalized a more hierarchical relationship between police and CSEs (Wilson Kovacs 2014).

Qualitative sociological research has made visible the experiential, deliberative and contingent aspects of crime scene work. This work may be particularly challenging in serious cases, where understandings of an incident and evidence may be complex, uncertain and fluid (Williams and Weetnam 2013). Qualitative research has challenged quantitative assessments carried out in the name of 'performance' and thus pointed to the need to re-think the nature of forensic practice. Without the application of subjective experience and embodied skills, there would arguably be no evidence for laboratories to analyze.

## The laboratory

Ethnographic laboratory studies are a key resource for social studies of science and technology (Latour 1987). Such an approach has also been valuable in illuminating how material collected from crime scenes is converted into forensic evidence. A criminal case may involve several different types of evidence, requiring different forms of scientific expertise. Forensic laboratories may therefore encompass various specialisms, using a range of scientific techniques. M'charek's (2000) participatory study of a Dutch forensic laboratory drew attention to the processes of communication and translation which enabled laboratory activities to become embedded in the wider criminal justice system. These processes relied on the agency of material and informational entities such as paperwork and the use of statistics for reporting the probative weight of evidence.

Like crime scene research, social research has critically charted how forensic laboratory practice is subject to managerialist gazes (Leslie 2010; Bechky 2021). Researchers have contrasted such regimes with portrayals which emphasized the importance of social relations in constructing knowledge overlooked by formalized technical protocols. Doak and Assimakopoulos' (2007a, 2007b) studies of forensic laboratories in the Republic of Ireland highlighted the role of informal social encounters in sharing knowledge. Negotiating the potentially overwhelming series of codified standard operating procedures (SOPs) was often circumvented by simply asking a colleague for guidance. More experienced scientists were highly valued and viewed as a key resource by their more junior colleagues. Scientists recognized which of their colleagues had particular capability in certain areas. Face to face consultations over evidential interpretation were found to be a habitualized feature of working life within the organization. Personal relationships were viewed as vital conduits for sharing best practice, often involving a degree of sharing tacit knowledge. Working friendships often amounted to coaching or mentoring relationships. Informal contexts, such as the meeting of acquaintances during coffee breaks, provided settings where discussions of best practice permeated casual conversations. The need to reciprocate instances of help was also regarded as highly important, as was the sharing of information and the need for open dialogue. Aware of the fact that their knowledge claims could be scrutinized in the courts, forensic scientists routinely conferred with colleagues to check whether they had followed the correct procedures and to discuss their personal judgements concerning evidence. Scientists relished the opportunity to have their judgments rigorously challenged by colleagues.

Studies have thus highlighted how social relations play a key role in developing intersubjective understandings of the value of evidence and enabling communication between practitioners. Kruse's (2013) study of a Swedish forensic laboratory highlighted how shared language and understanding maintained a sense of solidarity, which helped to project a communicable form of objectivity to the outside world of the courts.

As we shall see particularly in Chapter 7, social researchers have continued to look at how scientists have engaged in research on more advanced technologies and how this work has shaped relations between them and other stakeholders. As well as relations between scientists, integrating science and policing has been addressed by social researchers.

## Policing and science

Williams' (2004, 2007) earlier observations concerning the varied perceptions of crime scene work – as mere technical assistance or expert collaboration – were utilized by this author in subsequent work on general relations between science and policing (Lawless 2010, 2011). The integration of science and policing can be framed in terms of two contrasting normative interpretations. *Structural* integration, based upon the notion of technical assistance, describes a standpoint whereby science and technology are integrated into policing on the latter's terms. Forensic practitioners are regarded as having strictly limited areas of responsibility. Structural integration frames their duty as providing information which is then evaluated by police who are in control of casework. Science and technology is moulded to meet police practices and needs. Structural integration regards the application of new technology as relatively unproblematic, and its underlying scientific basis is generally not questioned.

An alternative standpoint, *procedural* integration, reflects a norm of expert collaboration between police and forensic practitioners. This recognizes that 'there is effective consideration of the potential for forensic science to contribute to criminal investigations and that all who can contribute are given the opportunity' (Fraser 2007: 397). Procedural integration places forensic practitioners and police on a more equal footing and acknowledges the distinct knowledge and skills of forensic practitioners to make meaningful contributions to casework. As well as emphasizing these relations, procedural integration is commensurate with the view expressed by some forensic practitioners that the interpretation of scientific results in the individual context of each case is the central defining activity of forensic science (Jackson et al. 2006; Barclay and McCartney 2007). This standpoint opposes the notion that policing merely moulds science and technology for its own purposes. Instead, procedural integration is commensurate with the idea that criminal investigation as a whole can be modelled more rigorously along 'scientific' lines. It thus projects a possible reconstruction of relations between forensic practitioners and police. This is reflected in initiatives such as the Case Assessment and Interpretation (CAI) framework which seeks to use statistical theory to break down the investigative process into a series of propositions (CAI is described further in Chapter 5, but see also Lawless and Williams 2010). This mode of integration questions the epistemological basis of forensic practice, such as the idea that evidence such as fingerprints can be reported in simple binary terms. It emphasizes instead epistemic risk, namely, the risk of assuming certainty from what may be uncertain information.

Structural and procedural integration are analytical distinctions, but they reflect co-existing standpoints which serve to shape forensic science. Their co-existence points to the way in which science and policing co-produce each other. This volume develops the idea of the co-production of science and social orderings in later chapters.

Advances in forensic science such as DNA profiling have been hailed as significant interventions. Forensic DNA and police DNA databases have been the subject of much sociological attention (see, for example, Williams et al. 2004; Lynch and McNally 2009). The ability to constantly monitor 'genetic suspects' (Hindmarsh and Prainsack 2010) endows law enforcement agencies with a significant degree of power. Persons included on DNA databases are aware that future activities may alert the attention of police if they are deemed to be linked to sites where suspicious events have taken place. By providing a means of ordering the future relationship between police and suspect, forensic science can therefore act as a source of social control. In their study of 'cold cases', Innes and Clarke (2009) described how forensic science facilitates police control of the past. The investigation of previously unsolved cold cases has benefitted greatly from scientific developments such as DNA profiling. Innes and Clarke argued that memory is significantly linked to social control in two ways. Memory can be thought of as an object *of* social control. Police cold case reviews allow institutional histories to be rewritten, from narratives of failure to success stories. The power of the police to reinvestigate, boosted by new forensic technology, accrues them greater power going forward. According to Innes and Clarke, cold case reviews represent a form of surveillance in which the past deeds of individuals can be reinvestigated at any time. Innes and Clarke also maintain that cold case reviews facilitate social control *through* memory. The potential to rewrite the past alters the conditions for the practice of social control in the present and future. The capacity to reframe the past functions to animate changes in the social order of the present, altering the conditions for how social control can be imagined and practiced. The tools which facilitate such social control, such as the National DNA Database of England and Wales (NDNAD), have been the subject of much ethical concern, as discussed in Chapter 7. That chapter discusses the rules which allow police to sample and retain biological material of individuals and new applications of DNA which may identify family relations or even claims to predict appearance.

## The courtroom

Social and legal research has attended to the complexities raised when scientific evidence is scrutinized in the courtroom (Jasanoff 1995). When forensic evidence is presented in court proceedings, the details of its creation may not necessarily be made fully clear to jurors, judges and lawyers. Here, claims of forensic evidence may be cloaked in rhetoric skewed towards either a prosecution or defence argument. Legal comprehension of science may lead to inconsistencies in the way scientific evidence is interpreted (Edmond 2000). Prosecutors may overlook the nuances or ambiguities surrounding a particular form of evidence. Defence counsel, on the other hand, may try and use seemingly trivial details to argue against the credibility of evidence and cast uncertainty over its status and integrity (Williams 2007; Lynch et al. 2008). Social researchers have explored how scientific knowledge sometimes rests uncomfortably in the arms of legal systems where procedure and vested interests predominate. These are environments in which lawyers, judges and juries may exhibit variable levels of scientific understanding (Edmond and Mercer 1997). Yet in contrast to claims of law struggling to keep up with scientific developments (Jasanoff 2008), forensic studies research has highlighted how law plays a significant and active role in the construction of scientific evidence by various courtroom actors, mediated by legal procedure (Edmond 2000).

In addition to other works, a 1998 special issue of the journal *Social Studies of Science* focused on the construction and deconstruction of the 'credible' status of scientific evidence in court. At the time, the O.J. Simpson case was still fresh in the mind. Courtroom actors such as Judge Lance Ito, who presided over that trial, were framed as key actors who could rule on what constituted convincing or credible evidence, in effect constructing the lens through which courts viewed it (Jasanoff 1998). The seemingly unquestionable 'black box' (Latour and Woolgar 1979) status of 1990's DNA evidence became a subject of particular interest for forensic studies. During the 1980s and 1990s, DNA was regarded in US and UK courts as an immutable form of evidence which virtually guaranteed a guilty verdict (Lynch et al. 2008). Earlier studies described how this image was underpinned by various framings and other practices. The status of DNA was found to depend on how courts understood various claims to a witness's expertise and whether it was regarded as 'relevant' to justifiably scrutinize DNA evidence (Halfon 1998; Lynch 2004). Elsewhere, expert communities were themselves found to work within legal strictures to project credibility. Cole's studies of fingerprint examiners (Cole 1998, 2001) argued that this expert community formulated rules and norms of testimony which maintained the image of a unified and credible scientific discipline for several decades.

Studies of adversarial proceedings charted how the 'expert' status of scientific witnesses was performatively or ritualistically bestowed by counsel using their examination to highlight a witness's academic credentials, in terms of their academic rank or number of published papers (Lynch 2004). Opposing counsel sought to contest the claims of relevance to specific witnesses. A number of studies around this time suggested that scientific expertise could be regarded as a contingent, contextualized and somewhat slippery category (Edmond and Mercer 1997; Lynch and McNally 2003; Bal 2005). These studies showed how, through adversarial examination and cross-examination, the 'expert' status of a witness was closely intertwined with the specific issues under discussion which might be pertinent to a particular case. Legal proceedings were framed as liminal moments, where the 'expert' or 'non-expert' status of a witness was decided through the cut and thrust of prosecution and defence counsel (Lynch 2004) or in other ways, such as the appeals system (Lynch and McNally 2003; Lynch et al. 2008).

The immutable black-box status of DNA came under challenge as the 1990s wore on, partly through the efforts of some defence lawyers to scrutinize the practices underpinning the production of this evidence. These lawyers familiarized themselves with scientific papers, visited laboratories and talked to scientists. Armed with this knowledge, they then sought to deconstruct the status of DNA in court. The seeming similarities with the methods of science and technology studies (STS) researchers was duly noted (Lynch 1998). Forensic studies delved further into the complex interplay of constructive and deconstructive manoeuvres. Lynch and McNally's (2003; see also Lynch et al. 2008) study charted how courts in one English criminal case, *R v Adams*, negotiated the respective roles and limits of science and law. This involved deliberations over the place of statistical reasoning versus 'common sense' or personal experience. Forensic studies examined how boundaries between the respective roles of science and law were drawn by courts and of the limits of science in relation to intersubjective commonsense reasoning. Bal's (2005) study of a grisly case in the Netherlands highlighted how inquisitorial courts struggled with the bestowal of expert status. Dutch courts do not use a jury; instead, the judge is the fact-finder, hearing prosecution and defence arguments. Bal charted a case involving a woman who had been found dead in her home with a ballpoint pen case lodged in her eye, having penetrated her brain. Her son was accused of murder by allegedly firing the pen case with a crossbow, yet an alternative explanation was presented that the woman's death might have been caused by accidentally falling on the pen. Prosecution and defence disputed each other's accounts. Prosecution experts claimed that a supporter of the defendant, an eye surgeon, stepped outside the grounds of his expertise. Both sides, however, struggled to successfully replicate a possible murder scenario. In this case, the boundaries of expertise were disputed, yet the nature of what constituted a 'scientific' explanation was also contested. Some claimed that failure to replicate a murder was down to physical variables: an inability to duplicate the 'right' kind of pen or having to use pigs' heads instead of a human one in modelling experiments. Others reverted to a statistical explanation, claiming that they did not have the time or resources to replicate the scenario the requisite number of times to produce a 'successful' murder simulation. While the Dutch inquisitorial system assumed 'science' to have stable, essential epistemological qualities, this case destabilized these assumptions and exposed contested ideas about scientific experimentation itself.

Social researchers have thus been able to highlight the complexities when science became uprooted and placed into the courtroom. These studies sometimes contrasted the representations of science in court with the backstage work involved in the production of forensic evidence in the laboratory. These studies did not have an iconoclastic interest in denying scientific fact per se, but rather than arguing for particular epistemological and ontological characteristics of science, they sought to observe how 'scientific' evidence was constructed in the field.

Researchers would move on to studying how DNA evidence re-established its status in the face of courtroom challenges. The book *Truth Machine* (Lynch et al. 2008) presented a comprehensive account of the changing status of DNA evidence, together with the contrasting fortunes of other evidential forms such as fingerprints. The authors moved across and between spaces in criminal justice systems and highlighted interdependences between them. Through the examination of several case examples and fieldwork conducted in a forensic laboratory, the authors traced how, following periods of challenge, DNA evidence reasserted its credibility through an entanglement of various technical, legal and bureaucratic interventions, designed to anticipate and foreclose future legal challenge. Lynch et al. charted how the introduction of a host of seemingly 'quotidian tools', such as tamper-proof evidence bags and barcode readers, played key roles in reinforcing the integrity of evidence by maintaining chains of custody linking crime scenes with forensic laboratories. Meanwhile, in the laboratory, these authors highlighted the importance of other, seemingly mundane items such as laboratory coats and colour-coded pipette tips in avoiding contamination and thus (re)producing evidential integrity, which also served to pre-empt legal scrutiny. Technological developments, such as the emergence of polymerase chain reaction (PCR) machines, which effectively function as molecular photocopiers of DNA, and improved means of presenting DNA profile data were also found to play an additional role in rehabilitating the image of DNA. Lynch et al. argued that re-establishing the status of DNA occurred through a combination of technical and bureaucratic means, together with ongoing legal acceptance of this form of evidence. They argued it was this entanglement, rather than scientific progress per se, which maintained DNA's status. Other authors also sought to follow the production of evidence through criminal justice systems (Kruse 2016; Bechky 2021). Together these studies highlight how the production of DNA and other evidence relies on reconfiguring connections between spaces and linking the activities occurring at and between them.

## Custody

Another area of research has concerned prisoners' perceptions of forensic science. Prainsack and Kitzberger (2009) conducted a series of interviews with prisoners who had been jailed for a series of crimes, some of them serious in nature, in which DNA had played an important part in securing their conviction. The study found that the prisoners were largely convinced of the reliability and authority of DNA evidence. They saw DNA as impossible not to leave behind from a crime scene and viewed DNA technology as 'impenetrable and intimidating' (Prainsack and Kitzberger 2009: 51). Forensic DNA techniques were seen by some career criminals as overcoming their own criminal knowledge and skills which had allowed them to previously evade capture. These and other such studies (see, for example, Machado and Prainsack 2012; Machado et al. 2012) played a significant role in showing how forensic evidence can project power over subjects. Studies found support among respondents for the existence of DNA databases to exonerate individuals but also words of caution as respondents also believed that criminals would take more precautions to avoid depositing DNA at scenes (Machado et al. 2012).

These studies, however, also indicated a certain reflexivity on the part of these respondents. While they gained some knowledge of forensic science from television shows such as *CSI*, they consciously contrasted the portrayal of forensic evidence with their own experiences (Prainsack and Kitzberger 2009; Machado 2012). Studies found that at times respondents were sceptical of television portrayals (Machado 2012). Chapter 2 examines media depictions of forensic science in more depth.

## The Prüm regime

The international promise of forensic science has also attracted the attention of social science. One key example concerns the Prüm Treaty regime within the European Union (EU; Prainsack and Toom 2010, 2012). The Prüm Treaty formalized the exchange of certain forms of forensic data, namely, DNA, fingerprints and car registrations, between EU Member States and some other jurisdictions. Under the terms of the Prüm regime, DNA profiles obtained from crime scene traces stored in one national database may be compared against profiles stored in the databases of other Prüm states.

Prüm has been regarded as a vision, or imaginary, for a harmonized 'European' approach to criminal investigation (Prainsack and Toom 2012). Social researchers, however, have raised concerns that the Prüm system risks making wider groups of people vulnerable to becoming 'objects of surveillance and investigation because of the calculability of their criminal risks to others' (Lynch and McNally 2009: 284). The Prüm imaginary has also challenged, and been challenged by, operational practicalities and legislative norms in individual nations (Sallavaci 2018; Toom 2018; Machado and Granja 2019; Toom et al. 2019). As of March 2019, it was reported that only 24 out of 27 EU countries were fully operational with Prüm, the exceptions being Greece, the Republic of Ireland and Italy. The level of interconnectivity was reported by Toom et al. (2019) to vary across countries. In 2018, the Netherlands exchanged forensic DNA data with 23 countries, but Denmark exchanged with only 5 countries (Toom et al. 2019).

The manner in which police forces utilize transnational exchange and the impact on relations between police forces across borders are questions which researchers continue to pursue. Social researchers have called for more data regarding the number of arrests and convictions that have stemmed from transnational data exchange within the EU to better evaluate the impact and effectiveness of Prüm in addressing transnational crime. Authors have reported that 'publicly accessible information' to assess the effectiveness of Prüm has been 'limited, disjointed and largely unavailable' (Toom et al. 2019: 51). In the absence of such data, assessing the effectiveness of Prüm is difficult. This is complicated by different laws among Member States regarding sampling and retention of information and material. The Prüm regime's emphasis on certain forms of evidence over others could potentially shift the focus of international policing from certain crimes onto others. The question remains whether the exchange of certain data forms could divert transnational police activity towards certain physical crimes to people or property but away from other recognized transnational threats such as fiscal or computer crime.

The example of the Prüm regime nonetheless suggests further ways to consider how forensic evidence travels. How is evidence translated across jurisdictional spaces, and how does it inter-penetrate jurisdictions? What potentially unforeseen consequences for policing does the enactment of the Prüm vision hold?

The Prüm regime continues to invoke notions of a European imaginary of technological solutions to crime, even though it has been difficult to ascertain whether the reality matches with the ambition. It is, however, an instructive example to help consider how the promise of science and technology in the service of law enforcement is mobilized and justified.

## Aims and scope of this volume

Social research has often presented alternative views of forensic science compared to official narratives. In undertaking more in-depth studies, sociological research has uncovered and recovered underlying scientific controversies which have threatened the status of evidence such as DNA in the eyes of the law. It has also compared official accounts with those who engage in forensic work, such as crime scene examiners and forensic scientists employed in laboratories, and explored different aspects of professional identity. Key themes of forensic studies include the comparison of representations versus realities and expectations versus experiences.

Over time, forensic technology has evolved. This new volume considers forensic science alongside the growth of biometric technology as used in a wider series of domains. *Biometric data* has been defined as 'information about an individual's physical, biological, physiological or behavioural characteristics' which can be used 'on its own or in combination with other information … to establish the identity of an individual' (Scottish Biometrics Commissioner

Act 2020: 14). The reference to behavioural characteristics incorporates digital transactions such as social media activity within this definition. The increasing use and variety of biometric data arguably blur the distinctions between law enforcement, security and identity further. Biometric data have over time become increasingly prominent in verifying identity in other spaces and walks of life. Biometric identifiers are now incorporated into passports, and facial scanning is now a common and largely accepted feature of airports. Biometric systems are being used as a means of accessing electronic devices or for accessing buildings.

Social science has sought to conceptualize these and related developments and to address their social and ethical implications. New forms of DNA methods are emerging, alongside other technologies such as facial recognition. A multitude of digital data forms now exist, and digital forensics is now a priority area. These new data forms arguably reflect new relations between a variety of stakeholders. Biometric data systems extend across a wider array of spaces, as exemplified by the claims of the Prüm regime.

This volume compares representations, projections and expectations of forensic science and biometric data with how they are actually experienced. In doing so, this updated edition focuses on how different narratives of forensic and biometric technology co-exist and how the use of these systems reflects varying ways of interpreting, anticipating and imagining the relationship between these technologies and society at large.

The volume draws upon Sheila Jasanoff's concept of science-society 'co-production' (Jasanoff 2004), which posits a mutually dependent relationship between scientific knowledge and the wider representations, discourses, identities and institutions through which societies understand themselves. This volume explores the co-production of forensic and biometric data with society in the past, present and near future. The theme of expectations versus experience is addressed via the concept of sociotechnical imaginaries. The sociotechnical imaginary has been used to describe how governments and other actors project 'collectively imagined forms of social life and social order' (Jasanoff and Kim 2009: 120) through technological plans or visions. Through the sociotechnical imaginaries framing, social researchers have charted how technological plans co-produce social, cultural or political imperatives which reflect local, national or supranational identities (Smith and Tidwell 2016; Mager 2017; Levenda et al. 2019; Lawless 2020). Sociotechnical imaginaries project specific visions of collective progress and social good, such as in the harnessing of science and technology to address crime and maintain national security. Alternative, contesting imaginaries may, however, reflect different concerns about technology, such as their potential social and ethical risks.

Forensic and biometric technology has previously been examined via the notion of the imaginary (Williams 2010; Donovan 2015; Markó 2016; Lawless 2021). This work has focused on how science and technology has been mobilized to justify certain policy decisions. This revised volume uses the notion of the imaginary as a point of departure through which to explore in more depth how forensic science and biometric technology are framed. It compares these framings with other critical perspectives and the experiences of those who engage more directly in forensic science and with biometric systems.

Rather like their topic, social studies of forensic science display a markedly interdisciplinary character, bringing together social science with legal scholarship and often displaying a fine-grained attention to scientific and technical detail. STS, an interdisciplinary field which applies various social scientific perspectives to science, has played an influential role. Social studies of forensics have tended to wear their sociological leanings relatively lightly, yet one can discern the influence of the interactional tradition of sociological thought. Rather than emphasizing the causative effects of social structures, interactional perspectives seek to study society from the bottom up. Interactional studies tend to focus on the observable relations between actors and the practices through which these relations are maintained or challenged. Through these kinds of observations, social forensic studies have been able to illuminate the ways in which actors negotiate and construct (or reconstruct) collective understandings of forensic science and evidence.

This is not to say, however, that social structures and inequalities have been overlooked. Indeed, new forensic and biometric methods, such as some DNA and facial recognition technologies, have raised much concern over their potential to discriminate via questionable reliability or erroneous scientific assumptions. The application of forensic science raises issues related to social justice, such as concerns about the disproportionate number of certain ethnic groups on national DNA databases (Duster 2004; Skinner 2013). New DNA technologies potentially raise the fear that new science may perpetuate old prejudices.

This edition is intended to reflect how forensic studies has evolved over time. Caution is exercised here against a too-heavy reliance on any particular sociological theory or method. Instead, this edition seeks to contribute to existing literature by providing an updated focus on the ways in which various stakeholders in forensic science interact. This leads to a detailed, sociologically informed consideration of how forensic science engages with society at large.

This volume also focuses on how forensic science is shaped by the projection of various ideas about what it is. While contestable, these assumptions exert influence on shaping the kinds of systems and structures in which forensic practices occur. These practices may in turn challenge relations between the actors and institutions who are stakeholders in forensic science. This volume aims to facilitate further understanding of how forensic science projects and embodies relations between knowledge, authority and societal participation.

In what subsequently follows, the place of forensic science in casework is explored across a variety of spaces. The book explores the power and resistances that descriptions of forensic knowledge exert across a variety of dimensions and directionalities. This includes structural, hierarchical (or 'topdown') dimensions and challenges to formalizations and orthodoxy observable through interactions. It also encompasses a focus on the tensions between law and science, two equally powerful but epistemologically distinct forms of authority (Jasanoff 2008). In focusing on all of these dimensions, the volume indicates a problematic relationship between the practice of representing forensic science and evidence and its perceived 'realities'.

This book draws from research by the author, who has been conducting sociological study of forensic science for sixteen years. A variety of sources are used. This includes a variety of documentary material ranging from academic, scientific and technical publications plus policy documents and other forms of informally published material (socalled grey literature). Numerous parliamentary inquiries into forensic science and biometrics have generated a considerable amount of relevant information and insight. Media representations such as news reports and websites were also examined in the course of preparing this volume. The book also draws upon interviews involving a variety of members of the forensic stakeholder community. This is complemented by fieldwork conducted by the author and attendance and participation at a wide range of meetings, conferences and seminars.

This book often centres its focus on the jurisdiction of England and Wales. This represents a rich source of subject matter. It is here where the use of DNA has been pursued with particular vigour, albeit not without controversy. Having been the site of the first forensic application of DNA in 1988, this jurisdiction has sometimes proclaimed itself as something of a 'world leader' in the development and use of forensic science

(British Broadcasting Corporation 2015). England and Wales also instituted one of the world's first national DNA databases. This jurisdiction has seen the application of market policies to the provision of police scientific support. These have, however, led to unanticipated effects such as the closure of the Forensic Science Service (FSS), once the largest external provider of forensic science in England and Wales. This jurisdiction's adversarial legal system, with its sometimes idiosyncratic posture to science, also provides plenty of material of interest to sociology.

While focusing primarily on England and Wales, the book does extend further afield. Forensic science transcends jurisdictional boundaries, and Scottish and Northern Irish justice has also embraced science, albeit though differing modes of provision. Hence, when discussing forensic science, it is sometimes equally appropriate to refer to the 'UK', except when policy and legal matters are discussed specifically in relation to England and Wales. Forensic science also owes a great deal to developments elsewhere in the world. Developments in countries which share the adversarial tradition have had some bearing on perceptions of forensic science in England and Wales and vice versa. These are discussed where appropriate. While this volume does not tend to focus on inquisitorial jurisdictions, it is acknowledged that they, too, represent a rich source for social research (see, for example, Bal 2005; Toom 2012). The international dimensions of forensic science extend to those jurisdictions and, together with political developments in spaces like the EU, represent opportunities for further research (Prainsack and Toom 2010, 2012). The final chapter encompasses developments elsewhere, taking a cue from studies in Southern Africa and Latin America.

A brief note on terminology. It should be noted that 'forensic practitioner' is used here as an all-encompassing term to describe all forensic practice, although this term has been the subject of some debate, as outlined in Chapter 3. More specific terms such as 'crime scene examiner' and 'laboratory scientist' are used when appropriate.

## Contents of this volume

The book proceeds as follows. Chapter 2 focuses on forensics in the media. Media representations of forensic science are a useful starting point, whether they are consciously fictional or whether they make claims to reality. This chapter suggests that media portrayals of forensic science challenge the distinction between fact and fiction, with implications for the development and provision of forensic technologies to the police and for wider understandings of science. Chapter 3 presents an overview of the emergence of forensic science as both profession and scientific discipline. In addition, Chapter 3 describes how discussions within the fora of scientific societies make visible contested assumptions about certain forms of forensic practice and the professional identity of forensic science in general. Chapter 4 focuses on forensic and biometric policy. It describes the history of moves in England and Wales to introduce a degree of marketization to the provision of forensic services but questions to what extent a cohesive UK imaginary can be discerned given more recent developments. Chapter 5 compares the expectations constructed by formalized depictions of forensic reasoning with the casework experiences of practitioners. Through a description of the CAI framework applied to the evaluation of evidence, Chapter 5 challenges the relationship between forensic theory and practice, suggesting that the epistemic identity of contemporary forensic science may be reflexively reconstructed in contingent, localized circumstances. This contrasts with idealized philosophical and technical statements concerning the perceived 'essence' of forensic reasoning.

Chapter 6 uses an example of a contested forensic DNA method to investigate how law–science engagements shape the perceived scientific and legal status of emerging forensic technology. Chapter 6 indicates that law–science coproduction can exhibit complex and potentially counterintuitive effects. Chapter 7 continues focusing on the issue of how new forensic technologies become known but shifts the emphasis to wider social and ethical matters. Chapter 7 suggests that techniques such as familial searching, genealogical analysis and DNA phenotyping continue to pose questions of social and ethical concern alongside legislation for DNA sampling and retention. Chapter 8 addresses social and ethical issues relating to the emergence of facial recognition technology, which is finding increasing use but not without controversy. Chapter 9 discusses digital forensics, now recognized as a priority for criminal investigations. Finally, Chapter 10 advances more critical ways of conceptualizing relations between expectations and experiences of forensic science, by showing how relations between science and society can be framed in different ways by different sociotechnical imaginaries.

Social research has highlighted the various ways in which forensic scientific knowledge is produced. Organizational structure, culture, rules and procedures, networks, interrelationships, representations and discourses all play a part in constructing forensic science. This volume comprehensively explores this diversity.

## Bibliography

Adderley, R. and Bond, J. (2007) 'The effects of deprivation on the time spent examining crime scenes and the recovery of DNA and fingerprints', *Journal of Forensic Sciences*, 53 (1): 178–182.

Adderley, R. and Bond, J. (2008) 'Predicting crime scene attendance', *Policing: An International Journal of Police Strategies and Management*, 31 (2): 292–305.

Adderley, R., Townend, M. and Bond, J. (2007) 'Use of data mining techniques to model crime scene investigator performance', *Knowledge-Based Systems*, 20 (2): 170–176.

Bal, R. (2005) 'How to kill with a ballpoint pen: credibility in Dutch forensic science', *Science, Technology and Human Values*, 30 (1): 52–75.

Barclay, A.D.B. and McCartney, S. (2007) 'Forensic science and miscarriages of justice', Paper presented at the 3rd National Forensic Research and Teaching Conference 2007, 5–7 September, Staffordshire University.

Bechky, B.A. (2021) *Blood, Powder, and Residue: How Crime Labs Translate Evidence into Proof.* Princeton, NJ: Princeton University Press.

British Broadcasting Corporation. (2015) 'Forensics in Crisis', BBC Radio 4 documentary, first broadcast 27 April 2015; online at: http://www.bbc.co.uk/programmes/b05r3tf1 (accessed 5 August 2015).

Cole, S.A. (1998) 'Witnessing identification: latent fingerprinting and expert knowledge', *Social Studies of Science*, 28 (5–6): 687–712.

Cole, S.A. (2001) *Suspect Identities: A History of Fingerprinting and Criminal Identification.* Cambridge, MA: Harvard University Press.

Delina, L.L. (2018) 'Whose and what futures? Navigating the contested coproduction of Thailand's energy sociotechnical imaginaries', *Energy Research & Social Science*, 35: 48–56.

Doak, S. and Assimakopoulos, D. (2007a) 'How forensic scientists learn to investigate cases in practice', *R&D Management*, 37 (2): 113–122.

Doak, S. and Assimakopoulos, D. (2007b) 'The tacit dimensions of collaborative network traffic', in L. CamarinhaMatos, H. Afsarmanesh, P. Novais and C. Analide (eds), *Establishing the Foundations of Collaborative Networks.* Dordrecht and New York: Springer, pp. 425–433.

Donovan, K. (2015) 'The biometric imaginary: bureaucratic technopolitics in post-apartheid welfare', *Journal of Southern African Studies*, 41 (4): 815–833.

Duster, T. (2004) 'Selective arrests, an everexpanding DNA forensic database, and the specter of an early twentyfirst century equivalent of phrenology', in D. Lazer (ed.), *DNA and the Criminal Justice System: The Technology of Justice.* Cambridge, MA: MIT Press, pp. 315–344.

Edmond, G. (2000) 'Judicial representations of scientific evidence', *Modern Law Review*, 63 (2): 216–251.

Edmond, G. and Mercer, D. (1997) 'Scientific literacy and the jury', *Public Understanding of Science*, 6 (4): 329–357.

Erlich, H., Stover, E. and White, T.J. (2020) *Silent Witness: Forensic DNA Evidence in Criminal Investigations and Humanitarian Disasters.* Oxford: Oxford University Press.

Fraser, J. (2007) 'The application of forensic science to criminal investigation', in T. Newburn, T. Williamson and A. Wright (eds), *Handbook of Criminal Investigation*, Cullompton, UK: Willan, pp. 381–402.

Fraser, J. and Williams, R. (2009) 'The future(s) of forensic investigations', in J. Fraser and R. Williams (eds), *Handbook of Forensic Science*, Cullompton, UK: Willan, pp. 602–622.

Halfon, S. (1998) 'Collecting, testing and convincing: forensic DNA experts in the courts', *Social Studies of Science*, 28 (5–6): 801–828.

Hindmarsh, R. and Prainsack, B. (eds). (2010) *Genetic Suspects: Global Governance of Forensic DNA Profiling and Databasing.* Cambridge, UK: Cambridge University Press.

Innes, M. and Clarke, A. (2009) 'Policing the past: cold cases, forensic evidence and retroactive social control', *British Journal of Sociology*, 60 (3): 543–563.

Jackson, G., Jones, S., Booth, G., Champod, C. and Evett, I.W. (2006) 'The nature of forensic science opinion – a possible framework to guide thinking and practice in investigation and in court proceedings', *Science & Justice*, 46 (1): 33–44.

Jamieson, A. (1999) 'Let me through, I'm a ummmm …', *Science & Justice*, 39 (2): 71–72.

Jasanoff, S. (1995) *Science at the Bar: Law, Science and Technology in America.* Cambridge, MA: Harvard University Press.

Jasanoff, S. (1998) 'The eye of everyman: witnessing DNA in the Simpson trial', *Social Studies of Science*, 28 (5–6):713–740.

Jasanoff, S. (ed.). (2004) *States of Knowledge: The Co-Production of Science and Social Order.* London: Routledge.

Jasanoff, S. (2008) 'Making order: law and science in action', in E.J. Hackett, O. Amsterdamska, J. Wajcman and M. Lynch (eds), *Handbook of Science and Technology Studies*, 3rd ed. Cambridge, MA: MIT Press, pp. 761–786.

Jasanoff, S. and Kim, S.-H. (2009) 'Containing the atom: sociotechnical imaginaries and nuclear regulation in the US and South Korea', *Minerva* 47 (2): 119–146.

Kruse, C. (2013) 'The Bayesian approach to forensic evidence: evaluating, communicating and distributing responsibility', *Social Studies of Science*, 43 (5): 657–680.

Kruse, C. (2016) *The Social Life of Forensic Evidence.* Berkeley, CA: University of California Press.

Latour, B. (1987) *Science in Action: How to Follow Scientists and Engineers Through Society.* Cambridge, MA: Harvard University Press.

Latour, B. and Woolgar, S. (1979) *Laboratory Life: The Construction of Scientific Facts.* Beverly Hills, CA: Sage.

Lawless, C.J. (2010) 'Managing epistemic risk in forensic science: sociological aspects and issues', *Sociology Compass*, 4 (6): 381–392.

Lawless, C.J. (2011) 'Policing markets: the contested shaping of neoliberal forensic science', *British Journal of Criminology*, 51 (4): 671–689.

Lawless, C.J. (2013) 'The lowtemplate DNA profiling controversy: biolegality and boundary work among forensic scientists', *Social Studies of Science*, 43 (2): 191–214.

Lawless, C.J. (2020) 'Assembling airspace: The Single European Sky and contested transnationalities of European air traffic management', *Social Studies of Science*, 50 (4): 680–704.

Lawless, C.J. (2021) 'The evolution, devolution and distribution of UK biometric imaginaries', *BioSocieties*. First published 5 May 2021. doi:10.1057/s41292-021-00231-x.

Lawless, C.J. and Williams, R. (2010) 'Helping with inquiries, or helping with profit? The trials and tribulations of a technology of forensic reasoning', *Social Studies of Science*, 40 (5): 731–755.

Leslie, M. (2010) 'Quality assured science: managerialism in forensic biology', *Science, Technology and Human Values*, 35 (3): 283–306.

Levenda, A.M., Richter, J., Miller, T. and Fisher, E. (2019) 'Regional sociotechnical imaginaries and the governance of energy innovations', *Futures*, 109: 181–191.

Ludwig, A., Fraser, J. and Williams, R. (2012) 'Crime scene examiners and volume crime investigations: an empirical study of perceptions and practice', *Forensic Science Policy and Management*, 3 (2): 53–61.

Lynch, M. (1998) 'The discursive production of uncertainty: the O.J. "Dream Team" and the sociology of knowledge machine', *Social Studies of Science*, 28 (5–6): 829–868.

Lynch, M. (2004) 'Circumscribing expertise: membership categories in courtroom testimony', in S. Jasanoff (ed.), *States of Knowledge: The Co-Production of Science and Social Order*. London and New York: Routledge, pp. 161–180.

Lynch, M., Cole, S.A., McNally, R. and Jordan, K. (2008) *Truth Machine: The Contentious History of DNA Fingerprinting*. Chicago: University of Chicago Press.

Lynch, M. and McNally, R. (2003) '"Science", "common sense", and DNA evidence: a legal controversy about the public understanding of science', *Public Understanding of Science*, 12 (1): 83–103.

Lynch, M. and McNally, R. (2009) 'Forensic DNA databases and biolegality: the coproduction of law, surveillance technology and suspect bodies', in P. Atkinson, P. Glasner and M. Lock (eds), *Handbook of Genetics and Society: Mapping the New Genomic Era*. Abingdon: Routledge, pp. 283–301.

Machado, H. (2012) 'Prisoner's views of CSI's portrayal of forensic identification technologies: a grounded assessment', *New Genetics and Society*, 31 (3): 271–284.

Machado, H. and Granja, R. (2019) 'Risks and benefits of transnational exchange of forensic DNA data in the EU: the views of professionals operating the Prüm system', *Journal of Forensic and Legal Medicine*, 68: 101872.

Machado, H. and Prainsack, B. (2012) *Tracing Technologies: Prisoners' Views in the Era of CSI*. Farnham: Ashgate.

Machado, H., Silva, S. and Cunha, M. (2012) 'Multiple views of DNA surveillance: The surveilled, surveillants and the academics', in G. Walle, E. Herrewegen and N. Zurawski (eds), *Crime, Security and Surveillance: Effects for the Surveillant the Surveilled*, Haia: Eleven International Publishing, pp. 177–192.

Mager, A. (2017) 'Search engine imaginary: visions and values in the co-production of search technology and Europe', *Social Studies of Science* 47 (2): 240–262.

Markó, F.D. (2016) '"We are not a failed state, we make the best passports": South Sudan and biometric modernity', *African Studies Review*, 59 (2): 113–132.

M'charek, A. (2000) 'Technologies of population: forensic DNA testing practices and the making of differences and similarities', *Configurations*, 8 (1): 121–159.

M'charek, A. (2008) 'Silent witness, articulate collective: DNA evidence and the inference of visible traits', *Bioethics*, 22 (9): 519–528.

Prainsack, B. and Kitzberger, M. (2009) 'DNA behind bars: other ways of knowing forensic technologies', *Social Studies of Science*, 39 (1): 51–79.

Prainsack, B. and Toom, V. (2010) 'The Prüm regime: situated dis/empowerment in transnational DNA profile exchange', *British Journal of Criminology*, 50 (6): 1117–1135.

Prainsack, B. and Toom, V. (2012) 'Performing the union: the Prüm decision and the European dream', *Studies in History and Philosophy of Science C: Studies in Biomedical and Biological Sciences*, 44 (1): 71–79.

Sallavaci, O. (2018) 'Strengthening cross-border law enforcement cooperation in the EU: the Prüm network of data exchange', *European Journal of Criminal Policy and Research*, 24: 219–235.

Scottish Biometrics Commissioner Act. (2020) Edinburgh: Scottish Parliament.

Skinner, D. (2013) 'The NDNAD has no ability in itself to be discriminatory: ethnicity and the governance of the National Forensic DNA Database', *Sociology*, 47 (5): 976–992.

Smith, J.M. and Tidwell, A.S.D. (2016) 'The everyday lives of energy transitions: Contested sociotechnical imaginaries in the American West', *Social Studies of Science*, 43 (6): 327–350.

Toom, V. (2012) 'Bodies of science and law: forensic DNA profiling, biological bodies and biopower', *Journal of Law and Society*, 39 (1): 150–166.

Toom, V. (2018) *Cross-Border Exchange and Comparison of Forensic DNA Data in the Context of the Prüm Decision*. Report on Behalf of European Parliament's Committee on Civil Liberties, Justice and Home Affairs: Policy Department for Citizen's Rights and Constitutional Affairs. Brussels: European Parliament.

Toom, V., Granja, R. and Ludwig, A. (2019) 'The Prüm decisions as an aspirational regime: reviewing a decade of cross-border exchange and comparison of forensic DNA data', *Forensic Science International: Genetics*, 41: 50–57.

UK Government. (2021) 'Forensic Science Regulator: About Us', online at: https://www.gov.uk/government/organisations/forensic-science-regulator/about (accessed 14 August 2021).

Wayment, R.C. (1982) 'The role of the civilian scenes of crime officer', *Journal of the Forensic Science Society*, 22 (4): 406–407.

Williams, R. (2003) 'Residual categories and disciplinary knowledge: personal identity in sociological and forensic investigation', *Symbolic Interaction*, 26 (4): 515–529.

Williams, R. (2004) *The Management of Crime Scene Examination in Relation to the Investigation of Burglary and Vehicle Crime*. Home Office Online Report, online at: http://www.homeoffice.gov.uk/rds/pdfs04/rdsolr2404.pdf (accessed 24 October 2014).

Williams, R. (2007) 'The problem of dust: forensic investigation as practical action', in D. Francis and S. Hester (eds), *Orders of Ordinary Action*, London: Ashgate, pp. 195–210.

Williams, R. (2008) 'Policing and forensic science', in T. Newburn (ed.), *Handbook of Policing*, Cullompton, UK: Willan, pp. 760–793.

Williams, R. (2010) 'DNA databases and the forensic imaginary', in R. Hindmarsh and B. Prainsack (eds), *Genetic Suspects: Global Governance of Forensic DNA Profiling and Databasing*. Cambridge: Cambridge University Press, pp. 131–152.

Williams, R., Johnson, P. and Martin, P. (2004) *Genetic Information and Crime Investigation: Social, Ethical and Public Policy Aspects of the Establishment, Expansion and Police Use of the National DNA Database*. Wellcome Trust Report. London: Wellcome Trust.

Williams, R. and Weetnam, J. (2013) 'Enacting forensics in homicide investigations', *Policing and Society*, 23 (3): 376–389.

WilsonKovacs, D. (2014) 'Backroom boys': occupation dynamics in crime scene examination', *Sociology*, 48 (4): 763–779.

Wyatt, D. (2014) 'Practicing crime scene examination: trace and contamination in routine work', *Policing and Society*, 24 (4): 443–458.

# 2 Forensics in the media

## Introduction

A relatively small sample of people engage with forensic science in their everyday lives. As opposed to forensic practitioners and other professional stakeholders, public engagement may largely be restricted to those who attract police attention or those unfortunate to be victims of crime. A wider proportion of society may experience forensic science only through media depictions, be they fictional portrayals or news reports. Many of these depictions, such as television drama, have proved to be very popular. The influence of media portrayals should not be downplayed given that members of the public in certain jurisdictions may find themselves called for jury service. They may have to comprehend scientific evidence having only previously viewed it through the prism of the media, which may present more or less accurate accounts of science. Even in parts of the world where jury systems are not in use, media representations of forensic science may promise an appealing vision of equitable, incorruptible justice.

## Forensic fiction

> Between ingenuity and the analytic ability there exists a difference far greater, indeed, than that between the fancy and the imagination, but of a character very strictly analogous. It will be found, in fact, that the ingenious are always fanciful, and the *truly* imaginative never otherwise than analytic. But it is by these deviations from the plane of the ordinary that reason feels its way, if it all, in its search for the true. (Poe 1841: 3)

Edgar Allan Poe's story 'The Murders in the Rue Morgue' is generally considered one of the first modern detective stories (Thomas 1999). In this tale, the narrator tells of his introduction to his some-time acquaintance Auguste Dupin, a gentleman of 'peculiar analytical ability' (Poe 1841: 4). This fantastical tale tells of Dupin's efforts in reconstructing and solving the mystery involving the gruesome deaths of a reclusive mother and daughter. From a tuft of hair recovered from the death grip of the mother and subsequently from fingermarks left on her body, Dupin is able to identify an escaped orang-utan as the culprit.

In the years following publication of 'The Murders in the Rue Morgue', several leading authors of the time followed Poe's lead, including such luminaries as Charles Dickens, Wilkie Collins and Mark Twain. Sir Arthur Conan Doyle's creation Sherlock Holmes is a particularly celebrated figure. The enduring popularity of the Holmes stories reflects a continuing fascination with the work of the detective, be it a member of the police or, like Dupin and Holmes, a talented outsider. Holmes was presented as an otherworldly figure, possessed of reasoning abilities seemingly beyond the reach of most

DOI: 10.4324/9781003126379-2

and often one step ahead of the authorities. The exploits of fictional figures such as Holmes often pre-dated actual procedures in police practice and the advent of certain forensic technologies (Thomas 1999). Holmes maintained his own laboratory, and in one story Holmes formulates a highly sensitive test for blood traces (Doyle [1887] 1996).

Detective fiction remained popular as the nineteenth century turned into the twentieth. Authors such as Agatha Christie, Dorothy Sayers and Ngaio Marsh reflected the 'Golden Age of Detective Fiction' in the 1920s and 1930s (Symons 1972). While the 'whodunit' story became popular, the role of science was rather less foregrounded compared to the works of Conan Doyle.

Another key trend in crime fiction during the earlier part of the twentieth century was the emergence of the 'hard-boiled' or 'noir' genre in American fiction. While emphasising themes of betrayal, moral ambiguity and tragedy, tales such as *The Postman Always Rings Twice* and *Double Indemnity* focused more on the crimes themselves and perhaps less on the way in which they were solved – indeed, the genre often tended to make it quite clear who the perpetrators were. However, novels which described forensic methods, while sometimes lurid or sensationalist, were also very popular among US audiences at this time (Littlefield 2011). These books raised concerns over the effects such fiction exerted on public perceptions towards the use of science in policing. Fears that these fictional depictions of forensic science presented unrealistic portrayals of the power of science to solve crime pre-date similar concerns which have arisen in the early 21st century, as described later in this chapter.

*Police procedurals*

The emergence of radio as a popular medium brought about successful police dramas such as *Dragnet*, which introduced the 'police procedural' genre to audiences, focusing more directly on police work as opposed to the adventures of enthusiastic amateur detectives. Police procedural dramas, including *Dragnet* itself, subsequently translated into film and television. Many police procedural dramas tended to be based on actual or seemingly real crimes. They focused on the inner workings of police organizations, revealing routines and procedures previously hidden to audiences (Kirby 2013). US police procedurals became popular internationally.

While police procedurals often depicted forensic scientific methods, the *CSI* franchise is particularly notable for its heavy emphasis on science. The original incarnation of *CSI* first aired in 2000, depicting the work and lives of forensic practitioners in Las Vegas. The popularity of *CSI* led to spin-off series set in Miami and New York and spawned a host of similar shows such as *NCIS* and *Bones*. Around the same time that *CSI* first aired, UK audiences were presented with BBC's *Waking the Dead*, a long-running police drama with a strong focus on forensic science.

Why has forensic science endured as a popular trope? Fiction can be thought of as centring on the tension between certainty and uncertainty in the course of a narrative arc (Kirby 2013). A dramatic arc is about the resolution of conflict and the kinds of puzzles or challenges protagonists have to face along the way. Uncertainty creates the kind of dramatic tension needed to maintain the interest of the audience, normally with some kind of revelation or question to which audiences become interested in seeing fully answered. The prospect of uncertainties being resolved maintains the interest of the viewer. According to Kirby (2013), forensic science in fiction is generally a source of certainty and resolution. The science in shows like *CSI* is generally presented as immutable. Kirby (2013) argues that the necessary dramatic uncertainty in forensic dramas derives from 'the interpretation of the forensics by the show's characters' (101). In a show such as *CSI*, initial interpretations of evidence may lead the characters to follow mistaken investigative routes. It takes the discovery of further forensic evidence to allow the fictional investigators to piece together the correct version of events. Holding the science as certain while depicting the characters as fallible enables television writers to concentrate on character development, a key element of television drama.

Forensic and police dramas have, however, been accused of presenting skewed representations of crime. Many crime dramas focus on murders rather than the more routine types of crime like robbery or vandalism (Deutsch and Cavender 2008). Despite the development of the police procedural genre over time, some crime dramas continued to portray crime in a morally unambiguous fashion, in terms of portraying characters as intrinsically good or evil (Mawby 2003). This may perpetuate stereotypes about crime and criminality, suggesting that crime is committed by 'bad' people rather than crimes being committed through a complex combination of circumstances.

TV crime dramas have also been criticized for portraying negative stereotypes of ethnic minorities and for over-victimizing women (Nolan 2007). It has been observed that women are often portrayed as helpless and powerless victims in many police dramas, although they have been depicted as stronger protagonists in shows like *Prime Suspect, Cagney and Lacey* and *The Wire* (Cavender and Deutsch 2007; Jermyn 2013). TV dramas often show women to be victims of strangers, even though the majority of violent crimes tend to be committed by people who know the victim (Innes 2003). *CSI* was also accused of misleading portrayals of relations between crime scene examiners and the police, depicting the former as 'the dominant and driving force in the criminal investigation' (Nolan 2007: 577).

## *The 'CSI effect'*

Elsewhere, shows like *CSI* were criticized for portraying an oversimplified and unproblematic impression of scientific practice. Professor Dan Krane, a biologist based in Ohio, was quoted as saying:

> [You] never see a case where the sample is degraded or the lab work is faulty or the test results don't solve the crime. ... These things happen all the time in the real world. (Krane 2004, quoted in Stephens 2007: 593)

*CSI* and similar shows were accused of misrepresenting the realities of forensic science and practice. They were criticized for a seeming tendency to overlook other potential errors in handling evidence, such as mistakes in the chain of evidence process or administrative errors (Stephens 2007). Concerns were expressed over whether these simplistic portrayals contributed to pressures already facing forensic practitioners, particularly in North America, where some police laboratories struggled to maintain standards, due in part to an alleged lack of financial support. On one hand, forensic practitioners in North America were reported as feeling the pressure of heightened expectations on the part of publics, while also being accused of 'poor standards, mismanagement and egregious errors' (Stephens 2007: 600).

Studies also suggested that forensic dramas reinforced the apparent 'mystique' of certain forms of scientific evidence, most notably DNA (Nelkin and Lindee 1995). For example, Ley et al.'s (2012) study of *CSI* episodes indicated that DNA techniques were normally shown in a positive light, playing an instrumental role in over a quarter of analyzed cases and portrayed more favourably than other kinds of evidence such as eyewitness testimony. The positive depiction of DNA work was boosted by dialogue which portrayed genetic information in an essentialized light. Ley et al. accused *CSI* and other such dramas as promoting simplistic, deterministic and reductionist views about genetics regarding personal identity. Dramas depicted forensic DNA analysis as quick and unproblematically identifying suspects, in contrast with actual forensic practice, where analyses take longer and are potentially subject to logistical issues such as backlogs. Actual DNA analysis may also be complicated by the need to resolve mixed DNA profiles or interpret partial DNA profiles. Fictional dramas may therefore make forensic DNA work more straightforward and accessible than it actually is.

Other commentators have suggested that forensic dramas overlook the contentious scientific status of many forensic analyses. Many forms of evidential analysis, such as ballistics, bite-mark analysis, handwriting, tool-marks and fingerprinting, have been critiqued for originating in police contexts, where the standards associated with scientific research in domains such as universities have not been thought to apply (Cooley 2007; Difori and Stern 2007; Saks and Faigman 2008). Concerns have also been expressed that forensic dramas do not provide realistic accounts of the error rates of certain forensic tests (Difori and Stern 2007).

*CSI* producers showed a marked reluctance to acknowledge such concerns. Cooley (2007) recounted a conversation with one of the staff who worked on an episode of *CSI*:

> The writers visualized a script where prosecutors called upon Gil Grissom [CSI character] and his super-sleuth colleagues to help solve and prosecute a grizzly [*sic*] murder. Specifically, Grissom and his cohorts would present the key physical evidence, which would all but secure the depraved defendant's death sentence. ... I suggested a different script which left viewers wondering: (a) whether prosecutors actually convicted and sentenced to death the actual perpetrator; and (b) whether prosecutors relied too heavily on highly subjective and inadequately researched forensic techniques to secure a death sentence. Needless to say, the CSI writer did not find my alternative script particularly useful, and our conversation ended shortly thereafter. (Cooley 2007: 499–500)

The popularity of the show led commentators to question whether it potentially skewed the expectations of the public in their interactions with the criminal justice system. A great deal of literature subsequently discussed the possibility of what became known as the 'CSI effect' – the possible influence of media in shaping the perception of forensic science by lay audiences, including members of the public who may serve on juries.

The CSI effect attracted significant initial attention from the community of social and legal researchers and practitioners in the United States (see, for example, Cole and Dioso-Villa 2007; Cooley 2007; Dowler et al. 2006; Ghoshray 2007). Cole and Dioso-Villa (2007) outlined a number of distinct potential effects. Firstly, they described the 'strong prosecutor's effect' as referring to the possibility of juries wrongly acquitting defendants because of a lack of the kind of forensic scientific evidence which they might have seen on shows like *CSI*. Second, Cole and Dioso-Villa used the term 'weak prosecutor's effect' to describe how prosecutors were seemingly being forced to take pre-emptive action, to advise jurors about the dangers of relying too much on forensic science and to explain away the absence of forensic evidence. Third, their 'defendant's effect' suggested that the extremely positive portrayal of forensic scientists on *CSI* and similar shows could potentially enhance the credibility of forensic scientists who testify as expert witnesses. This positive view might not necessarily always be justified. Fourthly, Cole and Dioso-Villa coined the term 'producer's effect' to describe the argument, sometimes made by the makers of *CSI*, that such shows were actually educational and that they helped juries know more about forensic science.

Fifth, these authors described the increased interest in forensic science by students as the 'professor's version'.

A sixth claimed variant of the CSI effect, termed the 'police chief's version', described the perceived risk that criminals may gain a greater awareness of forensic science through shows like *CSI* and that they might use knowledge gained through watching them to conceive ways of avoiding detection. A study by Prainsack and Kitzberger (2009) of convicted Austrian prisoners' attitudes to forensic science provided a more complex picture than the police chief's version might suggest. While some of the Austrian prisoners possibly gained some degree of forensic awareness from *CSI*, they remained alert that it was a work of fiction. They balanced the portrayal of crime in *CSI* with their own experiences, with some recalling how their arrest had come about through non-scientific means.

Despite much academic discussion of these multiple CSI effects, their actual existence remains debatable. Academic legal research on the CSI effect has tended to be somewhat restricted in scope and little empirical data exists confirming the CSI effect has been a problem for courts (Cole and Dioso-Villa 2007, 2009; and see Schweitzer and Saks [2007] for an example of an empirical study of the CSI effect). Authors have debated the extent to which the CSI effect is a real and significant issue (Podlas 2006; Shelton et al. 2007), and more recent results continue to provide a mixed picture (Hawkins and Scherr 2017; Podlas 2017; Vicary and Zaikman 2017). Some suggested that *CSI* had 'heightened' the expectation of jurors on the part of science (Mann 2006). While some have adopted a more agnostic stance to the *CSI* effect (see, for example, Podlas 2006; Tyler 2006; Smith et al. 2011), others have framed it in a more positive light. Rather than seeking to establish the 'reality' of the CSI effect, Ghoshray (2007) suggested that the growing aura of forensic evidence perpetuated by *CSI*, together with emerging evidence of misconduct and lying from prosecution witnesses, meant that the 'reasonable doubt' doctrine had been strengthened within US criminal jurisprudence. While remaining agnostic on the actual existence of the CSI effect, Ghoshray viewed the heightened awareness of forensic evidence as 'empowering' juries in the face of the rest of the criminal justice apparatus rather than distorting their perceptions. Others asserted that forensic dramas might have exerted other positive effects. While sceptical of the existence of the CSI effect, Cole and Dioso-Villa (2009) suggested a 'self-denying prophecy' that made actors pre-emptively aware of the possibilities of placing too much faith on purportedly scientific evidence. They also claimed that it made visible wider anxieties concerning the status of law versus science as truth-generating processes (Cole and Dioso-Villa 2009).

There is, however, some evidence to suggest that fictional representations of forensic science have adversely impacted on front-line crime scene staff. Huey (2010) interviewed 31 Canadian police officers and forensic practitioners about their experiences of dealing with the public and focused on how the latter perceived crime scene work through the prism of television. This study drew on the concept of role strain, namely, the emotional challenge of maintaining one's professional identity in the face of opposing perceptions (Goode 1960). Huey's study related role strain to the emotional stresses police and forensic practitioners experienced in trying to meet the demands of their employers and the expectations of the public and the tensions between reality and expectations which arose in the course of their work. Role strain was viewed as linked to the challenges faced by staff when citizens queried the techniques used in investigations. One of Huey's respondents expressed this as a feeling that their expert status on crime scene analysis had been called into question due the popularity of forensic dramas:

> [*CSI*] makes us look like idiots when we go to scenes, because they all think that they know exactly where a fingerprint can be found and what technique to do.

Then you get to the house and they're like, 'He touched that.' 'You know what? I can't get a fingerprint off a couch.' 'Yeah, you can'. (Huey 2010: 63)

A significant number of practitioners interviewed by Huey said they used these encounters to educate the public. These respondents consciously contrasted *CSI* with the realities of their own work. Hence, these practitioners used *CSI* as a point of departure to allow practitioners to make distinctions between fiction and the actualities of crime scene work.

A focus on the CSI effect draws attention to the ways in which representations of forensic science challenge perceptions as to what constitutes 'real' forensic scientific work. The CSI effect is a contested phenomenon, but it has nonetheless attracted the attention of some news outlets who have reported it as real. The next section focuses on the portrayal of forensic science in news media. This section indicates how, even in the case of 'factual' media portrayals, certain boundaries between representation and actuality may be transgressed.

## Forensics and news media

Crime features regularly among news headlines. The relationship between crime, news media and culture represents a wide programme of study (see, for example, Cohen 1971; Ericson et al. 1987, 1991; Gorelick 1989; Dowler et al. 2006; Cavender and Deutsch 2007; Deutsch and Cavender 2008). News media sources act as key gatekeepers for determining what issues are perceived to be significant among societies (Galtung and Ruge 1965). Theories of newsworthiness and news values have aimed to capture how and why certain stories are deemed to be important (Galtung and Ruge 1965; Harcup and O'Neil 2001; Shoemaker 2006; Barnard-Wills 2011).

Condensing potentially complex scientific controversies into a three-minute news report, however, poses a notable challenge. News media may simplify forensic technology but can portray it in either a positive or negative light. Stories involving the successes of forensic techniques like DNA profiling may provide a comforting sense of resolution and reinforce the police's image as the guardian of public safety. On the other hand, concerns about the ethics surrounding such technology may reflect public fears over the possible rise of 'surveillance societies' (Lyon 1994, 2003) and the erosion of civil liberties. Alternatively, news reports of miscarriages of justice may point the finger at faulty scientific practice.

Particular cases may come to exert a strong hold on publics. The disappearance of Madeline McCann is one such notable case which attracted considerable media attention in the UK, Portugal and elsewhere. In their analysis of tabloid press coverage of the McCann case, Machado and Santos (2009) identified two distinct rhetorical forms framing DNA evidence which was recovered from a car during the investigation. The *strong accusation* rhetoric framed forensic genetics in positive and authoritative terms. This, however, oscillated between a *weak association* discourse which emphasized uncertainties over the interpretation of DNA. The media veered from presenting the story as leading to some kind of resolution through this DNA sample only for further uncertainties about the evidence to emerge. Machado and Santos (2009) suggested that this mixture of stated certainty and uncertainty was comparable with the dramatic narrative of a *CSI* episode.

It has been suggested that the UK has exhibited different media attitudes to scientific expertise, reflecting a possible 'anti-CSI effect' (Difori and Stern 2007), where court cases such as those involving Sally Clark and the Birmingham Six, later ruled as miscarriages, seriously eroded trust in expert witnesses. On the other hand, the UK came to be described in the early 21st century, in rather self-serving terms, as a 'world leader' in forensic science (British Broadcasting Corporation 2015). The UK media portrayed developments such as DNA profiling as a source of national pride. A closer look at one example involving a technology known as DNABoost indicates, however, that there may be more to news media reports than it may initially seem.

### DNABoost

In October 2006, the UK Forensic Science Service (FSS) announced the introduction of a new method, known as 'DNABoost', which was heralded as representing another step forward in DNA profile interpretation technology, a 'world first in bringing clarity to a type of sample that was previously difficult to interpret' (Morris 2006). DNABoost was portrayed as a cutting-edge, sensitive system which could separate and analyse complex mixtures of DNA profiles in cases where minute quantities of biological material had been transferred and deposited by touch. This was considered a breakthrough due to the significant difficulties posed to investigators in interpreting such DNA samples. DNABoost was piloted by forces in West Yorkshire, South Yorkshire, Northumbria and Humberside on crimes such as burglary, theft and assault, with hopes being expressed that the technique could eventually be applied to 'cold cases', namely, previously unsolved cases involving serious crimes such as murders and sexual offences (Cochlin 2007).

The FSS invested a considerable amount of effort to publicise this new technique. They hired Medialink, a company which specialized in converting messages from commercial organizations into news stories, to be distributed along a number of channels, including the Internet and broadcast media. In 2008, Medialink's website displayed the logos of a number of high-profile clients, such as Adidas, Ford, Nokia and HSBC (Medialink 2008). Information displayed on Medialink's website provided further details of the work carried out by the company on behalf of the FSS and suggested the possible strategy of the latter. As well as raising general awareness 'of the process [DNABoost] and of the FSS as an entity' (Medialink 2008), it stated that the FSS 'particularly wanted to encourage those police forces who were not taking part in the pilot scheme to buy the DNABoost service from them' (Medialink 2008). Medialink conducted 'an intensive media relations campaign, dubbing the breakthrough *CSI Britain*' (Medialink 2008, emphasis added) and 'successfully placed FSS spokesperson Paul Hackett on all major channels for live interviews and offered filming opportunities from the FSS Lambeth laboratories' (Medialink 2008). Medialink proclaimed their approach to be a considerable success:

> The story really captured journalists' imagination and dominated throughout the news day, right from breakfast to 10 o'clock bulletins. Medialink obtained some of the most coveted spots in broadcast, including the sofa on GMTV; Radio 4's *Today*, *Sky Sunrise*, *BBC Breakfast*, and by the end of the day the FSS had been contacted by all of their target police forces in the UK. Even Downing Street commented on the story! (Medialink 2008)

By placing news stories in all the major UK broadcast networks, the FSS was able to obtain extensive publicity for its product. The FSS was at the time being converted into an entirely commercial body and faced some competition from an increasing number of private firms. Hence, there may have been a heightened self-awareness on the part of the FSS to promote itself. However, the work of Medialink went beyond normal advertising. Rather than using commercials, news channels were used to act as a platform through which DNABoost was exposed to police forces. These news stories effectively functioned as covert advertisements for the product. DNABoost was packaged within a particular type of news story – crime – an issue of concern to publics as well as the police. This strategy seems to have worked. According to Medialink, every other police force in the country apparently contacted the FSS to inquire about DNABoost.

It is worth noting the prominence of the term *CSI Britain*. Aside from the possible patriotic connotations, with the FSS keen to position itself as a world leader in forensic science, it is interesting to note the association with the American TV series. One can only speculate as to the real motivations behind the use of such a term, but it does invoke certain other connotations. The term could be said to have lent a certain transatlantic glamour to the technique and could be viewed as reinforcing a sense that DNABoost represented state of the art technology. *CSI* Britain could be said to function as an instrumental signifier, linking a publicly recognized (but normally fictionally associated) trope with a sense that a British company was turning imagination into reality by bringing DNABoost technology to life in the fight against crime.

The DNABoost story, however, ended ignominiously. While DNABoost hit the UK headlines in October 2006, police trials did not commence until 2009, and they were halted almost as quickly as they began. This was due to ethical objections. It was found that the FSS had developed DNABoost using the DNA data of individuals placed on the National DNA Database (NDNAD; Tully et al. 2013; see Chapter 7). This transgressed rules preventing commercial companies from retaining NDNAD data for their own purposes.

DNABoost and the imagery surrounding it nonetheless challenged boundaries between news and advertising and fact and fiction. Media representations bestowed DNABoost with great potential, even though this was never realized in practice. *CSI* appears to have played a role in allowing Medialink to blur these boundaries, being used as a means of alerting the public's and police's imagination. While actual forensic scientists and practitioners may be critical of such dramas (Huey 2010; Kirby 2013), the FSS, via Medialink, displayed a keenness to associate themselves with the immutability and sophistication of fictional forensic science.

The notion that *CSI* and other such dramas somehow depart from the 'reality' of science, as suggested by the CSI effect, has been critiqued for upholding the modernist distinction between the inherent, natural 'reality' of 'science' on the one hand and the social basis of 'culture' on the other (Latour 1993). Instead, Mopas (2007) has suggested *CSI* is better conceived as challenging the boundary between science and culture. According to Mopas, *CSI* can be thought of as a device which can be used by different actors to promote their own interests; for example, to highlight awareness of the need to better fund forensic laboratories by negative comparisons to the flashy and sophisticated environs depicted in *CSI* or to encourage public interest in law. *CSI* can be used *either* to compare 'reality' with fiction or to align (if not directly associate) legal actors with the same conceptions of 'truth' and 'justice' seemingly projected by *CSI* (Mopas 2007).

Similarly, Medialink and the FSS appear to have used *CSI* to associate DNABoost with the positive portrayals of science found in this drama. Through this and by promoting DNABoost in news media, they also implied that fictional, idealized technology could not just become real but could be routinely used in UK police casework. The DNABoost example therefore raises issues about the relationship between representations and realities of forensic science. Was this 'scientific information' or simply one more form of media 'content'? Can 'fictional' and 'factual' forensic scientific content be easily distinguished?

## *The CSI effect in the news: the 'surfeit' model of public understanding of science*

The CSI effect itself became a subject of interest among news media. News reports raised concerns about the perceived inaccuracy of forensic dramas and the consequences for public understanding of science. Interest in the *CSI* effect led news media to compare fictional and actual forensic work which drew similar conclusions to those described in earlier academic literature. Cole (2015) undertook an analysis of media reporting of the CSI effect which summarized news media critiques. The most common critique from news sources focused on over-optimistic portrayals of the amount of time it took fictional laboratories to process evidence. Media sources were also found to focus on differences in capacity between fictional and real laboratories, highlighting the apparent discrepancies between the technologically sophisticated settings shown in dramas like *CSI* and the more modest facilities routinely found in real life. Differences in capacity also related to the amount of time fictional scientists could devote to a single case compared to real forensic practitioners. News media critiques of the CSI effect often highlighted the fact that real-life practitioners worked on multiple cases at any one time, limiting the amount of attention they could devote to a specific case. Cole found that news media commonly critiqued fictional portrayals for depicting sophisticated technology or complained that television dramas invented forensic technologies which simply did not exist. News media critiques often focused on the tendency of dramas to overstate the probative force of a single piece of evidence or to depict evidence as non-ambiguous. Other criticisms included claims that the drama overstated the frequency with which certain forms of forensic evidence were found at crime scenes (Cole 2015).

Cole (2015) also noted the number of accounts which criticized dramas for showing the CSI profession to be glamorous. A significant proportion of news reports of the CSI effect involved criticisms about 'role confusion', where dramas conflated the responsibilities of the forensic scientists and the police detective. CSI effect news stories were often found to 'debunk the notion that forensic analysts perform law enforcement tasks' (Cole 2015: 138). Cole found that CSI effect news stories often highlighted the tendency of dramas to depict forensic practitioners as all-around experts when in reality they often specialize in a single form of evidence. Finally, many CSI effect critiques also mentioned the tendency of television to show the work to be fun and engaging when in reality it was often tedious.

Cole and colleagues suggested that, through such reporting, the 'reality' of the CSI effect was itself perpetuated by the news media, reflecting a kind of 'looping' effect (Cole and Dioso-Villa 2007; Cole 2015). Fictional representations of forensic science were deemed newsworthy due to the apparent effect they exert on publics, even though the existence of the CSI effect was contested by academic researchers.

Academic study of the CSI effect took a further turn. Cole (2015) summarized three scholarly approaches to the CSI effect (Cole 2015). Cole observed one set of scholars viewing it as a real social problem (Lawson 2009). As Cole noted, however, such claims were not necessarily matched by a requisite level of empirical support. The second approach identified by Cole saw academics viewing the CSI effect as an 'empirical hypothesis to be tested through various social scientific methods' (Cole 2015: 133).

Cole identified a third perspective which took media depictions themselves as the central focus of analysis. This perspective regarded the 'problem' of the CSI effect as caused by publics being exposed to too much scientific information and imagery, rather than too little, perpetuating overfamiliarity with the subject and assuming that forensic scientific evidence provided absolute certainty. This contrasts markedly with previous social research on public understanding of science (PUS). Earlier PUS literature noted a tendency in official statements to assume that publics operated with a *deficit* of scientific knowledge but would readily accept science once they were sufficiently educated (Bodmer 1985; Miller 2001). Authors also observed how this so-called deficit model of PUS framed science in certain and unproblematic terms toward audiences by those in authority. In contrast, Cole and Lynch noted how the publics were themselves sometimes accused of mistakenly over-simplifying and over-familiarizing themselves with forensic science. This projected assumption of too much knowledge has been described as a '*surfeit*' of forensic scientific knowledge rather than a 'deficit' issue (Lynch 2009; Cole 2015).

Cole (2015) argued that the surfeit model is another form of hegemonic discourse about the public 'misunderstanding' of science. Cole added a note of caution for researchers, suggesting that some social scientists and media commentators 'have asserted their hegemony not only over the "reality" of forensic science, but also, recursively, over the "reality" of the "*CSI* effect" itself' (Cole 2015: 141). According to Cole, this suggests a dilemma. In examining the effect of media portrayals such as *CSI*, we encounter the assertion that these fictional dramas are 'unreal'. However, in comprehending this issue, social researchers are confronted with the dilemma of assuming whether the CSI effect is 'real' or whether the media are duping publics in claiming this 'reality'.

Such studies show how the line between representation and reality continues to pose complexities. Concerns about how the news media portray fictional portrayals of forensic science and its effect on laypersons are therefore themselves refracted through further lenses, including academic literature.

## *True crime documentaries*

In recent decades television true crime documentaries have become popular. True crime as a genre has long held appeal. While some true crime is arguably salacious, works such as Truman Capote's *In Cold Blood* and Norman Mailer's *The Executioner's Song* are widely regarded as major literary contributions. The 2015 Netflix documentary *Making a Murderer* is a particularly prominent example of the renewed popularity of true crime media in the 21st century. *Making a Murderer* told the story of Steven Avery, of Manitowoc County, Wisconsin, who had served eighteen years for sexual assault and attempted murder as a wrongful conviction. In 2007 he was convicted for the murder of photographer Teresa Halbach. Avery's nephew Brendon Dassey was convicted as an accessory to the crime.

*Making a Murderer*, which ran over two seasons, cast doubts over Avery's conviction for Halbach's murder, including questioning some of the forensic evidence linked to the case. It was claimed that Avery's DNA matched that found in bloodstains recovered from Halbach's car. Avery's blood had been stored by the police since the 1985 trial in which he was wrongfully convicted. The vial containing Avery's blood was found to have broken seals and a puncture in the stopper, which led to accusations of the evidence being planted at the scene. The documentary depicted how Avery's defence team sought to establish whether the blood found at the scene contained the laboratory preservative ethylenediaminetetraacetic acid (EDTA), supporting the claim of police misconduct. While this was never fully established, the documentary highlighted the uncertain and interpretative nature of forensic evidence to a global audience. The uncertainty over Avery's and Dassey's convictions raised in *Making a Murderer* become a major international talking point and led to widespread calls to review the case.

*Making a Murderer* was by no means a lone example of the true crime documentary, nor was it the first, as Stella Bruzzi pointed out (Bruzzi 2016). The 2004 documentary

*The Staircase* told the story of North Carolina author Michael Peterson, who was accused of murdering his second wife Kathleen in December 2001 and convicted in October 2003. The makers of *The Staircase* filmed the trial as it proceeded, and Peterson allowed filming within his house after the day's courtroom business had ended, seeming wholly at ease in front of the camera (Bruzzi 2016).

Like *Making a Murderer*, questions over forensic evidence were raised in *The Staircase*. Peterson claimed he had been relaxing by his pool during the early hours and had found his wife collapsed at the foot of the stairs. Peterson also claimed that his wife had taken alcohol and Valium. Her blood alcohol content was measured at 0.07%, just under the US legal driving limit. The autopsy report concluded that the victim had sustained severe injuries consistent with a blow from a blunt object. Peterson's defence disputed this claim via their expert witness, who claimed that blood spatter patterns suggested the victim had accidentally fallen down the stairs.

Podcasts have also become another popular channel for true crime, and shows such as *Serial* have also questioned official accounts of cases and the safety of subsequent convictions (Golob 2017). Buoziz (2017) claimed that true crime documentaries, be they in televised or podcast form, challenge the monopolies of institutional truth-making, in which the police serve as the main conduit of information available to journalists. Documentaries may present alternative biographies of suspects and convicted persons which differ from those offered up in court. These documentaries may tell alternative stories about evidence. The questions over the bloodstains in Halbach's car in *Making a Murderer* attest to differing prosecution and defence narratives concerning the origin of this material. This instance shows how a bloodstain has multiple identities, contested between the prosecution and defence. By assigning a particular narrative to a piece of evidence, this evidence can be framed variously as inculpatory or exculpatory. Assigning different biographies to different forms of evidence may complicate the work of reconstructing a series of circumstances. In the Peterson case, for example, the defence was able to construct evidence in a way which suggested innocence, while the prosecution looked to construct a narrative around other evidence.

Documentaries add another layer of narrative to the existing work carried out in the courts, and it is here where we should challenge the supposed sense of 'reality' which we may associate with the documentary genre. Bruzzi (2016) argued that rather than functioning as a mirror representing reality, true crime documentaries present highly constructed versions of 'realities'. Bruzzi draws attention to the ways in which documentaries are subject to selective editing, production techniques and formats. *Making a Murderer* drew upon a mixture of archive material and interviews with those surrounding the case to shape a narrative which cast doubt on Avery's and Dassey's convictions. The programme was criticized in some quarters as being unduly favourable to Avery and for omitting information which supported the prosecution's case (LaChance and Kaplan 2020). Part of *Making a Murderer*'s narrative does, however, include elements of social commentary, portraying Avery, Dassey and family as poor and working class in contrast to the victims. *Making a Murderer* frames its ensemble in Manitowoc County through an insider/outsider dynamic: lacking trust from the community led to social, political, and economic exclusion (Engel 1984; Del Visco 2016). As Avery himself is quoted as saying: 'Poor people lose. Poor people lose all the time' (Del Visco 2016: 213).

The documentary style of *Making a Murderer* contrasts with *The Staircase*, which was able to present the trial as it unfolded and which was notable for the level of access granted by Peterson, at that point a free man, which enabled the programme to present a more personal view of the individual at the centre of the case. *The Jinx* followed Robert Durst, a multi-millionaire charged with murdering his friend Susan Berman. Durst's first wife Kathleen McCormack had disappeared in mysterious circumstances in 1983, and Durst had been found guilty of manslaughter for dismembering his neighbour, although he pleaded self-defence. *The Jinx* was notable in that unlike *Making a Murderer* and *The Staircase*, director Andrew Jarecki featured prominently in front of the camera. In the final episode, Jarecki confronts Durst with seemingly incriminating handwriting evidence. Durst leaves him to visit the bathroom but mumbles words while seemingly forgetting his attached microphone. His words were regarded by some as tantamount to a confession.

Even a brief comparison is sufficient to highlight how these three documentaries employ different styles, emphases and formats (Bruzzi 2016). *The Jinx* features director Andrew Jarecki placing himself prominently within the series, as much a principal character as Durst. *The Jinx* is also notable for depicting real-life incidents through melodramatically stylized re-enactments which employ bombastic and intrusive musical scores. Bruzzi (2016) argued that this presentation appears to do a disservice to audiences who are not trusted with their own imaginations. This style nonetheless represents a meshing of the documentary format with the production values of a piece of entertainment.

In some cases, such as *Making a Murderer*, documentaries may go further and actually intervene in reality, as in leading publics to campaign for Avery's and Dassey's appeals. The finale of *The Jinx* could also be said to intervene by revealing footage which seemed to incriminate Durst. Rather than acting as a mirror to represent reality, true crime documentaries may indulge in stylized reconstructions intended to entertain as much as inform. At times documentaries help create reality, in the way in which audiences respond to them and even in the course of the programme-making process itself. This creation rather than reflection of reality can be termed 'performativity' (MacKenzie 2006). The apparent performativity of true crime documentaries rubs somewhat awkwardly against claims that these broadcasts somehow present a challenge to institutionalized truth-making. If shows like *Making a Murderer* are themselves performative, who can we trust? Further dimensions arise when we consider the status of the audience – what truths do they construct of the individuals featured in these shows, and how do audiences construct themselves – as sympathetic to people like Avery, as jurors or as aspiring forensic scientists? How does media construct the audience's viewing identity?

Academic literature which has addressed true crime documentaries has tended to focus on a relatively small array of examples, and the overall body of literature is still relatively small compared to that which has discussed forensic fiction and the *CSI* effect. The most popular true crime documentaries have tended to originate from the United States and often portray white men as suspects, involved in the deaths of white women. Academic commentary which focuses on these examples risk overlooking other documentaries which focus on other groups. In addition, studies of true crime documentaries from the non-English-speaking world have been even more thin on the ground, although Bruzzi (2016) has discussed an example from French media. This raises the question of whether popular true crime documentaries are insufficiently diverse and whether subsequent academic commentaries have overlooked matters of diversity in turn.

True crime documentaries have proved to be popular, but questions remain as to whether their portrayals of forensic science are accurate or educational. There have been more recent signs, however, of some greater access to police functions, including forensic science, in shows such as BBC's *Forensics: The Real CSI*, which claim to present 'fly on the wall' views of forensic practice and its limitations. As the number of channels and streaming services increases, more programmes are needed to fill the time, and with it a variety of depictions of forensic science.

## Conclusion

The relationship between fictional representations of forensic science and reality has long been complex and interdependent. Works of fiction, such as the exploits of Sherlock Holmes, influenced a number of actual pioneers of early forensic science (see Chapter 3). Since then, science has often been portrayed as offering straightforward, immutable solutions to the mysteries raised in the context of criminal investigation. Twenty-first century portrayals of forensic science have, however, raised concerns about what kind of effect they may exert on audiences and the possible consequences for criminal justice. The CSI effect is nonetheless disputed by academic researchers but has been reported as a real phenomenon by news media.

This 'media looping' draws attention to the strangely self-perpetuating tendency of the CSI effect. Media looping suggests that representations of forensic science may interact and intertwine, in turn raising complications for social researchers seeking to understand the relationship between scientific authority and publics. Fictional portrayals may be accused of distorting reality, but these accusations of distortions may be picked up by news media. The lines between the fictional and the factual can become blurred, as exemplified by the case of DNABoost. Even the veracity of true crime documentaries and podcasts should be critically challenged. The same evidence can tell more than story, and true crime media may interpret evidence in ways which might challenge other accounts. Rather than reflecting simple objectivity, forensic evidence can be seen to be subject to different framings. Documentaries and podcasts may adopt specific standpoints which embed and frame evidence through the use of varying narrative techniques, formats and production values. Through them, reality can be performed and constructed rather than merely reflected.

We have seen how some academic framings suggest that publics may have been over-exposed to forensic science via media, claiming that audiences operate with a *surfeit* of supposed knowledge rather than a *deficit* in scientific understanding. We shall return to the concepts of scientific deficits and surfeits later in this volume. For now, while the CSI effect remains a contested phenomenon, we can see how media may challenge the professional identities of forensic practitioners and the epistemic status of science. We shall focus on these themes in Chapters 3 to 5. Next, Chapter 3 sketches a historical overview of the professionalization of forensic practice.

## Bibliography

BarnardWills, D. (2011) 'UK news media discourses of surveillance', *Sociological Quarterly*, 52 (4): 548–567.

Bodmer, W. (1985) *The Public Understanding of Science*. London: Royal Society.

British Broadcasting Corporation. (2015) 'Forensics in Crisis', BBC Radio 4 documentary, first broadcast 27 April 2015; online at: http://www.bbc.co.uk/programmes/b05r3tf1 (accessed 5 August 2015).

Bruzzi, S. (2016) 'Making a genre: the case of the contemporary true crime documentary', *Law and Humanities*, 10 (2): 249–280.

Buoziz, M. (2017) 'Giving voice to the accused: *Serial* and the critical potential of true crime', *Communication and Critical/Cultural Studies*, 14 (3): 254–270.

Cavender, G. and Deutsch, S.K. (2007) 'CSI and moral authority: the police and science', *Crime, Media, Culture*, 3 (1): 67–81.

Cochlin, D. (2007) 'The new key to murder riddles', *The Journal*, 5 January.

Cohen, S. (1971) *Images of Deviance*. Harmondsworth: Penguin.

Cohen, S. (1972) *Folk Devils and Moral Panics: The Creation of the Mods and Rockers*. St Albans: Paladin.

Cole, S.A. (2015) 'A surfeit of science: the "CSI effect" and the media appropriation of the public understanding of science', *Public Understanding of Science*, 24 (2): 130–146.

Cole, S.A. and DiosoVilla, R. (2007) 'CSI and its effects: media, juries and the burden of proof', *New England Law Review*, 41: 435–470.

Cole, S.A. and DiosoVilla, R. (2009) 'Investigating the "CSI effect" effect: media and litigation crisis in criminal law', *Stanford Law Review*, 61: 1335–1373.

Cooley, C.M. (2007) 'The CSI effect: its impact and potential concerns', *New England Law Review*, 41: 471–502.

Del Visco, S. (2016) 'Legality and the spectacle of murder: s review of Netflix's *Making a Murderer* (2015–)', *Humanity & Society*, 40 (2): 212–214.

Deutsch, S.K. and Cavender, G. (2008) '*CSI* and forensic realism', *Journal of Criminal Justice and Popular Culture*, 15 (1): 34–53.

Difori, J.H. and Stern, R.C. (2007) 'Devil in a white coat: the temptation of forensic evidence in the age of CSI', *New England Law Review*, 41: 503–532.

Dowler, K., Fleming, T. and Muzzati, S.L. (2006) 'Constructing crime: media, crime and popular culture', *Canadian Journal of Criminology and Criminal Justice*, 48 (6): 837–865.

Doyle, A.C. [1887] (1996) *A Study in Scarlet*. London: Leopard.

Engel, D.M. (1984) 'The oven bird's song: insiders, outsiders, and personal injuries in an American community', *Law and Society Review*, 18: 551–582.

Ericson, R.V., Baranek, P.M. and Chan, J.L.B. (1987) *Visualizing Deviance: A Study of News Organizations*. Toronto: University of Toronto Press.

Ericson, R.V., Baranek, P.M. and Chan, J.L.B. (1991) *Representing Law and Order: Crime, Law and Justice in the News Media*. Toronto: University of Toronto Press.

Galtung, J. and Ruge, M. (1965) 'The structure of the foreign news: the presentation of Congo, Cuba and Cyprus crises', *Journal of International Peace Research*, 2 (1): 64–91.

Ghoshray, S. (2007) 'Untangling the CSI effect in criminal jurisprudence: circumstantial evidence, reasonable doubt, and jury manipulation', *New England Law Review*, 41: 533–562.

Golob, B. (2017) 'Un-making a murderer: new media's impact on (potential) wrongful conviction cases', *California Western Law Review*, 54 (1): 137–150.

Goode, W.J. (1960) 'A theory of role strain', *American Sociological Review*, 25 (4): 483–496.

Gorelick, S.M. (1989) '"Join our war": the construction of ideology in a newspaper crimefighting campaign', *Crime and Delinquency*, 35 (3): 421–436.

Harcup, T. and O'Neil, D. (2001) 'What is news? Galtung and Ruge revisited', *Journalism Studies*, 2 (2): 261–280.

Hawkins, I and Scherr, K. (2017) 'Engaging the CSI effect: the influences of experience-taking, type of evidence, and viewing frequency on juror decision-making', *Journal of Criminal Justice*, 49: 45–52.

Huey, L. (2010) '"I've seen this on CSI": criminal investigators' perceptions about the management of public expectations in the field', *Crime Media Culture*, 6 (1): 49–68.

Innes, M. (2003) *Investigating Murder*. Oxford: Oxford University Press.

Jermyn, D. (2013) 'Labs and slabs: television crime drama and the quest for forensic realism', *Studies in History and Philosophy of Science C: Studies in Biology and Biomedical Sciences*, 44 (1): 103–109.

Kirby, D. (2013) 'Forensic fictions: storytelling, television production, and forensic science', *Studies in History and Philosophy of Science C: Studies in Biology and Biomedical Sciences*, 44 (1): 92–102.

LaChance, D. and Kaplan, P. (2020) 'Criminal justice in the middlebrow imagination: the punitive dimensions of *Making a Murderer*', *Crime, Media, Culture*, 16 (1): 81–96.

Latour, B. (1993) *We Have Never Been Modern*. Cambridge, MA: Harvard University Press.

Lawson, T.F. (2009) 'Before the verdict and beyond the verdict: the CSI infection within modern criminal jury trials', *Loyola University Chicago Law Journal*, 41: 121–172.

Ley, B.L., Jankowski, N. and Brewer, P.R. (2012) 'Investigating *CSI*: portrayals of DNA testing on a forensic crime show and their potential effects', *Public Understanding of Science*, 21 (1): 51–67.

Littlefield, M.M. (2011) 'Historicizing *CSI* and its effect(s): the real and the representational in American scientific detective fiction and print news media, 1902–1935', *Crime Media Culture*, 7 (2): 133–148.

Lynch, M. (2009) 'Science as a vacation: deficits, surfeits, PUSS, and doing your own job', *Organization*, 16 (1): 101–119.

Lyon, A.D. (1994) *The Electronic Eye: The Rise of Surveillance Society*. Cambridge: Polity Press.

Lyon, A.D. (2003) *Surveillance After September* 11. Cambridge: Polity Press.

Machado, H. and Santos, F. (2009) 'The disappearance of Madeleine McCann: public drama and trial by the media in the Portuguese press', *Crime, Media, Culture*, 5 (2): 146–167.

MacKenzie, D. (2006) *An Engine Not a Camera: How Financial Models Shape Markets*. Cambridge, MA and London: MIT Press.

Mann, M. (2006) 'The CSI effect: better jurors through television and science?', *Buffalo Public Interest Law Journal*, 24: 211–237.

Mawby, R. (2003) 'Completing the halfformed picture? Media images of policing', in P. Mason (ed.), *Criminal Visions*. Cullompton, UK: Willan, pp. 214–237.

Medialink. (2008) http://www.medialink.tv (accessed 5 January 2008).

Miller, S. (2001) 'Public understanding of science at the crossroads', *Public Understanding of Science*, 10: 115–120.

Mopas, M. (2007) 'Examining the "CSI effect" through an ANT lens', *Crime, Media, Culture*, 3 (1): 110–117.

Morris, N. (2006) 'British police forces to trial new DNA evidence procedures', *New Criminologist*, 4 October; online at: http://www.newcriminologist.co.uk/news.asp?id=-1830012562 (accessed 30 October 2008).

Nelkin, D.M. and Lindee, M. (1995) *The DNA Mystique: The Gene as a Cultural Icon*. Ann Arbor: University of Michigan Press.

Nolan, T.W. (2007) 'Depiction of the "CSI effect" in popular culture: portrait in domination and effective affectation', *New England Law Review*, 41: 575–590.

Podlas, K. (2006) 'The "CSI effect": exposing the media myth', *Fordham Intellectual Property, Media Entertainment and Law Journal*, 16: 429–465.

Podlas, K. (2017) 'The "CSI Effect"', 22 August 2017, online at: https://oxfordre.com/criminology/view/10.1093/acrefore/9780190264079.001.0001/acrefore-9780190264079-e-40 (accessed 26 August 2021).

Poe, E.A. (1841) 'The murders in the rue morgue'. Philadelphia, PA: *Graham's Magazine*.

Prainsack, B. and Kitzberger, M. (2009) 'DNA behind bars: other ways of knowing forensic technologies', *Social Studies of Science*, 39 (1): 51–79.

Saks, M.J. and Faigman, D.L. (2008) 'Failed forensics: how forensic science lost its way and how it might yet find it', *Annual Review of Law and Social Science*, 4: 149–171.

Schweitzer, N.J. and Saks, M.J. (2007) 'The CSI effect: popular fiction about forensic science affects public expectations about real forensic science', *Jurimetrics*, 47 (3): 357–364.

Shelton, D. E., Kim, Y. S. and Barak, G. (2007) 'A study of juror expectations and demands concerning scientific evidence: does the "CSI effect" exist?' *Vanderbilt Journal of Entertainment and Technology Law*, 9 (2): 331–368.

Shoemaker, P.J. (2006) 'News and newsworthiness: a commentary', *Communications*, 31: 105–111.

Smith, S. M., Stinson, V. and Patry, M. W. (2011) 'Fact or fiction? The myth and reality of the CSI effect', *Court Review: The Journal of the American Judges Association*, 47: 4–7.

Stephens, S.L. (2007) 'The "CSI effect" on real crime labs', *New England Law Review*, 41: 591–608.

Symons, J. (1972) *Bloody Murder: From the Detective Story to the Crime Novel: A History*. London: Faber & Faber.

Thomas, R. (1999) *Detective Fiction and the Rise of Forensic Science*. Cambridge: Cambridge University Press.

Tully, G., Sullivan, K., Vidaki, A. and Anjomshoaa, A. (2013) *Taking Forensic Science R&D to Market*. Horsham: Electronics, Sensors, Photonics Knowledge Transfer Network.

Tyler, T.R. (2006) 'Viewing *CSI* and the threshold of guilt: managing truth and justice in reality and fiction', *Yale Law Journal*, 115 (5): 1050–1085.

Vicary, A. and Zaikman, Y. (2017) 'The CSI effect: an investigation into the relationship between watching crime shows and forensic knowledge', *North American Journal of Psychology*, 19 (1): 51–64.

# 3 Shaping forensic science as discipline and profession

## Introduction

The previous chapter indicated how portrayals of contemporary forensic science challenge the distinction between fiction and fact. Some early key pioneers of forensic science were themselves influenced by the exploits of fictional characters such as Sherlock Holmes. As this chapter recounts, figures such as Edmond Locard and Hans Gross made major contributions to shaping forensic science through their writings and also through establishing laboratories and institutions. In doing so, these individuals helped to shape forensic science as both a scientific discipline and a profession.

Professions and professionalism and the nature of scientific disciplines are enduring themes of sociological interest. Various perspectives have been advanced in the course of exploring how professions emerge and the ways through which specific professional groups are distinguished. Sociological research has sought to investigate how the notion of 'a profession' is collectively shared and shaped by those who claim membership of a professional community and what differentiates those communities. Some studies of professions have been associated with the functionalist tradition of sociology (Merton [1942] 1973; Parsons 1964; Brante 1988). Broadly construed, functionalist approaches have theorized that professions are constitutive of social progress and order (Brante 1988). Such perspectives have viewed science as possessing a particular kind of value consensus emphasizing rationality. In this way, science has been viewed as the central driver of professional development and thus the engine of social advancement.

Other sociological perspectives have adopted different positions. So-called 'cynical' or 'neo-Weberian' perspectives (Brante 1988) have focused on the interests of collectives identifying as professional groups. These perspectives suggest that professions actually arise through practices of inclusion and exclusion, by communities claiming a certain 'professional' status (see, for example, Parry and Parry 1977). Similarly, some sociological studies have explored how scientific controversies and debates present challenges to expert communities. These may represent moments where the membership of such communities is reconstituted through attempts to establish 'consensus' around a particular scientific issue. Researchers such as Collins (1985) have argued that scientific consensus emerges through the scientific claims of certain individuals being accepted within expert communities while others become marginalized. Sociological studies have also explored how actors may draw distinctions between 'science' and 'non-science' through distinctly social practices, a phenomenon which has been termed 'boundary work' (Gieryn 1983). Some of this work suggests that, rather than being a strictly philosophical question, the demarcation of science from non-science is better understood as an empirical matter and as the result of practices of inclusion and exclusion by communities who claim scientific expertise.

DOI: 10.4324/9781003126379-3

This chapter considers what implications the development of forensic science holds for sociological perspectives on the professions and science. The chapter sketches a history of the development of forensic science in the UK and elsewhere and the role played by various organizations and bodies. As indicated here, a significant part of the development of recognized forensic 'expertise' and practice (which remains contested to a degree) is linked to its recognition by the wider community of criminal justice stakeholders. In the UK, the organization of forensic science by government bodies has played a role in shaping ideas about what constitutes forensic science. However, the formation of distinct scientific bodies and learned societies, with attendant activities such as peerreviewed journals and conferences, has also significantly shaped forensic science as both discipline and profession.

While focusing mostly on the UK, the chapter also describes related developments in other parts of the world, including the United States and Europe. Forensic science has maintained some commitment to the principle that its practitioners can identify with a global community. This is consistent with observations of other scientific communities, which have been identified as seeking to transcend national borders in the course of discussing their work (Merton [1942] 1973). Hence, a discussion of the emergence of forensic science as profession and discipline must acknowledge its international dimensions.

The chapter begins with a brief overview of the emergence of forensic science in the UK, outlining the increasing distinction which arose between forensic science and medical interventions in law. The establishment of a network of laboratories in England and Wales, which gave rise to the Forensic Science Service (FSS), is briefly described. While the UK Home Office played a significant role in instituting forensic science in England and Wales, other interventions, such as the formation of scientific societies, have also been key to shaping contemporary forensic science as practice and profession. Over time, concerns about potential miscarriages of justice have subjected forensic science to increased scrutiny, accompanied by debates over standardization and accreditation. Such debates have sometimes reflected different attitudes regarding what professionalism means in the context of forensic science.

## Science vs medicine in law

Emerging fields of science were used to inform legal proceedings from as early as the late eighteenth century. During this time, for example, scientific methods were used to attempt to establish the provenance of postal seals. Evidence from the nascent field of chemistry found use in the nineteenth century in a range of cases, including those involving alleged food adulteration through to terrorist bomb plots (Ward 1993).

The 1829 Metropolitan Police Act, introduced by Sir Robert Peel, is largely credited with creating the first modern police force (Emsley 2008; Rawlings 2008). In addition to creating the Metropolitan Police, this Act gave provision for the creation of police surgeons, who were primarily charged with providing medical treatment to police officers. Police surgeons were, however, often available to carry out postmortems on bodies in suspicious cases and became important figures in the process of criminal investigation. During the nineteenth century, civilian medical practitioners also assisted police in their inquiries, largely on an ad-hoc basis. Terms such as 'medical jurisprudence' or 'forensic medicine', sometimes used interchangeably and open to interpretation, came to describe these forms of investigative assistance (Ward 1993).

The systematic application of medicine to the law in the nineteenth century was, however, stymied by a number of factors. In addition to a lack of substantial state support, Ward (1993) identified the absence of specialist journals or societies as belying a lack of shared collective identity. Medical applications to law exhibited a 'confusion of titles' (Ward 1993: 68). Terms such as 'medical jurisprudence' and 'forensic medicine' competed with others, including 'legal medicine' and 'juridical medicine'. Likewise, practitioners described themselves variously as 'medical witnesses', 'medical experts', 'medical jurists', 'toxicologists' or 'medicolegists'. Group identity may also have been held back by fierce personal rivalries between those claiming to represent medicine in law (Ward 1993). Specialized education centres, enabling research as well as teaching, were slow to emerge. Insufficient financial incentives served to dissuade many medical practitioners from being involved in the law (Ward 1993).

There did, however, come to be growing interest in the potential of science to contribute to the management of criminality over the course of the nineteenth century. The latter part of this century saw the rise of systematic procedures for identifying recidivists (Cole 2001). The technique of anthropometry, involving a series of bodily measurements to catalogue individuals, became widespread. Fingerprinting also emerged around the same time, originally in colonial Bengal through the work of William Herschel. Fingerprint laboratories subsequently became established in most industrialized countries.

Towards the turn of the century, the use of bodily data such as fingerprints was generally directed towards the management of criminals and inquiries concerning the nature of criminality rather than the investigation and reconstruction of criminal offences. The earliest known identification using fingerprints was performed by detective John Maloy in Albany, New York, around 1856. The first European identification followed in Paris in 1902 (Cole 2001). The 1905 trial of brothers Alfred and Albert Stratton for the murder of a couple during a robbery of an art shop in Deptford, London, brought fingerprint evidence to the attention of English law. While the jury found the Stratton brothers guilty, Judge Channell, who sentenced them to death, took the opportunity to express some concerns about the reliability of using latent prints in criminal investigation: 'When proper impressions are taken, the system is extremely reliable, but it is a different thing to apply it to a casual mark made through the perspiration of a thumb' (Cole 2001: 174).

The potential of scientific techniques for criminal reconstruction and investigation, as opposed to the mere cataloguing of bodily data, therefore took some time to be recognized (Cole 2001). Some, however, were keen to promote the investigative potential of science. The Austrian Hans Gross was a proponent of teaching what he termed 'criminalistics' (Roux and Robertson 2009: 576), a term now used predominantly in the United States to describe the analysis of trace and transfer evidence. Gross regarded the scientific method as a much more robust template for criminal reconstruction than other forms of evidence such as eyewitness testimony. He published a series of influential works including *Criminal Reconstruction: A Practical Textbook for Magistrates, Police Officers and Lawyers*. This volume provided a key early resource for investigators (Williams 2008). Gross also established one of the early academic schools for forensic science in Graz, Austria, although not before the first such institution, the Institute of Forensic Photography, subsequently the Institut de Police Scientifique (School of Forensic Science), was established at the University of Lausanne, Switzerland, by Professor Rudolphe Reiss in 1909 (Roux and Robertson 2009). This institute was the first to offer degrees in forensic science and its members were also involved in criminal casework (Chisum and Turvey 2007).

Another key figure in the development of forensic science was the Frenchman Edmond Locard. He studied at the Lyon Institute of Forensic Medicine under its director Dr Alexandre Lacassagne, who himself was a fervent believer in the value of combining science with the systematic study of criminal behaviour. Inspired by the work of Hans Gross and also by the Sherlock Holmes stories, Locard travelled the world to study how large urban police forces integrated scientific method and trace evidence analysis into their investigative procedures. Locard was disappointed, however, to find that the methods of many forces were somewhat unsophisticated, with reconstructive methods often largely non-existent. He did, however, take inspiration from his visit to the School of Forensic Science in Lausanne. Following his visit, Locard returned to Lyon and managed to persuade the authorities to furnish him with two rooms in the attic of the Law Courts. It was here that Locard was able to create what is generally regarded as the world's first police crime laboratory.[1]

He worked on several areas, including the analysis of dust and the interpretation and analysis of handwriting, bloodstains and fingerprints (Chisum and Turvey 2007). His work became widely disseminated via his numerous books and articles. Locard was also instrumental in helping to establish an early professional body for forensic scientists, the International Academy of Criminalistics, founded in 1929. Locard's name also endures through a wellknown forensic scientific axiom: Locard's exchange principle. Locard's principle has been passed down extensively throughout the forensic science community over time (Wyatt 2014).

During the early twentieth century, police forces in England and Wales were free to choose which experts to assist them with their investigations. Medical pathologists such as Sir Bernard Spilsbury often made the headlines for their testimony in some notorious cases of the day. Spilsbury attracted particular attention for his role in the Dr Crippen murder trial of 1910, although his style of testimony would later be the subject of critical scrutiny (Burney and Pemberton 2010, 2011). A rising property crime rate in 1920s London posed challenges for the Metropolitan Police Service (MPS). In 1931, Lord Trenchard became MPS Commissioner. Trenchard had previously been in charge of the Royal Air Force and had a reputation for foresight and vision (Emerson 1995). Trenchard was instrumental in establishing the Metropolitan Police Laboratory at Hendon, North London. It was not long, however, before the new facility came under threat. Lord Trenchard's successor, Sir Philip Game, was opposed to relying on a single facility and preferred that the MPS had freedom to choose which experts they wished (Stockdale 1997). Game was, however, prevented from doing so by the Home Office, who thought his proposal to be 'retrograde' (Emerson 1995).

Elsewhere in the UK, a number of scientists based at academic institutions become known for their role in police work, such as the chemist Professor F.G. Tryhorn based at Hull, Dr Wilson Harrison at Cardiff and the botanist Dr H.S. Holden at Nottingham (Emerson 1995). Concerns were sometimes expressed, however, that external experts, while enthusiastic, sometimes strayed outside of their specific fields of expertise (Ambage 1987).

The formation of a network of regional forensic laboratories across England and Wales was, at least initially, largely imposed from above. Key to its formation was Sir Arthur Dixon, principal assistant under secretary of state and head of the Home Office Police Department between 1919 and 1941 (Ambage 1987). Dixon regarded English police forces as markedly slow to embrace the potential of science for detection. He viewed science as a means of increasing detective capacity and of facilitating cooperation (and hence efficiency) within and between forces, many of which exhibited rather parochial tendencies. In the early 1930s, the British police was highly fragmented, comprising 181 separate forces in the UK, including a combination of city, borough and county forces (a wave of amalgamations, from the Second World War onwards, would eventually reduce that number to 43 forces in England and Wales; Ambage 1987; Mawby and Wright 2008). Dixon's plan envisaged a national system of scientific support to police. Rather than training detectives in scientific methods themselves, Dixon thought that policemen should be instructed in various areas, including the assistance experts could provide to investigating officers, what kind of evidence detectives should look for, what to do and what not to do at crime scenes, and the methods by which potential evidential materials should be recovered and packaged for expert analysis (Ambage 1987).

In 1938, the Home Office Departmental Committee on Detective Work and Procedure reported to the Home Secretary, Sir Samuel Hoare (Ambage 1987). The committee's report argued for the readier availability of experts able to testify in court via a system which could circumvent the high fees often charged by independent experts. In endorsing a network of specialist forensic science laboratories, the committee made a series of recommendations for the Home Office's role in shaping the service. It recommended precisely what kind of personnel should man each site and that scientists should be recruited by the Home Office rather than police forces (Ambage 1987).

Senior police figures across British forces displayed a mixture of attitudes to science during the 1930s (Ambage 1987), with at least some displaying reluctance to embrace new methods. The Home Office, however, pressed ahead and in 1939 established a network of regional forensic science laboratories to ensure police forces had equal access to scientific assistance. This network was effectively the forerunner to the Forensic Science Service (FSS). The Metropolitan Police Laboratory (MPL) remained open but outside of this network. In 1941 the Home Office had suggested that the MPL be removed from police control and become the regional laboratory for the southeast, but this was successfully resisted (Emerson 1995). The MPL was eventually amalgamated into the FSS in 1995, although the MPS has since continued to invest in its own inhouse scientific facilities.

Professor Stuart Kind, the founder of the Forensic Science Society (FSSoc, later the Chartered Society of Forensic Sciences, CSFS), saw the Home Office as instrumental in the development of forensic science as a discipline through its creation of the regional laboratories system (Kind 1999). The gradually increasing awareness among police of the potential of science also played a role in promoting forensic science, 'being persuaded, largely by example, to use the laboratories and to familiarize themselves with the use of scientific aids and with the employment of experts for the analysis of evidential materials' (Ambage 1987: 166). It should be pointed out, however, that attitudes on the part of police forces to the potential contribution of science appear to have varied significantly, even through to the late 1980s.

In hindsight, the nature of some expertise which emerged in English forensic science during the postwar years appears to have been based on some rather questionable foundations, if one follows the reflections of figures such as Kind. Kind himself recalled one occasion, as director of the Northern Region Forensic Science Laboratory in Newcastle Upon Tyne, which involved delegating a colleague to the scene of a fire (Kind 1999: 122):

> Because we were a small laboratory we were very much at the mercy of the pattern of case work and the contingent demands which were placed upon us by the local police forces. We had, so to speak, no slack which could be taken up in times of emergency. There were only three experienced fire examiners in the laboratory and, with the requirements of courts, scenes, leave and other factors, we were sometimes in the position of being asked to dispatch someone to the scene of a suspicious fire but having noone available. In one such case pressure was being placed upon me to send a scientist to a fire scene but I had noone to send. Thinking about the problem as I walked down the laboratory corridor I saw a member of my staff approaching from the opposite direction. He was a very competent young chemist but he was inexperienced in fire scene examination. But stimulated by my own early experiences as a

'fire examiner' the following exchange took place:DIRECTOR [KIND]: M ... I want you to go to a fire at A ...

M: But I am not a fire examiner.

DIRECTOR [KIND]: I've got news for you.

Under the regional forensic science laboratories system, facilities were established first at Nottingham, followed by Cardiff, Bristol, Birmingham and Preston. While there was a push from central authority, cooperation between this network of laboratories was minimal. During the earlier days of the regional system, each laboratory was strictly controlled by their directors, who, it seems, discouraged communication with the other laboratories in the network. Stuart Kind accounted for the suspicion and enmity between these individuals (Kind 1999):

> The problem was that most of the directors were former academics who viewed each other with the deepest possible suspicion. Each was determined to keep his own laboratory as a little kingdom independent of the others. (155)

In Scotland the forensic science sector comprised police laboratories for each force. Strathclyde established the first in 1943, followed by Aberdeen (1969), Lothian and Borders (1975) and Tayside (1989; Emerson 1995). Scottish police forces became unified under the name of Police Scotland in 2013. In Belfast a laboratory was opened in 1956, albeit under the control of the Ministry of Commerce.

The 1970s saw significant investment in instrumentation, which gave forensic scientists the ability to offer the police and the courts more and more information from less and less sample. This then resulted in further increased demand, which allowed the FSS to pursue a greater degree of research and development activity (Pereira 1995).

Women have endured mixed fortunes in pursuing careers in forensic science. While women found early employment in US fingerprint bureaux (Cole 2001), women who joined the FSS faced considerable challenges in terms of career progression. Barbara Pereira, a former controller of the FSS, recounted how, as a junior 'reporting officer', she had to deal with attitudes within maledominated environments in the post–Second World War era. She recounted having to deal with doubts being expressed over whether women could cope with the rigours of cross-examination. The irregular hours associated with criminal investigation were also regarded as inhibiting women, who were still viewed by many as central to homemaking. Over time, however, many women have been recognized for their major contributions to forensic science in the UK (Pereira 1995).

British forensic science owes its development to a great extent to interventions from central authority, in the form of the Home Office, which was instrumental in shaping a network of laboratories from which the FSS would emerge (Kind 1999; Williams 2008). One should, however, be cautious in framing the FSS, and forensic science generally in England and Wales, as being overwhelmingly the product of government action. While the Home Office sought to establish a certain order to police scientific support, providing a national network to offset the ad-hoc employment of scientific expertise by local forces, the FSS never at any point represented the totality of scientific support available to the police. Rather, it was the case that the FSS 'ran alongside' (Ward 1993: 246) the capacity of the police to source expertise from wherever they saw fit. While the FSS came to be viewed as a vital source of scientific support, it was not the only channel the police could rely on for external expert input.

Nor should it be assumed that the emergence of a regional network fostered any great sense of collegiality. Indeed, the picture portrayed by commentators like Kind suggests a marked rivalry and lack of communication between laboratories. It was this reluctance to interact that contributed to the formation of the Forensic Science Society, later the Chartered Society for Forensic Science, in 1959. In addition to government interventions such as the FSS, scientific associations have played an important role in the professionalization of forensic science, as outlined further in the next section.

## Forensic scientific societies

Sociologists have suggested that learned societies may function as a means of controlling the membership of expert communities and thus shape scientific disciplines (Gieryn 1983). Learned societies may marginalize those whose scientific views are perceived to contest a certain disciplinary consensus. Thus, it is possible to assert that the emergence of a scientific discipline may result from who is excluded from that discipline as much as it develops through the activities of those who are accepted as members of an expert community.

A wide number of professional associations now represent various forensic specialisms. The increasingly global reach of forensic methods is reflected in the emergence of corresponding international organizations. Scientific societies are able to promote interaction among individuals claiming expertise in what may be narrow or esoteric specialisms and who may experience a degree of isolation. Forensic societies may also serve to identify commonalities among seemingly disparate groups of practitioners. Through the publication of specialist journals, such bodies may promote the sharing and critical scrutiny of knowledge claims. By offering membership in the form of chartered status or accreditation, these bodies also define certain forms of expertise through who they include or exclude. The potentially changing aims and membership of scientific societies may indicate possible changing attitudes within disciplines.

Space precludes an in-depth description of the numerous organizations representing various forensic specialisms. It is worthwhile, however, to briefly focus on a number of notable institutions which are relatively wide in scope and are hence relatively more visible. Doing so facilitates understanding of how the contours of forensic practice have been shaped, even in the face of heterogeneous claims to expertise.

One of the most enduring professional organizations is the International Association for Identification (IAI), founded in 1915 by Inspector Harry Caldwell of the Oakland (California) Police Department's Bureau of Identification (IAI 2015). The IAI publishes the *Journal of Forensic Identification* and operates a number of accreditation programmes for crime scene work, forensic art and photography and analysis of bloodstain patterns, footwear and fingerprints.

Some sociological studies have, however, taken a critical view of the way in which the IAI has upheld the status of fingerprint analysis. Cole (1998), for example, highlighted a case in which the IAI revoked the membership of a fingerprint examiner whose testimony had been judged as 'erroneous' by a Minnesota court. Cole observed how the IAI attributed cases of perceived error in fingerprint examination to individual examiners rather than questioning the technique itself. Cole argued that in this case, perceived 'honest' mistakes (Cole 1998: 702), rather than alleged misconduct on the part of the examiner, led to their exclusion from the IAI. His observations suggest that such a response can be regarded as an attempt to maintain a unified front, conveying an image of a cohesive and thus credible discipline.

The American Academy of Forensic Sciences (AAFS) is another longstanding forensic society. The AAFS was founded in 1948, following the First American Medicolegal Congress held in St Louis, Missouri (Uberlaker 2011). The founders desired 'to further the ends of Justice by maintaining a greater correlation between Science and Law' (Turner 1948: 108). The following aims were envisaged for this body:

(1) To promote the use of scientific methods and knowledge in the solution of legal problems and controversies, (2) to develop and extend a better understanding of the application of legal doctrines to scientific professions, (3) to improve professional qualifications of scientists engaged in the assistance of the courts and attorneys, and (4) to plan, organize, and administer meetings, publications, reports, and other projects for the stimulation, and advancement of the above purposes, and the standardization and improvement of scientific techniques, tests, and criteria. (Turner 1948: 107)

The AAFS now comprises over 7,000 members drawn from across the United States, Canada and over 70 other countries worldwide (AAFS 2015). It represents a diverse membership, representing numerous forensically related medical and scientific fields, plus lawyers, educators and others (National Research Council 2009). Since 1956 the AAFS has published the peerreviewed *Journal of Forensic Sciences*. It promotes research, education and training and operates accreditation schemes. These include a system for accrediting education programmes (AAFS 2015).

One notable episode in the history of the AAFS concerns controversies surrounding the definition of forensic science used by the organization. In 1969, the AAFS Executive Committee voted in favour of accepting a definition of forensic science that included the words 'social behavioural' (Field 1998: 41). The programme for the Annual Meeting of the AAFS held in 1970 prominently featured the following statement:

Forensic Science is the study and application of the sciences to law, in the search for truth in civil, criminal and *social behavioural matters*, to the end that injustice shall not be done to any member of society. (Quoted in Field 1998: 41, emphasis added)

The inclusion of references to 'social behavioural matters' was viewed by some AAFS members as a sign of willingness to embrace a broad view of the sciences and to facilitate a more inclusive approach to membership. Other members appear to have favoured a more exclusive attitude which limited recognition to a narrower range of scientific disciplines. At the 1971 Annual Meeting, the AAFS voted to accept a definition of forensic science as 'the application of those portions of all the sciences as they relate to the law'. This was considered sufficient to allow the AAFS to accept a wider range of disciplines into its fold, including the social and behavioural sciences (Field 1998: 53). This inclusive definition was not accepted, however, before a motion to adopt a more restrictive definition was rejected: 'Forensic science is the application of the *physical and medical* sciences as they relate to the law' (Field 1998: 53, emphasis added). Signs that a wider set of disciplines eventually gained acceptance included the incorporation of clinical psychologists into the AAFS in 1985 and the emergence of an AAFS Psychiatry and Behavioural Sciences Section in 1986 (Field 1998).[2]

In the UK, the FSSoc, now the CSFS, was formed in 1959, due in no small part to the activities of Stuart Kind. As well as promoting interaction between regional laboratories, FSSoc aimed to keep scientists informed about research developments of relevance to forensic science (Kind 1999). Promoting research was therefore viewed as a key priority (Ambage 1987; Kind 1999). FSSoc emerged largely through the initiative of Kind but not without some considerable opposition from his superior at the time, the director of the Harrogate Laboratory in Yorkshire. While Kind initially struggled to encourage forensic scientists to join, he managed to enlist another regional director in a manner which reflected the personal rivalries of the time:

A colleague from another laboratory joined our small group, and, wonder of wonders, persuaded his own director to enrol in our growing band. My delight at this event was sharpened by the knowledge that the director concerned, and my own, enjoyed an acute and mutual loathing. (Kind 1999: 156)

The Forensic Science Society was intended as a means for FSS scientists to have a voice independent of the Home Office. In providing such representation for the forensic scientific community, FSSoc also facilitated a degree of unity among a disparate group of experts. It also represented a means by which scientists could distinguish themselves from their medical and legal colleagues while retaining a perceived equality of status (Ambage 1987).

The CSFS, as FSSoc is now known, currently represents members drawn from 60 countries (CSFS 2014). Some of the stated aims of the CSFS are 'to provide education and development for forensic practitioners, to support research and development in forensic science and practice, and to promote and develop regulation in forensic science and practice' (CSFS 2014). It runs a series of accreditation systems, including proficiency standards across a range of techniques, and accredits university courses. CSFS also publishes the peerreviewed journal *Science & Justice* (formerly the *Journal of the Forensic Science Society*).

The year 1959 saw the inauguration of another professional body, the British Academy of Forensic Sciences (BAFS). A forensic pathologist, Francis Camps, was instrumental in the emergence of BAFS. Once considered rival organizations, a certain distinction in membership between the two societies emerged over time. While BAFS attracted some forensic scientists, it came to be dominated by medical and legal professionals (Ambage 1987). Hence, a distinction between 'forensic medicine' and 'forensic science' was perpetuated by the existence of the FSSoc (now CSFS) and BAFS. Some areas, such as forensic pathology, continued to be associated with the label 'forensic medicine' as opposed to more distinctly analytical fields. Today, BAFS continues to incorporate forensic specialisms with clear medical links, including pathology. The journal title published by BAFS titled *Medicine, Science and the Law* reflects this ongoing tradition.

Numerous professional bodies exist at the international level. For example, the International Society for Forensic Genetics (ISFG) aims to 'promote scientific knowledge in the field of genetic markers as applied to forensic science' (ISFG 2014). Founded in 1968, the ISFG draws its membership from 60 states worldwide. The ISFG publishes a peerreviewed journal *Forensic Science International: Genetics* and hosts a regular conference.

Some other international organizations represent forensic science in broader terms; for example, the European Network of Forensic Science Institutes (ENFSI), formed in 1992 (Willis 2009). With membership across 30 states, ENFSI aims to ensure 'the quality of development and delivery of forensic science throughout Europe' (ENFSI 2014). ENFSI also seeks to promote compliance with international scientific standards and best practice across its members. It organizes courses and training for forensic practitioners in support of its aims. A number of working groups focus on specific forensic specialisms.

It is worth noting differences between the memberships of such organizations. The ISFG comprises a combination of academic researchers working in the field of genetic methods which may have forensic application, together with forensic scientists who may be employed in casework. ENFSI, on the other hand, is a network of largely police institutions. Hence, international forensic societies may represent partially overlapping sets of institutionalized interests.

From this brief overview it is possible to discern a sense of how certain forensic scientific societies have evolved to represent certain groups. Organizations may define forensic science through the eyes of their members, whether possessing a medical or scientific background, or based in academic laboratories or police institutes. Such organizations may represent changing or partially overlapping sets of forensic practitioners. Their backgrounds may in turn shape perspectives on the role of science in the service of the law. Debates about how to define forensic science, such as those within the AAFS in the late 1960s and early 1970s, were interdependent with attitudes regarding who was considered appropriate to include within forensic communities. The plethora of specialisms which claim forensic application exposes potential socioepistemic differences and points to an epistemological identity which demonstrates a notable degree of fluidity. Practices of inclusiveness or exclusiveness may reflect attempts to shape the profession, but the inclusion or exclusion of certain groups through society membership may also simultaneously influence the epistemological character of forensic science.

## Standardization and accreditation

Despite the emergence of the FSS to promote the use of forensic science and the work of the FSSoc to facilitate greater collegiality, concerns about the police use of science endured. In the 1970s and 1980s, forensic science appeared to be a lowpriority form of evidence, with police officers tending to favour confessions and eyewitness testimony. One experienced forensic scientist, interviewed in 2008, claimed that the police in the 1970s would only use forensic science if it could implicate a suspect directly with a crime and support a prosecution. Kind (1999) even alleged that the police would, if needed, rely on entirely erroneous scientific practice to do so.

Cases such as the Birmingham Six exposed serious issues regarding the police use of science and the quality of forensic scientific work performed. In 1991, following Sir John May's inquiry into the miscarriage of justice surrounding the Maguire Seven and also reflecting concerns about other miscarriages, a Royal Commission was tasked with examining the criminal justice system in England and Wales. The commission, chaired by Lord Runciman, reported in 1993. It examined a number of criminal justice issues, including forensic science and the role of professional expert witnesses.

The Runciman Commission endorsed regulation of the forensic science sector, proposing a Forensic Science Advisory Council (Roberts 1996). The aim of accrediting the opinions and interpretational judgement of expert witnesses represented a major challenge, not least because the law sought to retain independence in determining admissibility in court. A key issue concerned the maintenance of standards to guard against miscarriages while also allowing the courts to benefit from the experience of experts and to 'prevent a stifling rigidity in the production of scientific evidence' (Roberts 1996: 52). Runciman recommended oversight be extended to all suppliers of forensic science, not just the FSS, which at the time was still an agency of the Home Office (Viscount Runciman of Doxford 1993).

As the 1990s progressed, the practices of forensic scientists in various jurisdictions came under concerted scrutiny. There came to be a growing perception that standards of forensic laboratory work needed to be raised (Stockdale 1997). Laboratories across the UK, Europe, the United States and Australia came to participate in various accreditation programmes to meet international standards. Standardization was viewed as facilitating best practice and enabling better quality of communication between laboratories within and across jurisdictions. This was also viewed as necessary given the recognition of the increasingly international character of crime. In order to meet the requirements of accrediting bodies, laboratories considered the increased use of standard operating procedures (SOPs) to ensure scientific methods were followed in a consistent and accountable manner, performed by trained personnel and via apparatus which had been clearly validated. This regime also sought to ensure best practice in the recording and reporting of results (Willis 2009). During the 1990s, the UK forensic community debated plans to introduce a system of national vocational qualifications (NVQs) as a means of accrediting personnel. FSSoc introduced vocational qualifications in the areas of firearms, documents, fingerprints and crime scene examination (Lees 1997). While some welcomed the move towards vocational qualifications (Emerson 1995), others were more sceptical towards them and to standardization in general (De Forest 1998; Jamieson 1999). Concerns were expressed that standardization might erode job satisfaction if it led to too much routinization of practice (Anon. 1997).

As well as publishing peerreviewed scientific papers, the FSSoc journal *Science & Justice* provided a forum in which opinions about standardization were expressed. The editorial section of *Science & Justice* gave forensic scientists a platform to reflect on the nature of forensic science and practice. One such editorial from 1998 spoke of fears of a situation 'where the forensic scientist is little more than a technician operating in a reactive mode, allowing nonscientists to define and circumscribe the scope of the scientific investigation' (De Forest 1998: 1). The editorial contrasted this scenario with an alternative whereby criminal investigations could be fully subject to a scientific gaze, which took a balanced and unbiased approach to the case and evaluated all evidence in a holistic manner. The association of science with holism was framed in terms of the former bringing crucial added value to the way in which investigations could be conducted:

> If meaningful scientific questions are not framed with respect to possible physical evidence, the potential value of this evidence will not be realized, and little or misleading information will be developed. (De Forest 1998: 1)

De Forest asserted that forensic science, even in drawing from several other sciences and forms of expertise, could still be regarded as entailing a distinct set of cognitive activities. De Forest drew comparisons with medicine, itself viewed as a distinct professional discipline despite also drawing upon a variety of other forms of knowledge:

> By analogous reasoning medicine could be carried out by biochemists, anatomists, physiologists, pharmacologists, etc. working together. We would find this ludicrous. Why? Is this because of historical factors or our familiarity with medicine? ... Forensic science uses the scientific knowledge developed in other disciplines, but uses it in different ways to solve the complex and varied problems encountered. The problems and the thought processes necessary to deal with them are distinctly different. No other science is concerned with the process of individualization, for example. (De Forest 1998: 2)

Other commentators, such as Allan Jamieson of the Forensic Institute, also reflected on the nature of the forensic scientific profession. In a later editorial in *Science & Justice* Jamieson wrote:

> One of the hallmarks of a profession, as opposed to a skilled trade, is the degree to which the professional routinely makes decisions on the basis of expertise and ability in complex situations where there may be no, or little, previous history. For example, although a lawyer dealing with a particular case may have dealt with similar cases before, the circumstances will not be identical to those previously encountered and he will have to make decisions on how best to handle the case in hand, based on expertise, experience and applied intelligence. The degree to which these decisions require the bringing together of rules, knowledge and intelligence, determine the separation of the skilled manual worker from the professional worker. (Jamieson 1999: 71)

In this editorial, Jamieson also suggested that forensic science was 'yet to achieve an identity' (Jamieson 1999: 71). Jamieson, however, drew attention to the use of the term 'forensic practitioner' as a means of including scientists within a broader group of workers who might be subject to NVQ accreditation, putting together scientists with technical operatives:

> By including Scenes of Crime Officers, Fingerprint Officers and similar (most employed by the Police) that have few widely recognized professional measures and can be encompassed in the term 'forensic practitioner', a lever is found to engage similar competence tests in the professional scientific areas. (Jamieson 1999: 71)

It is worth noting, however, the distinction made between 'skilled workers' and 'professions' and how NVQs are seen to apply to the former but not the latter. One can detect here contested lines being drawn over the nature of forensic work. Other professions, such as medicine and law, Jamieson claimed, had been reluctant to embrace forms of accreditation such as NVQs or competency testing. In the editorial Jamieson asserted that forensic scientists should be regarded as professionals due to their cognitive abilities, which he saw as being irreducible to manual technical skills:

> What makes the scientist an expert is not their mechanical skill, but the ability to use scientific method and knowledge to deliver an opinion on the support that particular physical evidence gives to a hypothesis. ... Given the requirement of the scientist as an expert in assessing and delivering opinion on evidence, is it then necessary that they should know how to do these manual things? (Jamieson 1999: 72)

Jamieson's words here suggest a boundary of professionalization being drawn around laboratory scientists. The label of 'forensic practitioner' is here considered a misnomer, and it is suggested instead that scientists display a distinct skill set compared to other forensic workers.

Jamieson also expressed suspicion that the competency testing regime was a tool of commercial organizations to push an agenda of increased throughput for the sake of profit. In doing so he questioned whether the apparent desire of large forensic organizations to train scientists 'in weeks rather than months' was consistent with the status of a profession (Jamieson 1999: 71).

Jamieson ended this editorial by advocating further reflection about what made forensic science a 'profession'. Yet one can also detect here a certain desire for differentiation within the forensic community:

> What I am advocating is that we determine the key features that make forensic science a profession and not a trade. That forensic scientists (you know who you are, even if managers struggle with the definition) stand up and identify themselves as professionals; *distance themselves from those who are not.* (Jamieson 1999: 72, emphasis added)

One can only speculate what is meant by 'distancing', although it could suggest a differentiation between scientific 'professionals' and manually skilled 'practitioners'.

Efforts to accredit forensic practitioners in England and Wales exhibit a chequered history. The Council for the Registration of Forensic Practitioners (CRFP), instituted in 1999, attempted to collate a single register of practitioners and to establish a unifying code of practice. It was, however, largely perceived to be a failure (Kershaw 2009), being wound up in 2006 due to a lack of support from its key stakeholders, which included the

MPS and the Home Office. The CRFP was largely unknown to its key intended end users, namely, the legal profession. Perhaps fatally for the CRFP, registration was not mandatory. The assessment process for CRFP involved an indirect, paperbased system and was not equipped to produce direct evidence of practitioner competence. The CRFP procedure was criticized for being haphazard, poorly managed with delays and blighted by poor communication (Kershaw 2009).

Opinions continue to be expressed among members of the forensic community about the extent to which individual competence can be assessed. As an experienced Regulator observed, this issue may become directly linked with notions of 'professionalism':

> How good is this person at their job? Are they fit to practise, at least to the threshold standard? Are they fit to do that today? Organizational quality systems need to address issues of places, processes and people. For the 'people' part, what is needed, but is rarely offered in traditional approaches, is a method of assuring the current competence of individual practitioners that seeks not to tick boxes but to assess the individual's approach to the sequence of thoughts and actions that make up the professional process. Professionalism is about a great deal more than the ability to complete a set series of tasks. It is about the ability to relate apparently unconnected facts, thoughts and concepts derived from different sources. It encompasses the willingness and the capacity to think beyond the immediate task in hand and outside received patterns. It is driven, above all, by a passion for the truth. (Kershaw 2009: 553)

Forensic science encompasses a potentially wide series of practical and cognitive activities. Yet establishing an agreed notion of 'professionalism' in forensic science remains a subject of debate.

## Conclusion

In its earlier days, forensic science in the UK was employed in a very reactive fashion, and there appears to have been at times some rather loose conceptions of 'expertise', if Stuart Kind's recollection of his fire examination case is representative. The early days of the FSS seem marked by personal rivalries and isolation which were not addressed until the emergence of the FSSoc. The trappings of a scientific discipline (journals, a learned society, conferences, etc.) may have strengthened the status and identity of forensic science in the UK. Recent engagement with other leading scientific societies, such as the Royal Society and the Royal Statistical Society (see Roberts and Aitken 2014) also indicates a degree of recognition from the wider scientific community. Yet while the emergence of bodies like CSFS and its activities suggest a maturing field, the existence of other organizations like the BAFS also indicates that different claims to the identity of forensic science possibly endure.

The historical outline described in this chapter suggests a difficult fit for both functionalist and "neo-Weberian" approaches. The functionalist preoccupation with scientific rationality is challenged by the way in which forensic science emerged. Functionalism regards science as the core of professionally mediated social progress, controlling the application of knowledge 'to social order (law) [and] effectiveness in governmental and private collectives (administration)' (Brante 1988: 121). While the UK Government provided a significant impetus in promoting forensic science via a network of laboratories, the kind of 'expertise' offered to police forces sometimes seemed rather questionable. A clearly 'rational' epistemological core seems therefore to have been lacking from some early forensic practices. Even in the contemporary age, epistemological differences exist among some forensic practitioners, with some advocating 'conditional' statistical approaches for interpreting evidence, while others have espoused the virtues of personal experience (Biedermann et al. 2012; Bodziak 2012). That forensic science, and earlier forensic medicine, has at times been marked by intense personal rivalries suggests a lack of collegiality which might puzzle functionalists.

More recent debates involving definitions of 'forensic practitioners' versus 'scientists' suggest the possible drawing of professional boundaries which might instead support a "neo-Weberian" thesis. The account presented here also, however, poses problems for "neo-Weberian". The latter views the emergence of professions as a process of inclusion and exclusion, of clear 'winners' and 'losers'. Looking back over the recent history of forensic science, it is difficult to ascertain any clear victors. While some techniques gained predominance over others and some, such as anthropometry, have faded from view, a wide variety of forensic disciplines continue to exist, all potentially able to contribute to criminal justice. Even fingerprinting, whose status as an epistemologically robust forensic technique has been challenged in recent decades, remains a widely used form of evidence. The decision by the AAFS to widen its definition of forensic science to include social and behavioural sciences runs counter to the neoWeberian emphasis on exclusivity. Today forensic organizations appear to co-exist relatively peaceably.

That is not say that scientific claims are not potentially subject to socially mediated processes of acceptance or rejection. This, of course, is a routine aspect of court proceedings (see Chapter 6). But the winners and losers in cases may be highly case dependent. Having evidence accepted in one court case does not guarantee subsequent success in another (Lawless 2013). Courtroom decisions are unpredictable and may confound those with a strictly scientific background. Understanding the way in which forensic 'winners' or 'losers' are determined poses a challenge to sociological theories of professions. These decisions are made not by forensic scientists but shaped by lawyers and judges, who are placed effectively on the outside of forensic science looking in, albeit obscured by the potentially selective presentation of evidence and their own legal, rather than scientific, training.

Attempts to standardize and regulate forensic science via an external gaze differ somewhat from academic research science, where norms of best practice tend to emerge internally from expert communities, however construed. While difficulties have emerged in efforts to accredit forensic science, the advent of the Forensic Science Regulator, as described in Chapter 4, indicates a continuing desire to introduce more standardization.

While forensic science continues to debate its own professional identity, it may remain vulnerable to external interventions in the name of standardization, as suggested by Jamieson (1999). Sociological research indicates that the notion of 'professionalism' is increasingly subject to appropriation by organizations seeking greater standardization (Evetts 2011). This research suggests that an interest in measuring and demonstrating 'professionalism' may lead to increased auditing and monitoring practices within the workplace and vice versa. 'Thus, managerial demands for quality control and audit, target setting and performance review become reinterpreted as the promotion of professionalism' (Evetts 2011: 412). This kind of work suggests that the notion of 'professionalism' could potentially be conflated with regimes of standardization.

Across the UK, the state has far from retreated from intervening in forensic science. Chapter 4 explores more recent developments in forensic policy across the UK.

## Notes

1 However, as Chisum and Turvey (2007) pointed out, it should not be mistakenly regarded as the world's first forensic science laboratory, which appears to have been the French Institut de médecine legale de Paris, established in 1868. They use the term 'police crime laboratory' to differentiate Locard's establishment from the first forensic science laboratories, which were private, specialized and often housed in university departments. They take Locard's establishment to be a police crime laboratory in the sense that it was the first to be housed explicitly under the auspices of law enforcement and staffed by law enforcement agents (Chisum and Turvey 2007).
2 The AAFS and IAI display broadly similar functions. Historically, however, the IAI appears to have represented the interests of a defined 'identification profession'. It is notable that this profession was assumed to have been preordained, representing those employed in police laboratories involved in investigative work. The AAFS, on the other hand, appears to have had its sights originally aimed at the courtroom, emphasizing in the beginning interactions between science and lawyers.

## Bibliography

Ambage, N.V. (1987) *The Origins and Development of the Forensic Science Service 1931–1967*. PhD thesis, University of Lancaster.

American Academy of Forensic Sciences. (2015) 'Homepage', online at: http://www.aafs.org/ (accessed 12 August 2015).

Anon. (1997) 'Jobs for the boys', *Science & Justice*, 37 (3): 160.

Biedermann, A., Taroni, F. and Champod, C. (2012) 'How to assign a likelihood ratio in a footwear mark case: an analysis and discussion in the light of *R v T*', *Law, Probability and Risk*, 11 (4): 259–277.

Bodziak, W.J. (2012) 'Traditional conclusions in footwear examinations versus the use of the Bayesian approach and likelihood ratio: a review of a recent UK appellate court decision', *Law, Probability and Risk*, 11 (4): 279–288.

Brante, T. (1988) 'Sociological approaches to the professions', *Acta Sociologica*, 31 (2): 119–142.

Burney, I. and Pemberton, N. (2010) 'The rise and fall of celebrity pathology', *British Medical Journal*, 341 (7786): 1319–1321.

Burney, I. and Pemberton, N. (2011) 'Bruised witness: Bernard Spilsbury and the performance of early twentiethcentury forensic pathology', *Medical History*, 55 (1): 41–60.

Chartered Society of Forensic Sciences. (2014) 'About Us', online at: http://www.forensicscience society.org.uk/AboutUs (accessed 24 October 2014).

Chisum, W.J. and Turvey, B.S. (2007) *Crime Reconstruction*. Burlington, MA: Elsevier Academic Press.

Cole, S.A. (1998) 'Witnessing identification: latent fingerprinting and expert knowledge', *Social Studies of Science*, 28 (5–6): 687–712.

Cole, S.A. (2001) *Suspect Identities: A History of Fingerprinting and Criminal Identification*. Cambridge, MA: Harvard University Press.

Collins, H. (1985) *Changing Order: Replication and Induction in Scientific Practice*. Chicago: University of Chicago Press.

De Forest, P.R. (1998) 'Proactive forensic science', *Science & Justice*, 38 (1): 1–2.

Emerson, V.J. (1995) 'Forensic science: the past, the present and the future', *Science & Justice*, 35 (2): 151–155.

Emsley, C. (2008) 'The birth and development of policing', in T. Newburn (ed.), *Handbook of Policing*. Cullompton, UK: Willan, pp. 72–89.

European Network of Forensic Science Institutes. (2014) 'About ENFSI', online at: http://www.enfsi.eu/aboutenfsi (accessed 24 October 2014).

Evetts, J. (2011) 'A new professionalism? Challenges and opportunities', *Current Sociology*, 59 (4): 406–422.

Field, K.S. (1998) *History of the American Academy of Forensic Sciences: Fifty Years of Progress 1948–1998*. West Conshohocken, PA: ASTM International.

Gieryn, T. (1983) 'Boundary work and the demarcation of science from non-science: strains and interests in professional ideologies of scientists', *American Sociological Review*, 48 (6): 781–795.

GOV.UK. (2015) 'Forensic Science Regulator', online at: https://www.gov.uk/government/organisations/forensicscienceregulator (accessed 12 August 2015).

International Association of Identification. (2015) 'History of IAI', online at: http://www.theiai.org/history/ (accessed 21 May 2015).

International Society for Forensic Genetics. (2014) 'About', online at: http://www.isfg.org/About (accessed 12 August 2015)

Jamieson, A. (1999) 'Let me through, I'm a ummmm ...', *Science & Justice*, 39 (2): 71–72.

Kershaw, A. (2009) 'Professional standards, public protection and the administration of justice', in J. Fraser and R. Williams (eds), *Handbook of Forensic Science*. Cullompton, UK: Willan, pp. 546–571.

Kind, S. (1999) *The Sceptical Witness*. Newcastle Upon Tyne: Hodology Limited.

Lawless, C.J. (2013) 'The lowtemplate DNA profiling controversy: biolegality and boundary work among forensic scientists', *Social Studies of Science*, 43 (2): 191–214.

Lees, R.F. (1997) 'Random thoughts of a nonscientist', *Science & Justice*, 37 (3): 207–209.

Mawby, R.C. and Wright, A. (2008) 'The police organization', in T. Newburn (ed.), *Handbook of Policing*. Cullompton, UK: Willan, pp. 224–252.

Merton, R.K. [1942] (1973) *The Sociology of Science: Theoretical and Empirical Investigations*. Chicago: University of Chicago Press.

National Research Council. (2009) *Strengthening Forensic Science in the United States: A Path Forward*. Washington, DC: National Academies Press.

Newburn, T. (ed.) (2008) *Handbook of Policing*. Cullompton, UK: Willan.

Parry, N. and Parry, J. (1977) 'Social closure and collective social mobility', in R. Scace (ed.), *Industrial Society: Class, Cleavage and Control*. London: Allen & Unwin, pp. 110–121.

Parsons, T. (1964) *Essays in Sociological Theory*. New York: Free Press.

Pereira, B. (1995) 'Women and the development of forensic science', *Science & Justice*, 35 (3): 223–230.

Rawlings, P. (2008) 'Policing before the police', in T. Newburn (ed.), *Handbook of Policing*. Cullompton, UK: Willan, pp. 47–71.

Roberts, P. (1996) 'What price a free market in forensic science services? The organization and regulation of science in the criminal process', *British Journal of Criminology*, 36 (1): 37–60.

Roberts, P. and Aitken, C. (2014) *Practitioner Guide No. 3: The Logic of Forensic Proof: Inferential Reasoning in Criminal Evidence and Forensic Science*. London: Royal Statistical Society.

Roux, C. and Robertson, J. (2009) 'The development and enhancement of forensic expertise: higher education and inservice training', in J. Fraser and R. Williams (eds), *Handbook of Forensic Science*. Cullompton, UK: Willan, pp. 572–601.

Stockdale, R. (1997) 'Exploding myths', *Science & Justice*, 37 (2): 139–142.

Turner, R.F. (1948) 'The first American medicolegal congress', *Journal of Criminal Law and Criminology*, 39 (1): 104–110.

Uberlaker, D.H. (2011) 'The forensic sciences: international perspectives, global vision', *Journal of Forensic Sciences*, 56 (5): 1091–1093.

Viscount Runciman of Doxford. (1993) *Report of the Royal Commission on Criminal Justice*. London: Her Majesty's Stationery Office.

Ward, J. (1993) *Origins and Development of Forensic Medicine and Forensic Science in England, 1823–1946*. PhD thesis, Open University.

Williams, R. (2008) 'Policing and forensic science', in T. Newburn (ed.), *Handbook of Policing*. Cullompton, UK: Willan, pp. 760–793.

Willis, S. (2009) 'Forensic science, ethics and criminal justice', in J. Fraser and R. Williams (eds), *Handbook of Forensic Science*. Cullompton, UK: Willan, pp. 523–545.

Wyatt, D. (2014) 'Practising crime scene investigation: trace and contamination in routine work', *Policing and Society*, 24 (4): 443–458.

# 4 Forensic and biometric policy in the UK

## Introduction

Chapter 3 provided an outline of how forensic science in the UK and elsewhere has been organized through communities of practitioners. In doing so, the previous chapter explored how these groups have helped shape the professional and epistemic identity of forensic practice. UK forensic science has also, however, been concertedly scrutinized by governments, parliaments and policymakers. This chapter provides an updated chronology of forensic policy in England and Wales and, more recently, the devolved administration in Scotland. This takes in a number of developments. Forensic science in England and Wales has been subject to a degree of marketization of provision. A number of Commissioners and Regulators have been instituted to oversee aspects of forensic science and biometric technology. A series of parliamentary inquiries have, however, been critical of successive UK governments. By providing an overview of these interventions, this chapter maps a fragmented policy landscape and questions to what extent it is possible to characterize a clear and instrumental UK imaginary.

## Marketizing forensics

In 1987, a Home Office–commissioned survey conducted by accountants Touche Ross concluded that police management of scientific support was 'generally poor' (Touche Ross 1987). It portrayed an environment in which the range of forensic techniques available to police had significantly developed but where science had not been systematically utilized to address rises in serious crime. Touche Ross recommended the appointment of managers of scientific support in each force, to oversee the provision of all scientific services and the management of their own forensic science budgets. This step represented one sign of the growing devolution of budget responsibilities to operational law enforcement actors. Touche Ross also considered the scope for changes in the method of funding and organization of the FSS, the primary external provider of forensic science to the police at the time. The FSS was then a state agency, publicly funded by a central grant.

Forensic science in England and Wales became subject to a government gaze which promoted 'economy', 'efficiency' and 'effectiveness' (Home Office 1983), similar to that imposed on other public services. This so-called new public management encouraged an 'ethos of business management, monetary measurement and value-for-money' (Garland 2001: 116). Market competition was framed as a means of improving the provision of forensic science in terms of motivating providers to improve the efficiency of their work in terms of, for example, turnover of analyses and to reduce casework backlogs.

DOI: 10.4324/9781003126379-4

As discussed in Chapter 3, the 1993 Royal Commission on Criminal Justice addressed issues concerning forensic science. The Commission recognized the emergent policy discourses surrounding the possibility of market reform of forensic science. It offered 'cautious endorsement' (Roberts 1996: 41) of the further development of free market competition for forensic services. The Commission also recognized the growth in the number and variety of private firms offering scientific support to both prosecution and defence which reflected concerns about how the quality of forensic science could be maintained (Roberts 1996).

As the 1990s progressed, other private forensic science providers (FSPs) began to emerge in direct competition with the FSS, such as LGC, Scientifics Ltd and Forensic Alliance. During the same period, the FSS introduced productbased charging, where each 'product', such as a body fluid search, tool mark examination or cannabis identification, was defined as encompassing a wider set of activities. This new definition of product as activity was intended to more closely reflect the actual work performed, 'thus providing customers with a better understanding of the true costs of services and enabling them to make informed judgements about their value' (National Audit Office 1998: 30). As the pricing strategies of forensic service providers became more sophisticated, signs emerged that police forces were capitalizing on the new market conditions.

Some of the assertions about the benefits of an emerging marketplace were supported in the McFarland review of the FSS (McFarland 2003). The McFarland review addressed the 'effectiveness of the organization in meeting the needs of the criminal justice system in terms of the quality, timeliness and cost effectiveness of its services' (McFarland 2003: 3.1). McFarland reported that communication between the FSS and the police had improved and claimed the FSS was able to better educate police officers about the value of certain forms of evidence. McFarland also assessed the management and business structures of the FSS in the light of possible increased competition for forensic science services. FSPs were, at this time, offering volume discounts and loyalty schemes, which assured McFarland that a 'truly competitive market' was 'beginning to develop' in UK forensics (McFarland 2003: 3.3). The review argued that the introduction of 'best value' principles 'had encouraged the police to seek better value for money in the boughtin services' (McFarland 2003: 3.3) and that the police had become 'informed customers', playing off 'suppliers against each other' (McFarland 2003: 3.3). Police reported that they had begun to receive 'a more personalized and responsive service' from suppliers, which was interpreted as meaning that competition had started to yield the kind of benefits claimed by advocates of marketization, such as 'greater choice, value for money and improved service delivery' (McFarland 2003: 3.3).

A marketplace for forensic science in England and Wales emerged which encompassed a diverse array of FSPs with considerable variance in terms of their size, scope and product range (Fraser 2003). In 2005, the status of the FSS changed. It became a 'Government company', or 'Govco', still stateowned but obliged to run on a forprofit basis. The 'Govco' status was intended to be temporary, ahead of full privatization, but this process was never completed. A 2005 inquiry conducted by the House of Commons Science and Technology Select Committee (2005) expressed concern over the lack of independent oversight for this move.

The 2005 Commons inquiry also recommended regulation of the emerging forensic marketplace. The FSS faced increased competition at this time from the varied field of private FSPs. The position of Forensic Science Regulator (FSR) was instituted by the Home Office in 2007 in the light of increased liberalization of the forensic marketplace in England and Wales (McCartney and Amoako 2018). The FSR was briefed on 'ensuring the provision of forensic science services across the criminal justice system, and to develop a regime of quality standards, and to provide independent advice to the government and the criminal justice system' (UK Government 2020). The FSR was not, however, tasked with regulating pricing of forensic services or any other economic matters and was not granted any statutory powers when first instituted. The FSR became involved with efforts to accredit in-house police laboratories and external providers. The latter were accredited in accordance with international standards, but in-house laboratories run within police forces were not subject to the same regime.

In late 2009, it was reported that the FSS was experiencing severe financial difficulties and had become dependent on government assistance. By this time the FSS had implemented a 'transformation programme' which included the closure of three of its regional laboratories. The announced full closure of the FSS by the UK government in December 2010 was nonetheless unexpected. The decision stimulated considerable controversy, with many expressing fears about the future viability of police scientific support. Two inquiries were conducted by the House of Commons Science and Technology Select Committee in 2011 and 2013. These focused on the state of the forensic market in England and Wales, with the first of these specifically addressing the closure of the FSS (House of Commons Science and Technology Select Committee 2011a, 2013).

The 2011 inquiry found that the police were increasingly investing in their own laboratories. The overall size of the market was reported to be in serious decline, perceived to be caused in part by increased inhousing, with spending on external FSP services markedly decreasing (House of Commons Science and Technology Select Committee 2011a). Some respondents to the inquiry pointed out that forces may have viewed insourcing as a cheaper option in the light of wider budget cuts (House of Commons Science and Technology Select Committee 2011a). The Commons Committee criticized the trends toward in-sourcing. Such a shift, with police customers effectively becoming competitors to external providers, was viewed as undermining the very idea of a fully functioning market for forensic science. The Committee also reported 'almost unanimous alarm' (House of Commons Science and Technology Select Committee 2011a: 35) about the quality of forensic science performed in police laboratories, which were not subject to the same accreditation procedures as those of external FSPs. The inquiry asserted that this risked 'the introduction of bias based on selective forensic examination of exhibits, arising from the need to make savings' (House of Commons Science and Technology Select Committee 2011a: 43). The inquiry concluded by expressing concerns 'about the risks to impartiality of forensic evidence produced by non-accredited police laboratories' (House of Commons Science and Technology Select Committee 2011a: 43). A reliance on insourced forensic practitioners was seen to increase the risk of evidence collection being influenced by immediate policing concerns rather than working in the more balanced interests of justice.

The 2011 and 2013 Commons Committee inquiries also heard how FSPs had become subject to ever more complicated procurement regimes in the form of the National Forensic Framework Agreement (NFFA) and the later National Forensic Framework Next Generation (NFFNG). These differentiated forensic products in a manner which allowed many English police forces to pick and choose them from different providers (Lawless 2011). The increased complexity of procurement arrangements was, however, viewed as disadvantageous by some FSPs during the 2013 inquiry. According to one FSP, Forensic Access, different forces required services to be delivered in slightly different ways. A representative of another, Cellmark, claimed that 'some product specifications have become too complex in an attempt [...] to provide flexibility and attribute specific costs against each activity at a very detailed level' (House of Commons Science and Technology Select Committee 2013: para. 23). FSP representatives claimed that the

NFFNG had led to multiple protocols for specific pieces of evidence. The NFFNG broke down forensic tests into many more pricing points. Under this system, FSPs had to charge forces on the basis of specific practices that together constituted a specific forensic test. Each price point referred to a specific activity. The CEO of LGC reported that:

> We have some cases where a particular test that we are doing previously had four or five pricing points; there are now as many as 25 or 30. (House of Commons Science and Technology Select Committee 2013: Ev19, Q104)

Contributors to the 2013 Commons inquiry perceived NFFNG to have imposed a significant administrative burden. FSPs reported that it had increased the complexity of 'working out exactly what it is we are doing and what we should be charging' (House of Commons Science and Technology Select Committee 2013: 15). Concerns were expressed that the NFFA and NFFNG eroded a sense of partnership between the police and forensic scientists. The NFFA was reported as having maximized the 'commodification and disaggregation of supply' (House of Commons Science and Technology Select Committee 2011a: 22), with a number of different providers handling different tests in a single investigation. This, it was claimed, prevented the systematic exchange of 'contextual information and scientific results' (House of Commons Science and Technology Select Committee 2011b). The NFFA was perceived to have reduced the ability of scientists to use their initiative in the course of investigations, giving more relative power to the police. One witness to the 2011 inquiry alleged that all too often the police took the cheaper option in favouring basic analytical tests over the interpretive skills of forensic scientists: 'Getting a DNA profile does not necessarily solve a crime but is a lot cheaper than interpretation of how the DNA got there, which is the more important aspect of successfully solving a crime' (House of Commons Science and Technology Select Committee 2011a: 22). During the 2013 committee inquiry, another witness suggested that commercial arrangements hindered a balanced holistic approach to the interpretation of evidence:

> They would bring together all the evidence – the DNA evidence, the blood pattern evidence if it was there and so on – and interpret that in the round in the context of the defence and prosecution propositions. They are not doing that now. Because the DNA element of it is outsourced, you simply cannot bring that together and do that more rounded analysis. (Kenny, quoted in House of Commons Science and Technology Select Committee 2013: Ev4, Q12)

As the 2010s progressed, concerns grew over the increasing fragmentation of forensic provision in England and Wales. Before the advent of the NFFA and NFFNG, FSPs had been able to work together to agree on the best strategy for each case (House of Commons Science and Technology Select Committee 2013). FSPs were in a position to advise police on the choice of examinations and forensic tests that might progress a criminal investigation. As well as perceived to be more effective, the 'partnership approach' was viewed as having facilitated considerable trust between FSPs and the police. A representative of LGC perceived that NFFA and NFFNG had, in contrast, 'created a transactional customer/supplier relationship' (House of Commons Science and Technology Select Committee 2013: Ev82). This latter relationship was also seen to have eroded trust between FSPs and the police, with the seeming perception on the part of the police that 'forensic providers just want to do more work so that they get more money' (Tully, quoted in House of Commons Science and Technology Select Committee 2013: Ev3, Q9).

Forensic services nonetheless came to be regarded as now 'more focused on requirements of police forces' (House of Commons Science and Technology Select Committee 2013: para.111). An LGC representative reported that forensic scientists no longer worked alongside police forces to determine the strategy to be applied to a particular case. Instead, LGC had increasingly been asked 'to do particular tests which [its] forensic scientists may not be able to see the full context of' (Richardson, quoted in House of Commons Science and Technology Select Committee 2013: Ev19, Q107).

The shortterm nature of contracts was viewed as extremely disruptive for FSPs. A representative of the FSP Manlove Forensics stated that the procurement arrangements did not oblige forces to provide guarantees 'as to the actual volume of work each successful provider will ultimately receive' (House of Commons Science and Technology Select Committee 2013: para. 21). It was reported that successful FSPs often had 'a very short length of time to ramp up' (Tully, quoted in House of Commons Science and Technology Select Committee 2013: Ev9, Q45) for 'what are often huge amounts of work' (House of Commons Science and Technology Select Committee 2013: para. 21). The arrangements were viewed as precluding appropriate planning:

> Until they have been awarded the contract, they [FSPs] cannot gear up to do the work, because it often requires new people, new equipment, and so on. (Tully, quoted in House of Commons Science and Technology Select Committee 2013: Ev9, Q45)

Other firms losing work had to 'downsize very rapidly to minimize unnecessary overheads once the work has gone' (Science and Technology Select Committee 2013: 14). FSPs were experiencing 'large swings in workloads' which was regarded as 'very destabilizing' (House of Commons Science and Technology Select Committee 2013: 14). LGC, for example, lost out on tenders to competitors after investing significantly in capacity and personnel. While FSPs were obliged to undergo accreditation, slow progress was made within police laboratories to accredit common techniques such as fingerprint analysis (House of Commons Science and Technology Select Committee 2013).

## Biometrics: widening scrutiny

Around the same time, the roles of the UK Biometrics Commissioner (UKBC) and Surveillance Camera Commissioner (SCC) were brought into being by the 2012 Protection of Freedoms Act (PoFA; these two roles are discussed further in Chapters 7 and 8). Briefly, the UKBC became statutorily responsible for making decisions over whether to retain DNA and fingerprints from persons arrested in connection with certain offences. The primary role of the SCC was to ensure police had regard to a specific Code of Conduct for Surveillance Cameras and attendant technologies including facial recognition systems. In 2021 these two roles were combined into a single position, the UK Biometrics and Surveillance Camera Commissioner.

Previous UKBC postholders went beyond their statutory role to express opinions about other forms of biometric data and emerging technology in annual reports, evidence to parliamentary inquiries and in other outlets such as official websites. A notable example concerns facial data and recognition systems. UKBC postholders expressed concern about the retention of facial images from arrested persons, and the lack of police activity to delete data (Office of the Biometrics Commissioner [OBC] 2019). Concerns were also expressed about the emergence of facial recognition technology and the ways in which these systems were trialled and deployed by police (see Chapter 8). The emergence of machine learning was raised as a potential barrier to judicial scrutiny in UKBC statements (OBC 2018b). UKBC postholders were also openly critical of claims made by technology producers and functional over-reach (Policy, Ethics and Life Sciences Research Centre 2017). In 2020 the Office of the UKBC issued an opinion on the UK Government's track and trace system to monitor COVID-19, urging a consideration of retention periods for individual personal data (OBC 2020). SCC postholders were at times critical of the UK Government's approach to facial recognition (see Chapter 8).

A 2015 inquiry, *Current and Future Uses of Biometric Data and Technologies*, again conducted by the House of Commons Science and Technology Select Committee, addressed wider developments. It pointed to three perceived trends: the 'growth of unsupervised biometric systems, accessed via mobile devices, which verify identity … the proliferation of "second-generation" biometric technologies that can authenticate individuals covertly' and 'the linking of biometric data with other types of "big data" as part of efforts to profile individuals' (House of Commons Science and Technology Select Committee 2015: 3). The Committee expressed concern over the seeming silence of the UK Government regarding ethical and legal matters, particularly relating to privacy and autonomy, and assessed risks and benefits for individuals (House of Commons Science and Technology Select Committee 2015). While noting the revocation of some initiatives such as the identity card scheme and the destruction of the National Identity Register, the Committee claimed that use of biometrics had expanded in areas such as immigration and law enforcement:

> If the Government is to build public trust in biometric data and technologies, there is a need for open dialogue and greater transparency. We therefore recommend that the Government sets out how it plans to facilitate an open, public debate around the use of biometrics. (House of Commons Science and Technology Select Committee 2015: 3).

The Committee criticized the delay of a formal strategy for biometrics and called for the publication of such a biometrics strategy by no later than December 2015. Before this, the Home Office published a separate *Forensic Science Strategy* in March 2016. This proposed a statutory role for the Forensic Science Regulator, a police review of the case for moving fragmented provision into a Joint Forensic and Biometric Service, ongoing oversight of the health of the supply chain of forensic services, and pledged to work more closely with public research organizations to identify new opportunities for forensic science (Home Office 2016).

The *Forensic Science Strategy* was, however, strongly criticised. The House of Commons Science and Technology Select Committee (2016) claimed there had been 'evident failure to consult widely on the Strategy, and that it was too narrowly focused on police needs and interests' (House of Commons Science and Technology Committee 2016: 3). The Committee claimed that the plans for a Joint Forensic and Biometric Service lacked detail, particularly in the absence of a published biometrics strategy which would only emerge in June 2018 (see The Inquiries Continue). The Committee also criticized future procurement plans which allowed greater agency for individual forces, stating it was 'vague about how the intended locally-negotiated … procurement approach for police forces commissioning from the private sector will deliver the "more consistent national approach"' (House of Commons Science and Technology Select Committee 2016: 3). The Committee saw a similar lack of detail in the proposals for greater engagement with public sector research, seeing 'no mechanism for setting national forensic research priorities', and regarded as inadequate data-sharing efforts to identify research requirements (House of Commons Science and Technology Select Committee 2016: 3). Finally, the delay in granting the FSR statutory powers was criticised. The Committee questioned the *Forensic Science Strategy*'s overall fitness for purpose, regarding it merely as a 'plan to produce a strategy' rather than reflecting any substantive foresight (House of Commons Science and Technology Select Committee 2016: 3). The perceived failings of the *Forensic Science Strategy* were regarded as particularly serious given the difficulties experienced by the UK forensic market and concerns over the status of commercial forensic providers.

The FSR repeatedly raised concerns about the state of the forensic marketplace throughout the decade. In her 2017 annual report, the Regulator described the forensic landscape as a mix of commercial providers of varying sizes and in-house police provision. This report discussed the vulnerabilities of commercial FSPs to a changing and shrinking market and competitive procurement processes. The Regulator argued that driving down prices had risked providers exiting the market and compromising the quality of provision. Risks were envisaged in terms of an eroding skills base and shortages of qualified practitioners in areas such as toxicology (FSR 2018). The report also described the sudden loss of trading on the part of some providers and how such uncontrolled exits risked loss of data and chains of custody.

The FSR also identified issues concerning digital forensics, which came to be regarded as a key type of forensic analysis for which demand had grown among English police forces relative to other methods such as DNA and fingerprints (McCartney and Amaoko 2018). Accreditation of digital forensic providers emerged as a concern, given the potential for poor practice; for example, in terms of insecure data storage (fieldwork 2019).

While there were notable delays in police laboratories gaining accreditation, small providers, sole traders or so-called micro-providers were also slow to be accredited (McCartney and Amaoko 2018). Cost was regarded as a key barrier to accreditation in these smaller providers, and concerns were expressed that lack of accreditation had left some small providers out of touch with scientific developments (McCartney and Amaoko 2018). Crime scene examination represented another problem for the Regulator's accreditation plans.

## Transforming Forensics

Separately, police bodies instituted Transforming Forensics, described on the National Police Chief's Council (NPCC) website as a programme to design and build 'world leading and sustainable' forensic services (NPCC 2021). Transforming Forensics is overseen by the Police Reform and Transformation Board (House of Lords Science and Technology Committee 2019) and received £30 million from the Police Transformation Fund between April 2018 and March 2020. Transforming Forensics is intended to assist with meeting strategic aims such as the *Forensic Science Strategy* and to anticipate technological developments in areas such as DNA and digital forensics. It seeks to address the fragmentation of forensic support and emphasizes a need to develop a national network of forensic capability and collective support for practitioners. Transforming Forensics is also intended to help stabilize the forensic marketplace (House of Lords Science and Technology Committee 2019).

A Forensic Capability Network was framed as a central feature (Ashworth, cited in House of Lords Science and Technology Committee 2018) knitting together a central team and infrastructure to integrate capabilities, speak with a single voice on the forensic marketplace and research and development, pursue accreditation more efficiently and improve procurement practice.

It was claimed that Transforming Forensics was intended to link with private providers and academia (Ashworth, cited in House of Lords Science and Technology Committee

2018). Others, however, criticized this programme for an overly narrow focus on police rather than private providers (House of Lords Science and Technology Committee 2019) and that it diverted funds away from the latter to the former (Schudel, cited in House of Lords Science and Technology Committee 2019). UK police forces have not been mandated to take part in Transforming Forensics. Instead, it has been claimed that forces have had to be persuaded to take part (House of Lords Science and Technology Committee 2019). Transforming Forensics was considered by a 2019 Lords inquiry (see The Inquiries Continue) to have not adequately addressed fragmentation of forensic provision (House of Lords Science and Technology Committee 2019).

## The inquiries continue

A 2018 inquiry on biometric strategy and forensic services conducted by the House of Commons Science and Technology Select Committee again raised concerns about the state of the forensic market and acknowledged the actual or near collapse of some forensic providers. Around this time one major provider, Key Forensic Services, entered administration and had to be rescued by the police. This inquiry also raised the issue of an incident at Randox, a commercial forensic provider where it was found that 1,000 blood samples for drug testing had been tampered with. This inquiry repeated concerns about the level of accreditation among forensic laboratories and called on the UK Government to review the sustainability of the market.

The Committee also called for the revision of the 2016 forensic strategy and noted the delay in the publication of the biometrics strategy. The Committee paid particular attention to the issue of deleting custody photographs of persons arrested but subsequently not convicted of any offence. The inquiry was critical of the lack of an automated deletion facility for custody images for non-convicted persons and called for such plans to be outlined in the biometrics strategy. The Committee saw automated facial recognition as possibly advantageous for policing but also highlighted concerns about reliability and possible discrimination and bias (see Chapter 8). 'The forthcoming Biometrics Strategy should consider how image databases should be managed and regulated, potentially by a dedicated "Regulator" or by the Biometrics Commissioner with an extended remit' (House of Commons Science and Technology Select Committee 2018: 4).

The Home Office *Biometrics Strategy* was finally published in June 2018. This document focused mainly on three specific forms of biometrics: DNA, fingerprints and facial data. While voice data was also acknowledged, the role and status of other biometrics was less clear. The strategy outlined the re-organization of existing information flows to provide a more centralized means of distributing biometric data to responsible parties within the Home Office system to meet law enforcement and immigration objectives. This was regarded as ameliorating what had been regarded as a reactive and ad-hoc approach to biometric data. The *Biometrics Strategy* justified the centralization and rationalization of biometric data by claiming it would lead to increased transparency and 'increase confidence that legal standards and ethical implications have been taken into account as new uses are developed. This will include ensuring that services have in-built safeguards so that only necessary and proportionate access to biometric data is allowed, for specific roles and purposes' (Home Office 2018: 7).

The *Biometrics Strategy* emphasized the claimed efficiencies of a single biometrics platform. The claimed benefits for law enforcement and border control officials included a reduction in the need 'for people to go to custody to have their fingerprints checked and is helping identify, *much more rapidly*, suspects, offenders, those who are unlawfully in the UK and even people who have been seriously injured in public places' (Home Office

2018: 9, emphasis added). The *Strategy* claimed that visa applicants would experience 'an improved customer service and *faster processing* for lower risk customers' (Home Office 2018: 9, emphasis added).

The *Biometrics Strategy* also claimed that the Home Office would 'develop options to simplify and extend governance and oversight of biometrics through consultation with stakeholders over the next 12 months' (Home Office 2018: 13). A new oversight and advisory board was proposed 'to coordinate consideration of issues relating to law enforcement's use of facial images and facial recognition systems' (Home Office 2018: 14). The *Strategy* claimed that this board would represent views of a host of existing stakeholders, including the police and the Home Office. Regulatory actors already in place, such as the Surveillance Camera Commissioner, Biometrics Commissioner, Information Commissioner and the Forensic Science Regulator, would 'provide independent advice to the board with regards to legislation and standards', together with the involvement of the Biometrics and Forensics Ethics Group (BFEG), an independent group of experts who advise the Home Office (Home Office 2018: 14). While discussing governance and oversight involving existing actors, the *Biometrics Strategy* was criticized by the UKBC for not proposing any new legislation to govern the use of biometric data (OBC 2018a).

The *Biometrics Strategy* could nonetheless be considered an imaginary of sorts. It promised a re-organization of certain biometric data forms to allow them to be used more efficiently to transform certain Home Office functions relating to law enforcement, immigration and nationality system applications. The *Biometrics Strategy* also embedded a series of Regulators and bodies within this imaginary, regarding them as key to overseeing the stated reforms (Lawless 2021).

In 2019 the House of Commons Science and Technology Select Committee conducted another inquiry, this time into the work of the UK Biometrics Commissioner and the FSR. This inquiry was again strident in its criticism of the perceived inactivity of the UK Government, stating that the forensic market was worsening and criticising the lack of activity on legislation to bestow statutory powers to the FSR. The Committee also acknowledged an incident involving Eurofins, a provider who suffered a cyber-attack and paid a ransom to unlock frozen data (House of Commons Science and Technology Select Committee 2019). This had a serious impact on forensic toxicology capacity, given that Eurofins was responsible for approximately 90 per cent of this work for English and Welsh police forces. The Committee reported that other providers were unable to step in to assist with this work.

This inquiry was also highly critical of the now-published *Biometrics Strategy*, claiming it 'was not worth the five year wait. Arguably it is not a "strategy" at all: it lacks a coherent, *forward looking vision* and fails to address the legislative vacuum that the Home Office has allowed to emerge around new biometrics' (House of Commons Science and Technology Select Committee 2019: 20, emphasis added).

The Committee, however, favourably compared the approach taken by the devolved Scottish Government (discussed in The Scottish Biometrics Commissioner):

> The UK Government should learn from the Scottish Government's approach to biometrics and commission an independent review of options for the use and retention of biometric data that is not currently covered by the Protection of Freedoms Act 2012. The results of the review should be published along with a Government Response, and a public consultation on the Government's proposed way forward should follow. This process should culminate in legislation being brought forward that seeks to govern current and future biometric technologies. (House of Commons Science and Technology Select Committee 2019: 3)

This inquiry once again raised the issue of deleting custody images of non-convicted persons and noted a lack of resources to manually identify and delete such images, as well as a lack of awareness among police to review such images every six years. This inquiry called for a moratorium on automated facial recognition until concerns over possible bias and effectiveness could be resolved and raised concerns over innocent persons images being used on watchlists. 'No further trials should take place until a legislative framework has been introduced and guidance on trial protocols, and an oversight and evaluation system, has been established' (House of Commons Science and Technology Select Committee 2019: 4).

The House of Lords Science and Technology Committee conducted its own inquiry into forensic science in 2018–19. This inquiry focused on a wide range of issues including the powers of the FSR, oversight and strategy, the state of the UK forensic marketplace, relations between stakeholders, legal engagement with science and technology, and digital forensics (House of Lords Science and Technology Committee 2019). The inquiry's final report made a number of recommendations, including an arms-length forensic science board 'responsible for the coordination, strategy and direction of forensic science in England and Wales' (House of Lords Science and Technology Committee 2019: 13), which would work with a wide array of stakeholders and 'aim to promote proper understanding of forensic science in the criminal justice system' (House of Lords Science and Technology Committee 2019: 13). The House of Lords Science and Technology Committee (2019) also recommended that the role and capabilities of the FSR be expanded to include 'responsibility for regulating the market.' (para. 72). Statutory powers for the FSR were also recommended, including the power to take enforcement action against forensic providers found to be non-compliant with quality standards (House of Lords Science and Technology Committee 2019). The House of Lords Science and Technology Committee (2019) also recommended that legal advocates undertake training in the use of scientific evidence in court and basic scientific principles. Finally, the Committee recommended a National Institute for Forensic Science be created to coordinate and direct forensic science research and development.

Draft legislation to grant the FSR statutory powers had existed for some time in the form of Private Member's Bills. Debating such a bill was, however, subject to delays. The Forensic Science Regulator Act was, however, finally passed in 2021. This Act obliges the Regulator to draft a code of practice, approved by the home secretary and parliament and subject to review. The legislation grants the Regulator considerable scope to identify actors to whom they regard the code applies. The Regulator is now able to issue compliance notices to those who they believe are in breach of the code, which prohibits further forensic science activity to be carried out (Act 6(4)) until the Regulator is satisfied compliance has been met. This includes the power to issue injunctions (Act 6(7)).

The House of Commons Science and Technology Select Committee held a follow-up hearing in 2021, featuring the outgoing FSR and UK Biometrics Commissioner. This heard that digital forensic activity, while now recognized as a priority area, suffered from numerous backlogs and delays. Toxicology was also singled out as exhibiting a lack of capacity. The former UKBC opined that 'the framework of governance for the police use of biometrics simply has not kept up with the development of new biometrics' (Wiles, quoted in House of Commons Science and Technology Select Committee 2021, Q26: 10). Police and the Home Office were also criticized for not developing a 'proper evidence base' or cost–benefit framework for the use of biometrics. The Home Office was additionally criticized for failing to update biometric and police databases and for failing to 'grasp the strategic significance' of emerging biometric technologies (Wiles, quoted in House of Commons Science and Technology Select Committee 2021, Q26: 10). Once again the Committee raised concerns about the ongoing lack of accreditation among police laboratories.

## The Scottish Biometrics Commissioner

As noted by the 2019 Commons inquiry, the Scottish Government had begun to pursue a distinct approach to biometric governance to the rest of the UK (Lawless 2021). Biometric data in Scotland are subject to a separate legal system and devolved oversight through the Scottish Government and a separate parliament based in Edinburgh. The administration has powers to address law enforcement matters separate from Westminster. In 2016 Her Majesty's Inspectorate of the Constabulary Scotland (HMICS) 'identified a need for improved legislation and better independent oversight around the police use of biometrics in Scotland' (HMICS 2016: 8). The HMICS proposed a Scottish Biometrics Commissioner (SBC) to independently oversee biometric databases and records held in Scotland and to anticipate future technological developments (HMICS 2016). On behalf of the Scottish Government, an Independent Advisory Group (IAG) was formed, including representatives from the legal system, policy and academia. The IAG addressed the use and retention of biometric data. It sought to establish an 'ethical and human rights based framework' which could be applied to 'existing, emerging and future biometrics' (Scottish Government 2018: 4). In March 2018 the IAG reported and made numerous recommendations. The IAG agreed with the need for an SBC and a code of practice to govern police use of biometrics. The IAG saw this as a response to potentially rapidly evolving technology which did not require constant legislation (Scottish Government 2018).

Draft legislation subsequently followed. The Scottish Parliament passed the Scottish Biometrics Commissioner Act in March 2020 with 110 votes in favour and none against. The first SBC was announced a year later. The Act requires the SBC to draft a code of practice with which Police Scotland, the sole national force, has to comply. The Act provides for a formal complaints procedure in the event of alleged police misuse of biometric data. When drafting the code, the SBC is legally obliged to consult with representatives from the Scottish Government, law and policing, the Information Commissioner, the Scottish Human Rights Commission and the Commissioner for Children and Young People in Scotland (Scottish Parliament 2020b). The Act also requires the SBC to be assisted by an advisory group. Under the legislation, the code applies only to police agencies. It does not, however, apply to other users of biometric systems such as local authorities, private actors or the Scottish Prison Service. This is despite the private provision of biometric systems being made evident during an earlier parliamentary inquiry into the legislation (Scottish Parliament 2019b). The role of private sector providers of biometric systems in this regime may, however, evolve. The Act allows the SBC to consult with 'such other persons' they consider 'appropriate' in the formation of the code (Scottish Parliament 2020b: 10(1)). This allows but does not compel the SBC to engage with the private sector, and the latter are not directly obligated to comply with the code. Police Scotland may be ultimately responsible for compliance if they were to contract out biometrics provision. The SBC Act obliges review of the code at regular intervals, although it is more flexible on when it should be revised.

The SBC Act represents a notably different vision of biometric oversight compared to elsewhere in the UK. This legislation appears intended to apply to and pre-empt technological developments. This contrasts with England and Wales, in which the use of biometric systems has sought to be justified with recourse to a series of pre-existing pieces of legislation. As Chapter 8 details further, however, this has made technology such as facial recognition vulnerable to legal challenges. The SBC Act is, however, largely centred on the police. Relationships between the SBC and other actors, such as commercial biometrics providers, private users and public institutions such as prisons, health providers or schools, could evolve in the future, but at time of writing this remains to be seen. It should be noted that the Scottish Parliament has addressed biometrics and digital data in other channels (Scottish Parliament 2019a, 2020a). The SBC legislation was scrutinized by the Scottish Parliament's Justice Committee (Scottish Parliament 2020a). The Justice Sub-committee on Policing also held inquiries into the use of digital forensics and facial recognition technology by Police Scotland (see Chapters 8 and 9; Scottish Parliament 2019, 2020b). It is conceivable that these committees may wish to hold the SBC accountable, and it is highly likely that the Scottish Parliament as a whole will do so. The SBC could be joined by developments elsewhere in the UK. In July 2020 the Northern Irish Justice Minister announced a consultation on its own Biometrics Commissioner (Northern Ireland Executive Department of Justice 2020).

## Conclusion

This chapter has traced a recent history of forensic and biometric policy and oversight in the UK. It has done so in order to outline the current landscape in which forensic science and biometric systems are embedded. This is a landscape which contains within it commercial providers, in-house police laboratories and a number of Regulatory bodies with varying powers and responsibilities. It is a landscape which has been scrutinized by a series of parliamentary inquiries, in both Westminster and devolved administrations. While this kind of science and technology shapes political thinking about law, security, rights and ethics, to name but a few concerns, policies have also intervened in the operation and deployment of forensics and biometrics. The UK context is particularly instructive given the contentious promotion of market-based forms of forensic provision in England and Wales. Here it is possible to discern the impact of certain policies on scientific practice. Marketization was claimed to improve the efficiency of scientific work and to provide police customers with more choice. This era, however, saw the loss of the FSS, once the largest and considered the leading provider. Parliamentary inquiries and other fora have heard how marketized arrangements led to a fragmentation of provision, which hindered collaboration between scientists to analyze evidence holistically. In-house police provision was seen as risking bias in forensic analysis. In more recent times, a number of strategies and plans have been published. It remains to be seen to what extent these visions reflect policing and scientific realities.

Over time, biometrics as construed in wider terms has overlapped with policy debates about forensic science, reflecting the potential of technology to intersect with a wider series of domains other than law enforcement. Differing approaches to the oversight of biometrics are evolving across different parts of the UK. The UK Government has proposed a *Biometrics Strategy* which seeks to develop a common technical platform and acknowledges the roles of a range of regulatory bodies and groups. No new legislation has been enacted, other than the Forensic Science Regulator Act, which may strengthen some powers. Scotland has, however, pursued a distinct vision, passing specific legislation to institute its own Biometrics Commissioner tasked with overseeing police use of data via a code of practice. This approach differs in that it seeks to anticipate new technological developments, rather than justifying them with recourse to existing legislation, as the UK Government has done in the case of facial recognition. The Northern Ireland Executive may also pursue its own path in the future.

Over time an array of actors, strategies, rules and regulations has evolved which has served to shape forensic science and biometric technology across the UK. This landscape only partially reflects responses to advances in science and technology. It is also partly the product of specific ideologies, such as that of 'new public management', and the role of the private sector. Distinct visions for biometric governance can be discerned in England

& Wales and Scotland in the form of the Home Office *Biometric Strategy* and Scottish Biometrics Commissioner, respectively. Rather than reflecting a unified, instrumental governmental vision, forensic and biometric policy is distributed across a range of different actors, who possess differing agencies, powers and standpoints. Forensic and biometric policymaking is negotiated and contested across these networks and encompass different ways in which science and technology is perceived.

A more holistic view of forensic science must, however, take into account other standpoints, such as the professional experiences of forensic practitioners. The next chapter takes a finer-grained view of forensic casework.

## Bibliography

Amankwaa, A.O. and McCartney, C. (2019) 'The UK National DNA Database: implementation of the Protection of Freedoms Act 2012, *Forensic Science International*, 284: 117–128.

Forensic Science Regulator. (2018) *Annual Report November 2016–November 2017*. Birmingham: Forensic Science Regulator.

Forensic Science Regulator. (2019) *Annual Report November 2017–16 November 2018*. Birmingham: Forensic Science Regulator.

Forensic Science Regulator. (2020) *Codes of Practice and Conduct for Forensic Science Providers and Practitioners in the Criminal Justice System Issue 5*. Birmingham: Forensic Science Regulator.

Fraser, J. (2003) 'Delivery and evaluation of forensic science', *Science & Justice*, 43 (3): 249–252.

Garland, D. (2001) *The Culture of Control: Crime and Social Order in Contemporary Society*. Oxford: Oxford University Press.

Her Majesty's Inspectorate of the Constabulary in Scotland. (2016) *Audit and Assurance Review of the Use of the Facial Search Functionality Within the UK Police National Database (PND) by Police Scotland*. Edinburgh: Her Majesty's Inspectorate of the Constabulary in Scotland.

Home Office. (1983) *Manpower Effectiveness and Efficiency in the Police Service*. Home Office Circular 114. London: Home Office.

Home Office. (2016) *Forensic Science Strategy: A National Approach to Forensic Science Delivery in the Criminal Justice System*. London: Home Office.

Home Office. (2018) *Biometrics Strategy: Better Public Services Maintaining Public Trust*. London: Home Office.

House of Commons. (2021) *Forensic Science Regulator and Biometrics Strategy Act*. London: Her Majesty's Stationery Office.

House of Commons Science and Technology Select Committee. (2005) *Forensic Science on Trial: Seventh Report of Session 2004–5*. London: Her Majesty's Stationery Office.

House of Commons Science and Technology Select Committee. (2011a) *The Forensic Science Service: Seventh Report of Session 2010–12*. London: Her Majesty's Stationery Office.

House of Commons Science and Technology Select Committee. (2011b) 'Written Evidence Submitted by Professor T. J. Wilson', online at: http://www.publications.parliament.uk/pa/cm201012/cmselect/cmsctech/855/855vw79.htm (accessed 12 August 2015).

House of Commons Science and Technology Select Committee. (2013) *Forensic Science: Second Report of Session 2013–14*. London: Her Majesty's Stationery Office.

House of Commons Science and Technology Select Committee. (2015) *Current and Future Uses of Biometric Data and Technologies: Sixth Report of Session 2014–15*. London: Her Majesty's Stationery Office.

House of Commons Science and Technology Select Committee. (2016) *Forensic Science Strategy. 4th Report of Session 2016–17*. London: Her Majesty's Stationery Office.

House of Commons Science and Technology Select Committee. (2018) *Biometric Strategy and Forensic Services: Fifth Report of Session 2017–19*. London: Her Majesty's Stationery Office.

House of Commons Science and Technology Select Committee. (2019) *The Work of the Biometrics Commissioner and The Forensic Science Regulator: 19th Report of Session 2017–19*. London: Her Majesty's Stationery Office.

House of Commons Science and Technology Select Committee. (2021) *Oral Evidence: Biometrics and Forensics: Follow-Up*. 30 June 2021.

House of Lords Science and Technology Committee. (2018) *Corrected Oral Evidence: Forensic Science*. 4 October 2018.

House of Lords Science and Technology Committee. (2019) *Forensic Science and the Criminal Justice System: A Blueprint: 3rd Report of Session 2017–19*. London: Her Majesty's Stationery Office.

Lawless, C. (2011) 'Policing markets: the contested shaping of neoliberal forensic science', *British Journal of Criminology*, 51 (4): 671–689.

Lawless, C. (2021) 'The evolution, devolution and distribution of UK biometric imaginaries', *BioSocieties*. First published 5 May 2021. doi:doi:10.1057/s41292-021-00231-x.

McCartney, C. and Amoako, E.N. (2018) 'The UK Forensic Science Regulator: a model for forensic science regulation?', *Georgia State University Law Review*, 34 (4): 945–981.

McFarland, R. (2003) *Review of the Forensic Science Service*. London: Her Majesty's Stationery Office.

National Audit Office. (1998) *The Forensic Science Service*. London: Her Majesty's Stationery Office.

National Police Chief's Council. (2021) 'Transforming Forensics', online at: https://www.npcc.police.uk/NPCCBusinessAreas/ReformandTransformation/Specialistcapabilitiesmain/SpecialistCapabilitiesProgrammeTransformingForensi.aspx (accessed 6 July 2021).

Northern Ireland Executive Department of Justice. (2020) 'Long Announces Consultation on Biometric Proposals', 3 July 2020; online at: https://www.justice-ni.gov.uk/news/long-announces-consultation-biometric-proposals (accessed 27 August 2021).

Office of the Biometrics Commissioner. (2018a) 'Biometrics Commissioner's response to the Home Office Biometrics Strategy', 28 June 2018; online at: https://www.gov.uk/government/news/biometrics-commissioners-response-to-the-home-office-biometrics-strategy (accessed 27 August 2021).

Office of the Biometrics Commissioner. (2018b) *Commissioner for the Retention and Use of Biometric Material: Annual Report 2017*. London: Her Majesty's Stationery Office.

Office of the Biometrics Commissioner. (2019) *Commissioner for the Retention and Use of Biometric Material: Annual Report 2018*. London: Her Majesty's Stationery Office.

Office of the Biometrics Commissioner. (2020) *Biometrics Commissioner Statement on the Use of Symptom Tracking Applications*, 21 April 2020; online at: https://www.gov.uk/government/news/biometrics-commissioner-statement-on-the-use-of-symptom-tracking-applications (accessed 3 October 2020).

Policy, Ethics and Life Sciences Research Centre. (2017) 'Securitization and Forensic Genetics', Northumbria University, 24 March 2017, online at: https://www.ncl.ac.uk/peals/research/forensicgenetics/#seminar5, accessed 3 October 2020.

Roberts, P. (1996) 'What price a free market in forensic science services? The organization and regulation of science in the criminal process', *British Journal of Criminology*, 36 (1): 37–60.

Scottish Government. (2018) *Independent Advisory Group on the Use of Biometric Data in Scotland*. Edinburgh: Scottish Government.

Scottish Parliament. (2019a) *Report on Police Scotland's Proposal to Introduce the Use of Digital Device Triage Systems (Cyber Kiosks)*. Justice Sub-committee on Policing. 1st Report, 2019 (Session 5). Edinburgh: The Scottish Parliament.

Scottish Parliament. (2019b) *Scottish Biometrics Commissioner Bill Stage 1 Report*. Edinburgh: The Scottish Parliament.

Scottish Parliament. (2020a) *Facial Recognition: How Policing in Scotland Makes Use of This Technology*. Justice Sub-committee on Policing. 1st Report, 2020 (Session 5). Edinburgh: The Scottish Parliament.

Scottish Parliament. (2020b) *Scottish Biometrics Commissioner Act*. Edinburgh: The Scottish Parliament.

Surveillance Camera Commissioner. (2019) *The Police Use of Automated Facial Recognition Technology with Surveillance Camera Systems*. London: Her Majesty's Stationery Office.

Touche Ross. (1987) *Review of Scientific Support for the Police*. London: Home Office.

UK Government. (2020) 'Forensic Science Regulator', online at: https://www.gov.uk/government/organisations/forensic-science-regulator (accessed 3 October 2020).

# 5 Reconstructing a reconstructive science
Probability and performativity in forensic investigation

### Reflections on the epistemological identity of forensic reasoning

The history of forensic science and criminal investigation is marked by numerous claims made about their epistemological status. Variously descriptive and/or prescriptive, some claims have sought to define forensic activity in terms of specific notions of the 'scientific method'. In some cases, the alignment of criminal investigation with scientific ideals may have reflected a certain reforming intent (Gross [1893] 2016). Early pioneers, such as the French police scientist Edmond Locard, made claims about the supposedly unique character of forensic scientific reasoning. One of the most wellknown early examples is Locard's 'exchange principle':

> The principle is this one. Any action of an individual, and obviously, the violent action constituting a crime, cannot occur without leaving a mark. What is admirable is the variety of these marks. Sometimes they will be prints, sometimes simple traces, and sometimes stains. (Locard 1934: 7–8)

Although Locard extensively catalogued the analysis of evidential materials, it is not clear whether he conducted experiments that directly demonstrated the veracity of the exchange principle. While Locard's 'exchange principle' may be epistemologically questionable, it continues to be taught on training courses for crime scene examiners who appear to have readily accepted and even internalized Locard's claims (Williams 2007; Wyatt 2014).

A desire to isolate the unique epistemological character of forensic science possibly reflects interests in establishing an image of scientific credibility. Professor Paul Kirk of the University of California, Berkeley, is regarded as another influential figure. His 1963 paper, 'The Ontogeny of Criminalistics', proclaimed it to be the 'science of individualization' ('criminalistics' being a term sometimes used to describe the analysis of trace evidence; Kirk 1963: 236). Since then, discussions of the cognitive and ratiocinative character of forensic science have often centred on particular philosophical interpretations of the scientific method (Williams 2008). For example, Jamieson (2004) sought to frame forensic science as congruent with the hypotheticodeductive method, proceeding via the formulation, testing and possible elimination or acceptance of hypotheses.

Other contrasting claims have been made concerning the epistemological nature of forensic reasoning. Some of these relate to the concept of philosophical *abduction*, which is frequently associated with Charles Sanders Peirce and often affiliated with philosophical pragmatism (Eco 1983; Truzzi 1983; Nordby 2000). Peirce differentiated between three different forms of reasoning: deduction, induction and abduction. The first of these is generally taken to involve arguments in which the premises are claimed to support a

DOI: 10.4324/9781003126379-5

conclusion in such a way that it is impossible for the premises to be true and the conclusion false (Hurley 2000). Induction, on the other hand, involves an argument in which the premises are claimed to support a conclusion in such a way that it is improbable for the premises to be true and yet the conclusion false.

Abduction is often regarded as a less clearly defined notion, but Walton (2004) cited three key characteristics. First, abduction may be thought of as a means of narrowing down a multiplicity of alternative explanations for an event by selecting one or a few particular hypotheses. Second, it can be conceived of as a process of guessing or choosing the right guess – a fallible process in which wrong hypotheses can be chosen as often as correct ones. Third, it is often involved when a new phenomenon is observed which is unable to be explained by current scientific understandings. On this basis it can be summarized that abduction generally involves the assessment, on the basis of observable signs, of an inferential hypothesis which can account for the observations, which may then be tested in some way to determine the extent of its explanatory power.

Abductive reasoning has been associated by some with applications of Bayes' theorem, an interpretation of probability theory regarded as a means of updating belief in the light of new data (Lipton 2004; Jackson et al. 2006). Discussions concerning the application of statistics and probability in legal reasoning date back at least to the early 1960s (Ball 1961; Finkelstein and Fairley 1970; Tribe 1971). Around the same time, the increased use of statistics, including Bayes' theorem, was being advocated within the US forensic science community as a means of improving the robustness of criminalistics techniques.

Some commentators advocated that applications of probability theory be adopted to help underpin a 'new paradigm' in forensic science, to bring it closer to accepted notions of conventional scientific propriety (Saks and Faigman 2008). In the UK, Bayes' theorem received continued attention as a basis for advancing epistemic reform in forensic science and practice (Evett and Joyce 2005). Bayesian reasoning was portrayed as promoting a more rigorous and conditional approach to the interpretation of forensic evidence. This was sometimes contrasted with the seemingly categorical, binary logic of older forensic practices in areas such as fingerprint analysis (Broeders 2006).

The use of Bayes' theorem was promoted in the UK through the work of Ian Evett and colleagues in the Interpretation Research Group at the Forensic Science Service (FSS; Evett 1986, 1987). This group became interested in the possibilities for Bayes' theorem to facilitate more robust means of testing hypotheses concerning criminal cases.

In England and Wales, the use of Bayes' theorem, however, suffered a setback via the appeal court verdict in the case *R v T*, heard in October 2010, where Bayesian methods used to assess the significance of a footwear print were ruled inadmissible (R v T [2010]). The alleged lack of transparency of reasoning and of a 'sound basis' upon which to make assessments were cited as reasons for rejecting this evidence (Hamer 2012). The *R v T* decision was controversial among the forensic community as it effectively discouraged expert witnesses from testifying in court using probabilistic terminology. It was perceived by some as a return to more subjective claims to expertise and something of a retrograde step given attempts to promote statistical methods in UK forensic science (fieldwork 2014).

The *R v T* court decision exerted a certain impact on the way experts could testify in court, but it did not blunt a desire among the forensic community to utilize the Bayesian approach in investigations, if not necessarily for courtroom testimony. Bayesian reasoning was defended in academic literature (Aitken 2012; Biedermann et al. 2012; Nordgaard and Rasmussen 2012) and continued to be promoted by statisticians to the legal community in England and Wales (Roberts and Aitken 2014). The 'likelihood approach' influenced by Bayes' theorem has continued to influence forensic science and practice.

Bayesian reasoning has been influential in promoting a more balanced form of evidence interpretation where both hypothetical prosecution and defence positions are taken into account. The rise of Bayesian methods also shaped working relations between forensic scientists and their chief clients, the police. Bayesian methods emphasize greater clarity for the kinds of questions police may wish to ask about evidence in relation to an investigation (interviews with Home Office representatives 2010, 2014). This led to changes to paperwork accompanying submissions of material to forensic scientists.

While more sceptical attitudes towards Bayes' theorem have been apparent in certain parts of the world such as the United States (Bodziak 2012), the theorem has nonetheless helped shape the modern disciplinary identity of forensic science to a significant degree, particularly in the UK, Europe and Australasia (Hamer 2012).

The emergence of Bayes' theorem in forensic science was accompanied by assertions that the central defining activity of the latter is best characterized as 'the interpretation of [scientific] results in the *individual context of each case*' (Barclay and McCartney 2007: 1, emphasis added). Such expressions align with the development of general principles to guide the course of forensic investigations (see, for example, Ribaux and Talbot Wright 2014).

The case assessment and interpretation (CAI) framework sought to introduce a more systematic, unified approach to forensic investigation through a set of guidelines for the evaluation and interpretation of evidence. CAI, based on Bayesian principles, emerged via the work of the FSS Interpretation Research Group during the early 1990s. It aimed to provide a more accountable framework for forensic reasoning, using statistical methods to evaluate hypotheses pertaining to criminal investigative casework. CAI was developed to identify the most promising lines of inquiry that could be pursued through certain evidential analyses. This aspect of CAI was a response to the growing budgetary devolution occurring in police forces at the time and hence reflected an imperative to streamline the resources of both forensic scientists and their chief 'customers', the police (Lawless and Williams 2010). CAI has been influential in both the UK and across Europe (interview with forensic scientist in Republic of Ireland 2010). The Association of Forensic Science Providers (AFSP), a group of private forensic firms and police organizations based in the UK and Republic of Ireland, endorsed CAI principles (AFSP 2009). In Europe, the European Network of Forensic Scientific Institutes (ENFSI) promoted guidelines for evaluative reporting similar to CAI concepts (ENFSI 2015). CAI has been the subject of numerous peerreviewed journal articles, and related methods have found their way onto the curricula of forensic science degree programmes.

However, the manner in which CAI has been used in actual casework merits further scrutiny. Precisely how has Bayes' theorem been used in forensic practice?

The following sections seek to illuminate this question through a further exploration of CAI, drawing upon a number of resources, including scientific articles from peerreviewed journals and published interviews. The following sections also utilize a number of qualitative semistructured interviews and group discussions conducted between 2006 and 2014. Respondents included forensic scientists working in the UK and the Republic of Ireland. This included consultations with two highly experienced forensic scientists (here forensic scientists 1 and 2) who had been involved with numerous highprofile criminal cases. These respondents had been involved with the development of Bayesian reasoning frameworks.

The next section introduces the rationale of CAI and key elements of the framework before describing issues arising from its use in casework practice. In doing so, it is possible to identify issues of significance for forensic science and sociology alike.

## Forensic science and Bayesian reasoning

CAI was formulated to guide the formation of sets of propositions to attempt to account for a specific investigation. CAI sought to meet two aims: first, to enable scientists and investigators to make more robust, testable and transparent judgments in the course of police casework and, second, to enable police clients to preassess the potential utility a particular scientific analysis might add to their investigations. This was originally intended to enable the police to make informed choices over how they allocated their forensic science budgets and marked a conscious attempt to help provide greater value for money (Lawless and Williams 2010).

CAI frames evidence interpretation as a collaborative course of action involving consultation and input from forensic practitioners from the outset. This approach was contrasted with an older, policeled model of investigation, in which suspects were identified through nonforensic means, with the collection and deployment of forensic evidence largely being informed by a concern to incriminate suspects (interview, forensic scientist 2 2008). This prosecutorial model was viewed as dangerously subjective and unscientific. Bayes' theorem was regarded as improving forensic reasoning by providing a mathematical framework for testing subjective intuitions:

> Interpretation is, of course, a part of everyday life and it is possible to visualize a kind of spectrum. At one extreme there is pure intuition, which defies rational analysis. At the other extreme is pure logic. Scientific judgement cannot be based on pure intuition or 'hunch' ... the scientist should, as far as possible, be able to rationalize the opinion that is presented. The opinion might be supported by data: there is, indeed, a kind of data spectrum ranging from the case where the opinion rests largely on an established data collection to the case at the other extreme where there are no data and the opinion is entirely based on experience. In any case, the expert opinion is necessarily subjective, but it should always conform to logical principles. Those principles are furnished by considering probability theory as a means of reasoning under uncertainty: this leads to the Bayesian view of evidence interpretation. ... (Evett et al. 2000: 234)

In this context, Bayesianism was framed as embodying certain key principles informing the correct practice of evidence interpretation:

- Interpretation of scientific evidence is carried out within a framework of circumstances, dependent on the *structure* and *content* of the framework.
- Interpretation is *only meaningful* when two or more competing propositions are addressed.
- The role of the forensic scientist is to consider the probability of the evidence *given* the propositions that are addressed. (Evett et al. 2000: 235, emphasis added)

CAI authors argued that the primary role of the forensic practitioner in a criminal investigation was to consider the repertoire of claims and allegations of investigators, advocates and witnesses which together comprise the framework of circumstances in which the practitioner operates (Cook et al. 1999). Construction of such a framework of circumstances was regarded as a necessary prerequisite for the development of propositions relevant to the evidence and the case. CAI authors stressed the need for scientists to take a 'balanced view' of each case, in line with what they regard as the principles of 'the Bayesian view of evidence, that it is not sensible for a scientist to attempt to concentrate on the validity of a particular proposition without considering at least one alternative' (Cook et al. 1998b: 153). At each stage of the process, scientists are obliged to consider two competing propositions, most commonly relating to a proposition relevant to a prosecution hypothesis and another relevant for a defence hypothesis. This involves identifying precisely what kind of propositions should be assessed. In some cases, the proposition of interest may appear to be somewhat removed from the crime under investigation, possibly relating to the investigation of the origins of transfer evidence; for example, 'these fibres came from this garment'. Such a proposition may relate to the crime due to the wider framework of circumstances. For example, the fibres in question may have been recovered from the scene of an apparent burglary. Subsequently, a possible suspect may be arrested wearing a garment which might match with the fibres recovered from the scene. Forensic scientists may wish to determine how significant any match may be, particularly if the garment in question is unusual or rare.

In older models of investigation, forensic evidence was only identified and analyzed if it was regarded as contributing toward the construction of a case against an individual already suspected by the police. The decision to carry out particular forensic tests was often the preserve of police officers themselves, who may have perceived certain items of evidence as yielding incriminating forensic information, regardless of their specific level of scientific understanding. CAI obliged investigators, however, to take a more neutral and balanced view of evidence, requiring them to consider defence and prosecution hypotheses in order to generate likelihood ratios (LRs). The generic LR formula is typically derived in the following way:

**Posterior probability** (Probability of a hypothesis given evidence)
= **Prior probability** (Probability of hypothesis) × Probability of evidence given hypothesis
Or, in mathematical terms:

$$P(H|E) = P(H) \times P(E|H)$$

In a forensic context, two hypotheses pertaining to prosecution (Hp) and defence (Hd) positions are considered using the Bayesiantype formula:

$$\frac{P(Hp|E) = P(Hp) \times P(E|Hp)}{P(Hd|E) = P(Hd) \times P(E|Hd)}$$

The ratio P(E|Hp)/P(E|Hd) is the *likelihood ratio* (LR). LRs can provide an indication of whether a piece of evidence favours a prosecution or defence argument P(Hp|E) or P(Hd|E). The generation of LRs involves the formulation of pairs of prosecution and defence propositions:

$$LR = \frac{\text{Probability of the evidence if prosecution proposition is true}}{\text{Probability of the evidence if defence proposition is true}}$$

This form enables the scientist to represent their expectations more precisely. For example, in an assault case it may be necessary to examine an item of a suspect's clothing to determine whether any fibres from the victim's clothing might have been transferred in the course of an assault being carried out. This might lead the scientist to express the following expectation: 'If $x$ numbers of transferred fibres are found, then the prosecution or defence hypothesis is $y$ times more likely'.

Through generating LRs, Bayes' theorem allows reasoners to express probabilistic assertions in terms of measures of belief and enables them to update their beliefs in the light of incoming information. The CAI method further organizes propositions into a hierarchy, classifying them as 'source' (relating to the origin of a piece of evidence), 'activity' (the manner in which that evidence was generated) and 'offence' (the extent to which evidence can indicate ultimate guilt or innocence). Through this system, investigators are able to assess the usefulness of a particular evidential analysis or 'product' (e.g., a DNA test or fibre match analysis) to the course of an investigation. CAI facilitated the use of probability theory to anticipate how much probative weight a specific 'product' may contribute to an investigation.

Level I, or the *source* level, relates to propositions concerning the origins of evidentiary material.[1] For example, a set of Level I propositions could be formulated to consider the origin of blood on the clothes of a suspect under suspicion in an alleged assault case. A prosecution hypothesis would seek to ascertain the probability that the blood came from the victim of an assault. A defence hypothesis may, however, seek to consider the probability that the blood originated from another individual not involved in the assault. In each instance, assessment of the sets of hypotheses at source level is based on strictly scientific observations, measurements and analyses. This may involve blood typing and possible DNA profiling in such a case.

Level II in the hierarchy, the *activity* level, involves a greater element of reconstruction of the events in each case. In the example of the alleged assault, the prosecution hypothesis may consider the probability that a suspect attacked the victim by kicking the latter in the head. The defence hypothesis, meanwhile, may be concerned with the probability that the suspect was *not* present when the victim was kicked in the head or the blood was transferred through nonviolent means. Blood pattern analysis might assist the investigators in addressing such questions.

A key difference between Level I and Level II propositions is that while the former may be addressed via strictly analytical means, Level II propositions cannot be addressed without taking a specific framework of circumstances into consideration (Cook et al. 1998a). The more information a scientist possesses in relation to the circumstances of the case, the more fully activitylevel propositions can be considered and the more bearing insights generated at Level I will have on consideration of Level II propositions. The transition from source to activity level necessitates greater interaction between police investigators and forensic scientists to enable them to generate more meaningful inferences.

The final level in the hierarchy, Level III, or the *offence* level, concerns the probability that a suspect has committed a criminal offence. Level III propositions are the domain of the jury, assisted by the judge (Cook et al. 1998a). Offencelevel propositions may also be construed as activitytype propositions. The key difference concerning the former, however, is that they concern the question of whether an actual crime has occurred. Offencelevel propositions are, however, ultimately beyond the role of the forensic scientist. They remain a theoretical component of CAI, with investigators generally focusing on source- and activitylevel propositions.

## Enacting Bayes' theorem

Applying CAI was regarded by a respondent as beginning right from the outset of an investigation:

> Say we just find a body in a field, what's gone on? How did the body get there? What happened to the body? So the scientist ... would be giving some kind of opinion, an investigative opinion ... as to what went on. So they say, 'Well looking

> at the tracks in the disturbance at the scene, I think the body's been dragged from that position to that position, I then think it's been turned over, you know, and all stuff like that'. (Interview, forensic scientist 1 2006)

At this initial stage, scientists will generally attempt to establish some form of reconstructive knowledge based on observations made of the scene. The respondent describes the scientist's initial evaluations of the scene, which they would then use to reconstruct a possible chain of circumstances that may have led to an incident. CAI allows them to test those evaluations, which may be subsequently supported or not through Bayesian calculations. As the interviewees' comments demonstrate, the ability to make reconstructive inferences in such cases was seen to depend on one's capacity to interpret a variety of visual cues. Another respondent referred to these as 'soft data' (interview, forensic scientist 2 2008). This kind of data may have subjective epistemological groundings, reflecting the experience and standpoint of the individual investigator. Forensic investigators may draw upon their memory of previous investigations of similar cases and also of a more generalized commonsensical life experience. In the following discussion, another forensic scientist recounted an incident in which a girl's body had been found in a ravine:

> I said we can tell the senior investigating officer something important ... because the scratches on the girl's knees were 'round the legs ... the scratches went round like that, and I said to the scientist, she's obviously been upright going down the bank, she's run down there, so that means it's an attack site. If she'd been dead and transported in [a car and the body then dumped in the ravine], and she'd have been dragged down the bank with scratches they would have gone down the length of the leg. (Interview, forensic scientist 2 2008)

The identification of these visual cues and the interrelationships between them at a crime scene may inform the generation of prior probabilities, and subsequently propositions, as investigators attempt to reconstruct a series of events. The recovery of items of possible evidence allows CAI to proceed from source level. Consideration of related propositions allows the scientist to begin to operate using Bayesian methods. However, in the transition to this mode, applying Bayesianism became increasingly problematic.

A key issue at the source level in the hierarchy of propositions concerns the availability of suitable background databases against which to assess the significance of particular pieces of recovered evidence through their frequency within populations of evidential forms (e.g., the recovery of a fibre from a particular manufacturer's garment which may be more or less common among a population of garments). In some cases, such as evaluating the significance of a DNA match, frequencies of genetic material which constitute profile data (alleles) are relatively well established and indeed are considered necessary resources upon which match probabilities are calculated. However, for many other forms of evidence, interviewees argued that the necessary data sets to aid scientists in assessing propositions were often lacking:

> ... we're dealing with likelihoods which is the probability of the evidence given propositions but there's huge areas where there just ain't the data. ... (Interview, forensic scientist 1 2006)

One apparent exception concerned the field of arson investigation. In this case there appeared to have been efforts to establish databases to aid investigators in making inferences regarding the cause of particular fires:

> ... they set their priors from a database of known previous fire causes. ... I can't quote you the figures but what they'll say is that from a known database the previous fires ... twenty per cent are caused by accelerants, twenty per cent are caused by electrical, twenty per cent are caused by smoking or whatever ... so they have a database ... which gives them priors. So it's testable, it's exposed, it's explicit, it can be challenged, but it's explicit, people can see the priors that we are using. Now we are far, far, far from that in other fields. (Interview, forensic scientist 1 2006)

Hence full implementation of Bayesian methods was regarded as being hampered by the absence of data to help generate accurate likelihood estimates. It was stated that in the absence of background data, recourse could instead be given to less explicitly rationalized means of estimating likelihoods:

> ... so people rely on their own experiences, they maybe kick it round with their colleagues and say, 'What do you think about the likelihood of getting this?' (Interview, forensic scientist 1 2006)

Hence, there was great potential for likelihood estimates to be based on a plurality of epistemic groundings. In the absence of standardized data, such estimates could be based on experiential or intersubjective understandings of the significance of evidence based on previous instances. Likelihoods could then be generated in the absence of transparent calculative procedures.

Even where more concrete statistical foundations could be encountered, the application of Bayesian methods faced a series of challenges in terms of constructing propositions. The next section discusses this issue in more detail and describes how potentially intractable issues were resolved.

## Managing ambiguity

The complexities involved in applying Bayesianism to investigation manifested themselves in a number of sources of ambiguity encountered during the process of constructing propositions. First, *intra-propositional* ambiguity concerns the potential semantic uncertainty relating to the wording of propositions. Second, *inter-propositional* ambiguity relates to uncertainty over the most appropriate proposition to address in relation to an activity. This could involve uncertainties over whether two pairs of propositions are actually mutually exhaustive and how they subsequently shape the perceived probative weight of evidence. Finally, *statistical* ambiguity involves uncertainty over the nature of data used to estimate prior probabilities and likelihoods.

*Intra-propositional* ambiguity commonly manifests itself via the use of vague terms in propositions. CAI authors cited the example of the word 'contact' as typical of the kind of phrases open to interpretation (Evett et al. 2000). For example, the phrase, 'Mr Smith had been in contact with broken glass' does not convey precisely what Mr Smith was doing that led him to be in contact. In this case he may have deliberately broken a window or, alternatively, he may have been an innocent bystander, located close to a window when it was broken by someone else:

> I think in everyday language there's more leeway and we probably understand what we mean ... but if we're trying to evaluate evidence, we've got to be very careful to specify the proposition and the alternative, quite crisply, because otherwise it's very

difficult, if not impossible, to assign any probability to the evidence given this woolly proposition. (Interview, forensic scientist 1 2006)

*Intra-propositional* ambiguity often arises through a lack of information at the activity level. If it is difficult to establish the precise series of events, scientists only have recourse to vague terms such as 'contact'.

*Inter-propositional* ambiguity exists where matching propositions are being formulated but where more than one possibility emerged when considering a particular activity based on the evidence. One example discussed in interviews involved the trial of Barry George for the murder of TV presenter Jill Dando and explanations for the presence of firearm discharge residue on the defendant:

> The propositions ... it was the result we've got ... is 'how likely is it to arise if it got into his pocket at the time he fired the weapon that killed Jill Dando' and 'how likely is it to have got into his pocket ... at some other time?' Now that does illustrate my difficulty with the process. One, why is that second proposition the one they used? Why isn't it 'anybody else in the street', why isn't it 'anybody else who has an interest in guns'? (Interview, forensic scientist 2 2008)

This example demonstrates the myriad factors that could be taken into consideration when constructing propositions. Most issues lie with the construction of alternative (generally defenceled) propositions. Prosecution propositions simply needed to account for the probability of a certain suspect committing a particular offence. However, in trying to construct an alternative account of events, any number of factors could be taken into consideration; for example, the timing of an activity. Another example given concerned a burglary:

> Say the guy's accused of burglary and there's a bloodstain at point of entry [a broken window]. He's interviewed and he states, 'No comment'. (Interview, forensic scientist 1 2007)

In this case the scientists were obliged to consider an innocent explanation themselves:

> Our [defence] alternative if we're trying to be at activity level could be to say, 'He's the man who broke the window but that blood there is nothing to do with him, it's someone else'. ... You always set an alternative that he hasn't done the burglary, nothing at all to do with it ... but why doesn't the scientist postulate, 'He didn't break the window but he did cut himself a week earlier and left the blood', and that would then increase the probability of getting a match dramatically but support a defence proposition. (Interview, forensic scientist 1 2007)

*Statistical ambiguity* relates to the intractable difficulties in determining which data to evaluate propositions. The construction of defence propositions in certain ways influences the perceived probative weight of a piece of evidence. This occurs even at source level:

> Let's say a crime was committed, a burglary, but there was a witness to say it was a very young woman in her teens, a young teenager, and the police attend, they find a footwear mark which they believe could be proven that it was the offender's footwear mark. They arrest the suspect, take her shoes, they're submitted and the scientist compares this and says, 'That's a good match, that's a small shoe, it's a woman,

it's a female's shoe and it's really, really unusual that'. So, you know, in the general population it would be unusual. ... But then you say, well let's have a think about this. What is the ... database? What is the alternative? Let's think of the proposition and the alternative. The proposition is this shoe made the mark and the alternative is this shoe didn't make the mark, it was made by the shoe of another young female. So you've conditioned your alternative and you're conditioning then the database because the database is young females who are likely to be in the pool of potential perpetrators. ... So the value of the evidence is not what the scientist first thought, this is a very unusual shoe. Sure, it's a very unusual shoe in the population of burglars, but in the population conditioned on the alternative, which is young females in this area at the time, it may be quite common. (Interview, forensic scientist 1 2006)

Here, the challenge for scientists was to consider whether the shoe match should be compared against a database of all shoes, men's or women's, or whether to compare against a population of women's shoes only. Such a decision influenced the extent to which the shoe match was perceived as significant. Hence, the significance of evidence could be regarded as relative to the kind of database used, which in turn reflected assumptions about gender and criminality.

Statistical ambiguity also related to the potentially intractable difficulties in obtaining specific data to test propositions. The following example describes a case involving the death of an elderly woman in the Netherlands. The woman was found dead in her greenhouse with two stab wounds to the neck, seemingly administered by a pair of scissors. The woman also had a history of substance abuse and had a high concentration of alcohol and diazepam in her system. Her husband, who also had a history of alcoholism as well as minor domestic violence, was placed under suspicion of her murder.

... the main reason why the police charged the husband with murder was that they couldn't see how anybody could accidentally fall and stab themselves in the neck fatally with scissors. ... (Interview, forensic scientists 2 2008)

Three senior forensic scientists, a psychiatrist, a pathologist and a lawyer all deliberated over this case using a Bayesian approach. Considerable difficulty was experienced in agreeing on which alternative propositions to formulate with regard to the case. However, it was felt that a possible alternative to consider was that the woman had died accidentally:

The first thing you do when you look at it is to try and get some figures about how likely it is that you would be stabbed in the neck fatally, or stabbed with scissors anyway ... and how likely you are to accidentally fall and stumble and kill yourself like that. ... (Interview, forensic scientist 2 2008)

Initial figures were obtained which seemed to suggest that a murder had occurred. These statistics indicated that the probability of a murder using scissors was 1 in 10,000 while the probability of an accident was three in four million. When combined, these figures returned a likelihood that indicated it was approximately 133 times more likely to have been murder.

But that's not the right population ... there are only seven hundred murders per year in the UK, so that's the population available for murder by scissors, so it's 1 in 10,000 ... times 700 ... of all murders, ... whereas it's the entire population that's available for falls onto scissors, so if that's three in four million, its 60 million times three in four million. When you work it out, by Bayes it turns out to be, instead of intuitively, that it's much more likely to be murder, *it's actually 640 times more likely to be an accident.* (Interview, forensic scientist 2 2008, emphasis added)

It was possible to question these results. As can be seen, the figures for murder were obtained for the UK, not the Netherlands, the latter having a lower population. Furthermore, the figures relating to accidental death were obtained from the coroner's office in Birmingham. However, the ambiguity became further compounded:

[A colleague] said, 'No, we need to know all 50-year-old plus ladies in the UK, how likely they are to fall'. And at that point we thought ... 'But we can't get that'. Can we? Because that includes all the falls that don't injure anybody, because by definition the ones that do injure somebody enough for them to go to hospital is a subset of that anyway. So it's actually, quite difficult. ...

And [the colleague] was adamant that that wasn't what we wanted to know, we wanted people who don't fall when they are drunk, and we missed that point. Because the alternative is that how likely is she to do that when she's ... fallen when drunk and he wanted to know how likely are you to fall and not injure yourself when you're drunk. And as well as how likely are you to just fall, and so he wants the proposition to be as close to the alternative as relevant ... as possible. (Interview, forensic scientist 2 2008)

This example provides an instance of statistical ambiguity and interpropositional ambiguity. Controversies over data were related to the kind of propositions the team sought to test. A number of other potential factors could have been considered in the analysis, affecting the kind of propositions that could be considered in turn:

Why was she the person who fell on the scissors? Right? As opposed to anybody else? We all found that very difficult ... by then we were definitely going backwards and forwards.

Yes, we probably were influenced by the fact that we could see some of the propositions we weren't going to get data on. And that wasn't sensible, was it? Really, we should have got the propositions right and worried about the data afterwards. ... (Interview, forensic scientist 2 2008)

There came to be a direct interdependence on the type of propositions constructed and the availability of the data. Propositions were formulated after it was determined which data were available, as opposed to agreeing on what propositions to test from the outset in accordance with formal Bayesian method. Hence, the calculations were marked by a notable degree of contingency. Eventually the Bayesian answer suggesting innocence was understood through nonmathematical means:

But if you think about it, you can think of an explanation really easily. I can demonstrate, I *Bayesianized* it. ... So if you think of yourself as tottering about, on your feet, and you trip as you're going through the doorway, you might stick out your hand to hold yourself up, I've got scissors in my hand, I spread my hand to try and catch something, this is an upright of the door frame, and I fall and I turn my head because I can see the blade coming, and I've stabbed myself in the left side of my neck, like that, with the scissor blades open, so my whole weight is going to push them into my neck ... the pathologists were thinking, 'How could you fall?' in, scissors in your right hand, and get stabbed there, with the scissors open, you can't. But, if you think of it that you trip and you open your hand ... you open your hand to support yourself, that does everything that's required ... you turn your head, see how wide apart they are, because she's spread her fingers. (Interview, forensic scientist 2 2008, emphasis added)

The important point to consider is that while Bayes' theorem may have been cited as a guide to reasoning towards an innocent explanation, other more practical modes of reasoning were employed to help establish precisely what happened. What was notable was the observation of the particular type of marks made by the scissors and how this informed a practical reconstruction of events. The forensic scientist in this case understood the Bayesian result through physically reenacting the possible events leading up to the woman's death. Although Bayes' theorem provided guidance to the investigators, suggesting a possible alternative explanation, an embodied, enacted form of reasoning was required to progress the situation.

The respondent's reference to 'Bayesianizing' the case is significant. The use of this term indicated the respondent's desire to shape the case into a 'Bayesian' form. Indeed, the reinterpretation of statistical data provided the original spur to the reinvestigation. Yet while it partially guided them towards a conclusion, other reasoning practices took over. As the other examples also demonstrated, attempts were made to provide the grounding for the application of Bayes' theorem, but this was much more problematic than first anticipated. With manifold intractable ambiguities, Bayesian theory resisted simple application and invited practices which appeared to deviate from what might be considered as appropriate reasoning behaviour but which led from the invocation of Bayesianism.

## Conclusion

The application of Bayesian reasoning to forensic science via initiatives such as CAI denotes a significant attempt to establish a common epistemological identity for forensic science. Certain principles concerning 'Bayesian reasoning' in the context of forensic science appear to have gained acceptance over time. These include the need to formulate explicit probabilistic estimates of belief concerning specific events, the requirement to think in terms of formulating multiple alternative propositions (involving propositions for prosecution and defence arguments), the need to take into account as much relevant information as possible when making calculations and a cautious approach to judgements based on personal intuition and/or subjective experience. These kinds of principles have been repeatedly cited in discussions pertaining to Bayes' theorem and the likelihood approach. These tenets were viewed as directly crucial elements in conveying what it meant to reason in a 'Bayesian' manner. Among its proponents, 'Bayesian reasoning' has generally been valorized ahead of other interpretations of probability theory.

CAI requires investigators to formulate mutually exclusive propositions. This, however, often exposes uncertainties concerning available data and ambiguities in determining which propositions should be formulated and evaluated.[2] In the examples presented here, ambiguities linked to propositions reasoners sought to address were compounded by the tendency for different propositions to skew the LR estimate in different ways. Proposition construction was furthermore influenced by the limitations of available data sets. Constrained by the data available to them, investigators interviewed in this research had to pragmatically modulate the propositions they intended to test. Hypotheses viewed as relevant to cases could not be formulated as the data needed to generate LR estimates were often not in existence. In the absence of data, forensic practitioners had to consider other, more testable propositions. Through applying CAI, investigators, rather than test what were viewed as the ideal propositions, became aware of the propositions that they *could* evaluate through identifying what data were available. Rather than guiding the reasoner in asking the 'right questions' (Evett and Joyce 2005: 37), the enactment of Bayes' theorem made visible which epistemological strategies were available to investigators. When investigators actively sought to evaluate propositions via Bayesian methods, they often employed various forms of subjective and intersubjective agency to circumvent data limitations. This plurality of agency, which included 'soft data' based on personal biographical experience, informal discussions with peers and embodied practice, presented a much more complex picture as conveyed than many theoretical accounts of Bayesian reasoning, which often describe 'subjective belief' in relatively opaque terms. More recently, Kruse's ethnographic study of Swedish crime scene examiners found they incorporated their subjective experience into the Bayesian model they were obliged to use in their work (Kruse 2020).

Rather than simply functioning as a means of calculating the probative potential of evidence, Bayes' theorem appears to play a more complex role in shaping forensic practice. The examples discussed in this chapter suggest that the application of Bayes' theorem does not entail a straightforward process of merely reading off data from a passive world. Instead, the use of 'Bayesian' reasoning, complicated by data constraints and propositional ambiguities, involves the coordination and configuration of various reasoning practices as investigators seek to reconstruct events. For it to occur, 'Bayesian' forensics has to exert a reconfiguration of relations and social arrangements. It shapes subjective and intersubjective agency, invokes the previous experiences of investigators and necessitates embodied performances.

The application of Bayes' theorem to criminal investigation could be said to exhibit a significant degree of performativity. The concept of performativity has for some time attracted philosophical and sociological attention (Austin 1962; Pickering 1994). Performativity has received concerted attention from science and technology studies (STS) researchers, who have made connections with economic sociology (MacKenzie 2003; MacKenzie and Millo 2003; Pinch and Swedberg 2008). STS research has suggested that financial models developed by economists are performative in that they do not describe economic activities but actively shape them instead (MacKenzie 2006). This view suggests that financial models are not devices which passively reflect the a priori economic behaviours of actors. Instead, mathematical formulae actively reconfigure relations between people, objects and technologies in order to enable them to function. Rather than representing reality, they bring certain realities into being.[3]

The subjective, intersubjective and embodied practices constituting forensic investigative activity contrast with the precise, clear, quantitative ratiocinations which one might typically associate with statistical formulae. What is also apparent in the instances described in this chapter is that reasoners sought to make 'Bayesian' reasoning *accountable* to themselves and one another through various means. Philosophical and scientific accounts of reasoning using Bayes' theorem are unlikely to capture such practices, yet these practices were vital in making 'Bayesian' reasoning feasible among groups of forensic reasoners and for them to make sense of certain states of affairs. In illuminating these phenomena, this chapter hints at the potential for qualitative ethnographic studies to uncover the finer practices which underpin performative aspects of consciously 'Bayesian' reasoning but which evade the gaze of philosophical accounts and models presented in technical journal articles.

A suitable framing for such studies is *ethnomethodology*, a branch of social research which, broadly construed, attends to the study of practical reasoning (Garfinkel 1974). Ethnomethodology does not ascribe any a priori framings to terms such as 'facts', 'evidence', 'ratiocination', 'common sense', 'science', etc. Instead, ethnomethodology focuses on how actors construct intersubjective understandings of these epistemological phenomena in localized settings. Two key ethnomethodological principles are *indexicality* and *reflexivity*. Indexicality may be used to describe the localized practices through which reasoners construct epistemological categories such as 'facts', 'evidence', 'reasoning', etc. Reflexivity describes the dependence reasoners ascribe to such categories, even though the practices through which such categories are constructed may evade philosophical and/or scientific idealizations.

The explicit mention by one forensic practitioner of 'Bayesianizing' their conclusions through embodied practice suggests one such instance of the codependency of indexicality and reflexivity. Here, the embodied practice of acting out the scenario of an accidental fall onto scissors led to an understanding of how the uncertainty surrounding the case could be resolved. The conscious linkage of this performance with the term 'Bayesianizing' resembles a means of retaining a relevance with the statistical processes which had led the investigator to question whether the incident was murder as indicated by their preliminary analysis. This performance of 'Bayesian' reasoning may be unfamiliar or even anathema to many philosophers of science. However, the reference to 'Bayesianizing' here indicates how a combination of practices, including statistical analysis and embodied performance, was justified or made accountable as an instance of a particular kind of 'forensic' activity.

Understanding the impact of Bayes' theorem on forensic science invites researchers to explore how the former configures and rearticulates the variety of objects and practices involved in criminal investigations. STS is wellplaced to pursue such studies and to explore questions of agency – how does evidence acquire meaning, and how is that meaning circulated and translated (Latour 1999; M'Charek 2000, 2008)? How are these meanings rendered and incorporated in investigations, and how can investigative reasoning practices be understood once made visible?

This chapter has indicated possibilities for reconciling performativity studies and ethnomethodology to explore epistemological practices of evidential interpretation in organizational settings. Some STS research which has adopted the performativity perspective has emphasized the role of materiality. Research has focused on the role of ostensibly quotidian objects, such as charts or forms, in creating the conditions of possibility for mathematical equations to function and to shape social and material realities (Latour 1999). While this applies to forensic science (M'charek 2000), it is also possible to see that the performativity of Bayesianism requires an attention to embodied activity and intersubjectivity.

The examples presented in this chapter suggest that Bayes' theorem, in exposing ambiguity and epistemic contingencies, shapes reasoning behaviours rather than reflecting them. Key areas for STS include *ontological* questions concerning the constitution of realities and the relations between humans and objects (Woolgar and Lezaun 2013). While notions of the practices or enactments through which realities are constituted feature prominently in such accounts, the interpretive and imaginative dimensions of such practices, and how reasoners make such practices accountable to themselves and peers, invite further scrutiny.

For now, however, it may now not seem so strange to consider the capacity of mathematical formulae to exert a kind of agency in the course of reconstructing an imagined series of events. The concept of performativity has significant utility in explaining how epistemological representations such as formulae can influence how investigative reconstruction proceeds in potentially unexpected ways. It is possible, therefore, to comprehend how statistical idealizations of evidence interpretation may construct forensic practices rather than represent them.

The contingent epistemological identity of forensic science and practice manifests itself in other ways. The next chapter moves on to explore how law–science interactions can represent moments in which the process of knowing evidence becomes redistributed. Law–science relations may be challenged in the course of their engagements, particularly in cases involving new, untested or contested scientific evidence.

## Notes

1 In addition to the three levels outlined above, another level, known as *sub-source*, has been proposed to describe the possibility of a further set of considerations that may be introduced by the existence of DNA evidence. The consideration of a *sub-source* level separates questions of match probability of DNA from the question of where it was recovered. The question of whether the DNA was recovered from blood, semen or another source may vary in importance depending on the nature of the crime or the other circumstances surrounding the incident. The use of a subsource level has been seen as a possible means of preventing the overprivileging of DNA profile data against other evidence in relation to the case.
2 Bayes' theorem has previously been criticized for being impossibly informationhungry (see Rawling 1999, for example).
3 MacKenzie (2006) summarized the central question facing research on the performativity of finance thus: 'Has finance theory helped to create the world it posited – for example, a world that has been altered to conform better to the theory's initially unrealistic assumptions?' (24).

## Bibliography

Aitken, C. (2012) 'An introduction to a debate', *Law, Probability and Risk*, 11 (4): 255–258.

Association of Forensic Science Providers. (2009) 'Standards for the formulation of evaluative forensic science expert opinion', *Science & Justice*, 49 (3): 161–164.

Austin, J.L. (1962) *How to Do Things with Words: The William James Lectures Delivered at Harvard University in 1955*. Oxford: Clarendon Press.

Ball, V.C. (1961) 'The moment of truth: probability theory and standards of proof', *Vanderbilt Law Review*, 14: 807–830.

Barclay, A.D.B. and McCartney, S. (2007) 'Forensic science and miscarriages of justice', Paper presented at the 3rd National Forensic Research and Teaching Conference 2007, 5–7 September, Staffordshire University.

Biedermann, A., Taroni, F. and Champod, C. (2012) 'How to assign a likelihood ratio in a footwear mark case: an analysis and discussion in the light of R v T', *Law, Probability and Risk*, 11 (4): 259–277.

Bodziak, W.J. (2012) 'Traditional conclusions in footwear examinations versus the use of the Bayesian approach and likelihood ratio: a review of a recent UK appellate court decision', *Law, Probability and Risk*, 11 (4): 279–288.

Broeders, A.P.A. (2006) 'Of earprints, fingerprints, scent dogs, cot deaths, and cognitive contamination – a brief look at the present state of play in the forensic arena', *Forensic Science International*, 159 (2): 148–157.

Cook, R., Evett, I.W., Jackson, G., Jones, P. and Lambert, J.A. (1998a) 'A hierarchy of propositions: deciding which level to address in casework', *Science & Justice*, 38 (4): 231–239.

Cook, R., Evett, I.W., Jackson, G., Jones, P. and Lambert, J.A. (1998b) 'A model for case assessment and interpretation', *Science and Justice*, 38 (3): 151–156.

Cook, R., Evett, I.W., Jackson, G., Jones, P. and Lambert, J.A. (1999) 'Case preassessment and review in a twoway transfer case', *Science & Justice*, 39 (2): 103–111.

Eco, U. (1983) 'Horns, hooves, and insteps: some hypotheses on three types of abduction', in U. Eco and T. Sebeok (eds), *The Sign of Three: Dupin, Holmes, Peirce*. Bloomington: Indiana University Press, pp. 198–220.

European Network of Forensic Scientific Institutes. (2015) *ENFSI Guideline for Evaluative Reporting in Forensic Science: Strengthening the Evaluation of Forensic Results Across Europe (STEOFRAE)*, online at: http://www.enfsi.eu/sites/default/files/afbeeldingen/enfsi_booklet_m1.pdf (accessed 10 August 2015).

Evett, I.W. (1986) 'A Bayesian approach to the problem of interpreting glass evidence', *Journal of the Forensic Science Society*, 26 (1): 3–18.

Evett, I.W. (1987) 'Bayesian inference and forensic science: problems and perspectives', *The Statistician*, 36 (2/3): 99–105.

Evett, I.W., Jackson, G., Lambert, J.A. and McCrossan, S. (2000) 'The impact of the principles of evidence interpretation on the structure and content of statements', *Science & Justice*, 40 (4): 233–239.

Evett, I.W. and Joyce, H. (2005) 'Career story: consultant forensic statistician', *Significance*, 2 (1): 34–37.

Finkelstein, M.O. and Fairley, W.B. (1970) 'A Bayesian approach to identification evidence', *Harvard Law Review*, 83 (3): 489–517.

Garfinkel, H. (1974) 'The origins of the term "ethnomethodology"', in R. Turner (ed.), *Ethnomethodology: Selected Readings*. London: Routledge Education, pp. 15–18.

Gross, H. [1893] (2016) *Criminal Investigation: A Practical Handbook for Magistrates, Police Officers and Lawyers*. Charleston, SC: BiblioBazaar.

Hamer, D. (2012) 'Discussion paper: the R v T controversy: forensic evidence, law and logic', *Law Probability and Risk*, 11 (4): 331–345.

Hurley, P.J. (2000) *A Concise Introduction to Logic*. Belmont, CA: Wadsworth.

Jackson, G., Jones, S., Booth, G., Champod, C. and Evett, I.W. (2006) 'The nature of forensic science opinion – a possible framework to guide thinking and practice in investigation and in court proceedings', *Science & Justice*, 46 (1): 33–44.

Jamieson, A. (2004) 'A rational approach to the principles and practice of crime scene investigation', *Science & Justice*, 44 (1): 3–7.

Kingston, C.R. (1965a) 'Applications of probability theory in criminalistics 1', *Journal of Criminal Law, Criminology and Police Science*, 60 (309): 70–80.

Kingston, C.R. (1965b) 'Applications of probability theory in criminalistics, 2', *Journal of Criminal Law, Criminology and Police Science*, 60 (312): 1028–1034.

Kirk, P.L. (1963) 'The ontogeny of criminalistics', *Journal of Criminal Law, Criminology and Police Science*, 54 (2): 235–238.

Kruse, C. (2020) 'Making forensic evaluations: forensic objectivity in the Swedish criminal justice system', in A. Adam (ed), *Crime and the Construction of Forensic Objectivity from 1850*. London: Palgrave Macmillan, pp. 99–121.

Latour, B. (1999) *Pandora's Hope: Essays in the Reality of Science Studies*. Cambridge, MA: Harvard University Press.

Lawless, C. and Williams, R. (2010) 'Helping with inquiries, or helping with profit? The trials and tribulations of a technology of forensic reasoning', *Social Studies of Science*, 40 (5): 731–755.

Lipton, P. (2004) *Inference to the Best Explanation*, 2nd ed. London: Routledge.

Locard, E. (1934) *La Police et les Méthodes Scientifiques*. Paris: Editions Rieder.

MacKenzie, D. (2003) 'An equation and its worlds: bricolage, exemplars, disunity and performativity in financial economics', *Social Studies of Science*, 33 (6): 831–868.

MacKenzie, D. (2006) *An Engine Not a Camera: How Financial Models Shape Markets*. Cambridge, MA and London: MIT Press.

MacKenzie, D. and Millo, Y. (2003) 'Constructing a market, performing theory: the historical sociology of a financial derivatives exchange', *American Journal of Sociology*, 109 (1): 107–145.

M'charek, A. (2000) 'Technologies of population: forensic DNA testing practices and the making of differences and similarities', *Configurations*, 8 (1): 121–159.

M'charek, A. (2008) 'Silent witness, articulate collective: DNA evidence and the inference or visible traits', *Bioethics*, 22 (9): 519–528.

Nordby, J.J. (2000) *Dead Reckoning: The Art of Forensic Detection*. Boca Raton, FL: CRC Press.

Nordgaard, A. and Rasmusson, B. (2012) 'The likelihood ratio as value of evidence – more than a question of numbers', *Law, Probability and Risk*, 11 (4): 303–315.

Pickering, A. (1994) 'After representation: science studies in the performative idiom', *Proceedings of the Biennial Meeting of the Philosophy of Science Association*, 2: 413–19.

Pinch, T. and Swedberg, R. (eds). (2008) *Living in a Material World: Economic Sociology Meets Science and Technology Studies*. Cambridge, MA and London: MIT Press.

*R v T*. [2010] All ER (D) 240 (Oct); [2010] EWCA Crim 2439.

Rawling, P. (1999) 'Reasonable doubt and the presumption of innocence', *Topoi*, 18: 117–126.

Ribaux, O., Crispino, F. and Roux, C. (2014) 'Forensic intelligence: deregulation or return to the roots of forensic science', *Australian Journal of Forensic Sciences*, 47 (1): 61–71.

Ribaux, O. and Talbot Wright, B. (2014) 'Expanding forensic science through forensic intelligence', *Science & Justice*, 54 (6): 494–501.

Roberts, P. and Aitken, C. (2014) *Practitioner Guide No. 3: The Logic of Forensic Proof: Inferential Reasoning in Criminal Evidence and Forensic Science*. London: Royal Statistical Society.

Saks, M.J. and Faigman, D.L. (2008) 'Failed forensics: how forensic science lost its way and how it might yet find it', *Annual Review of Law and Social Science*, 4: 149–171.

Tribe, L. (1971) 'Trial by mathematics: precision and ritual in the legal process', *Harvard Law Review*, 84 (6): 1329–1393.

Truzzi, M. (1983) 'Sherlock Holmes: applied social psychologist', in U. Eco and T. Sebeok (eds), *The Sign of Three: Dupin, Holmes, Peirce*. Bloomington: Indiana University Press, pp. 81–118.

Walton, D. (2004) *Abductive Reasoning*. Tuscaloosa: University of Alabama Press.

Williams, R. (2007) 'The problem of dust: forensic investigation as practical action', in D. Francis and S. Hester (eds), *Orders of Ordinary Action*. London: Ashgate, pp. 195–210.

Williams, R. (2008) 'Policing and forensic science', in T. Newburn (ed.), *Handbook of Policing*. Cullompton, UK: Willan, pp. 760–793.

Woolgar, S. and Lezaun, J. (2013) 'The wrong bin bag: a turn to ontology in science and technology studies?', *Social Studies of Science*, 43 (3): 321–340.

Wyatt, D. (2014) 'Practising crime scene investigation: trace and contamination in routine work', *Policing and Society*, 24 (4): 443–458.

# 6 Law–science interactions and new technology

## Introduction

Chapter 5 explored how forensic reasoning practices are produced and made accountable in the context of investigating criminal cases. This chapter moves on to consider how forensic epistemologies may be contested and negotiated between science and law. Establishing the credibility of evidential claims and the expert witnesses who testify them is complicated by the procedural and epistemological differences between science and law (Jasanoff 2008). Researchers have observed how courtroom interactions challenge the status of scientific expertise as an 'autonomous, objective entity which has authority independent of the institutional settings in which it is used' (Wynne 1989: 28). Instead, research has suggested that the legal recognition of scientific 'expertise' may be contingent, localized and case dependent. Scientific knowledge has been regarded as 'intrinsically vulnerable to systematically applied scepticism' (Wynne 1989: 38), as apparent in adversarial legal systems.

Forensic scientific methods and technologies are thus subject to multiple forms of scrutiny. While they may be assessed through scientific peer review, forensic methods and evidence may also be subject to the legal gaze. While forensic techniques may be considered valid in principle, their operational application is dependent on the competency of practitioners. Any perceived deviations or irregularities might render a method vulnerable to cross-examination, which could risk an evidential claim being rendered inadmissible.

Social researchers and legal scholars have cautioned against assuming certainty about how expert evidence may be received in specific courts hearing specific cases (Jasanoff 1998; Edmond 2000; Bal 2005). Perceptions of the credibility, competency or relevance of an expert witness may vary. Novel claims to scientific knowledge may be particularly vulnerable to criticism. The allpowerful, immutable image attached to early instances of forensic DNA evidence proved to be fragile once informed lawyers were able to expose irregularities and questionable practices involved in the production of such evidence (Aronson 2007; Lynch et al. 2008). Re-establishing the epistemic authority of forensic DNA has been found to involve a combination of bureaucratic and technical interventions to foreclose future legal challenges (Lynch et al. 2008).

The application of well-established scientific techniques for forensic use may entail extra adaptations and innovations, such as methods for interpreting complex DNA profiles. The original techniques for forensic DNA profiling originated in academic laboratories (Aronson 2007). In time, however, genetic technology found itself adapted further for use in criminal casework (Clayton 1998; Gill and Buckleton 2004). Research conducted by scientists working in organizations like the UK's Forensic Science Service (FSS) developed new methods to interpret DNA profiles recovered from

DOI: 10.4324/9781003126379-6

80  *Law–science interactions*

crime scenes. Scientists sought to enhance the utility of DNA profiling by devising methods to facilitate the interpretation of complex DNA profiles obtained from samples containing mixtures of DNA. Other research sought to improve the sensitivity of DNA profiling by developing methods to produce and interpret DNA profiles from particularly minute quantities of biological material. The generic term *low template DNA (LT-DNA) profiling* is now commonly used to describe the latter set of methods.

In what follows, this chapter recalls how methods to interpret LT-DNA profiles received scrutiny in a variety of arenas, including scientific communities, the media and the courts. In describing legal and scientific discussions surrounding these methods, this chapter traces an example of how emergent forensic technologies and the evidence produced by them become known. The chapter examines the resultant consequences for framings of the relationship between law, science and society at large.

## LT-DNA: jurisprudential and regulatory interventions

The modern history of the forensic use of DNA is generally accepted to have begun with the work of Professor Sir Alec Jeffreys at the University of Leicester (Gill and Buckleton 2004). Interest in the possibilities of analyzing particularly minute quantities of DNA developed as scientific procedures and instrumentation improved and awareness grew of the investigative potential of DNA. Aided by academic collaborators, forensic scientists developed techniques that they claimed could produce DNA profiles from material equivalent to that of a single human cell (Findlay et al. 1997).

The FSS was instrumental in introducing these kinds of methods into casework. The method which the FSS originally termed 'low copy number' (LCN) DNA analysis was first used in 1999 and featured over 40 times in UK criminal cases in the first eight years of its use (interview, US scientist 2007). This development is now more commonly referred to as 'low template' DNA profiling alongside methodological variants developed by other forensic organizations (Caddy et al. 2008). The perceived technical sophistication of the method attracted media interest. The FSS cited a number of successes in their corporate literature. The FSS website described how minute quantities of DNA were recovered from a microscope slide bearing evidence from a case involving the rape and murder of Marion Crofts in 1981. Having supposedly been left deliberately untouched in anticipation of future technological advances, a subsequent profile provided a match with Tony Jasinskyj in 1999, leading to his subsequent conviction and life sentence (FSS 2005). In another case, LT-DNA was used to obtain a profile from a microscope slide containing biological material retained from an unsolved rape case dating from 1995. When loaded onto the National DNA Database (NDNAD) of England and Wales, the DNA profile matched that of Mark Henson, who was convicted and sentenced to life imprisonment in 2005 (FSS 2005). LT-DNA evidence has been used in other jurisdictions. In Australia, it played an instrumental role in securing the conviction of Bradley Murdoch for the 2006 murder of British tourist Peter Falconio. LT-DNA evidence was also used to investigate the murder of the Swedish Foreign Minister Anna Lindh.

### *R v Hoey*

LT-DNA, however, became subject to notable legal and scientific scrutiny arising from the case *R v Hoey*. On 20 December 2007, Sean Gerard Hoey was found not guilty of all 58 criminal charges that were brought against him in relation to his alleged role in the bomb attack which took place in Omagh, Northern Ireland, in August 1998. This included 29 counts of murder corresponding to the number of victims of the attack, which caused the largest single loss of life during the Irish conflict. Particular prominence was attached to DNA evidence generated using LT-DNA methods. The prosecution had argued that LT-DNA data provided a match between the DNA of Hoey and minute quantities of genetic material found on the bomb timers used in the attack. This evidence was subject to a concerted challenge from the defence, whose witnesses disputed the reliability of the technique. Even two prosecution scientists, called to testify in support of the LT-DNA evidence, conflicted with each other during the trial.

The criticisms of DNA analysis from the presiding Judge Weir were based on two sets of objections. The first concerned alleged shortcomings in the ways in which the DNA evidence had been recovered, packaged, stored and transported in the course of its analysis. Via a series of thorough examinations of police and forensic laboratory records, the defence exposed several instances of what were seen to amount to inappropriate practices and which, in the view of the court, seriously compromised the integrity of the DNA evidence (R *v* Hoey (2007)).

The second set of objections raised by Weir focused upon the means by which the validity of the method had been claimed. He concluded that LT-DNA could not be regarded as having been appropriately validated by the scientific community (R *v* Hoey (2007)). In his view, two articles published by the developers of the FSS method were insufficient to constitute validation of the technique. Weir accepted the defence argument, which included references to the relative lack of uptake of LT-DNA in certain jurisdictions and the lack of international agreement on validation procedures, in contrast to established guidelines and definitions for the validation of conventional DNA tests (R *v* Hoey (2007)).[1] Experts testifying for the defence mounted a concerted challenge to the scientific basis of LT-DNA. Professor Dan Krane from Wright State University, Ohio, argued that the results of LT-DNA testing were susceptible to a far greater level of subjective interpretation than conventional forensic DNA analysis. He also voiced concerns over the relative ease by which LT-DNA samples could become contaminated. Attempts to assess the reproducibility of the results were also criticized. In an experiment performed at the Birmingham laboratory of the FSS, three LT-DNA tests were performed on the same sample. The consensus results obtained via the first two tests were not replicated by the third. 'Thus the normal approach used in the United Kingdom had unintentionally been demonstrated by its own proponents to be potentially (and in that particular instance actually) misleading' (R *v* Hoey (2007): para. 62.10). In his conclusion Judge Weir used the issue of the scientific validity of LT-DNA as indicating the possible need to reconsider the manner in which scientific evidence was assessed for admissibility.

Following the *Hoey* outcome, the Association of Chief Police Officers (ACPO) ordered a temporary suspension of LT-DNA use in criminal investigations in England and Wales. Forces in Scotland and Northern Ireland followed suit. The UK's Crown Prosecution Service also announced a review of all cases involving LT-DNA evidence.

The *Hoey* trial publicly exposed differences of opinion within the forensic scientific community about the validity of the technique. Concerns about LT-DNA had been voiced prior to the *Hoey* verdict (British Broadcasting Corporation 2005, 2007; Caddy et al. 2008). In response to these, a review was commissioned by the Forensic Science Regulator, with the findings being published a few months after *Hoey*, in April 2008 (Caddy et al. 2008). The report addressed a number of areas, including sample recovery and extraction, transfer and persistence of DNA, quantification and interpretation procedures, validation procedures and the place of LT-DNA within the wider criminal justice system. The report concluded that the scientific basis of LT-DNA techniques was 'robust' and 'fit for purpose' for forensic use (Caddy et al. 2008: 1). The report's authors were satisfied that all three companies supplying variants of the technique at the time had adequately validated their processes for analyzing DNA at low quantities (Caddy et al. 2008). They did, however, recommend the development of universal standards for the extraction and interpretation of profiles under low template conditions.

The reaction within the forensic scientific community to the report's findings varied. The report was hailed as providing a decisive endorsement of LT-DNA at a forensic practitioner conference attended by the author in 2008. However, it drew equally vehement criticism elsewhere (Jamieson and Bader 2008; Gilder et al. 2009). Critics argued that the report did not fully address many of the issues arising from the *Hoey* trial, such as the lack of international agreement, and that it did not acknowledge dissension within the scientific community over LT-DNA (Jamieson and Bader 2008; Gilder et al. 2009). It was also claimed that the report paid insufficient attention to certain scientific issues concerning profile interpretation.[2] Furthermore, even though the report expressed satisfaction with the manner in which LT-DNA had been validated, it was criticized for failing to reproduce any actual validation data.

> The Caddy report therefore only represented a partial resolution of the controversies surrounding LT-DNA. The manner in which the technique was assessed and the conclusions of the report were themselves a source of considerable dispute. Although the outcomes of the Caddy report shaped subsequent judicial decisions, they did not silence criticisms of the technique. Such criticisms maintained that 'the review [raised] important issues about what it [meant] for a forensic science technique to be validated', amid concerns over the way in which LT-DNA profiles had been interpreted in the past. (Gilder et al. 2009: 535)

## *R v Reed and Reed*

Issues relating to LT-DNA were raised again in the appeal of the murder case *R v Reed and Reed*. Brothers David and Terence Reed had been convicted of stabbing Peter Hoe to death in his house in Eston in North-East England. Two pieces of plastic, which the prosecution alleged were parts of knife handles, were found to yield the respective DNA profiles of the accused pair following LT-DNA analysis. Although the profiles were recovered from the plastic fragments, the nature of the biological material (blood, saliva, sweat, etc.) from which the DNA originated could not be established. The Reeds appealed on the basis that the evidence of reporting forensic scientist Valerie Tomlinson was inadmissible. Tomlinson had asserted that the DNA of the accused was deposited onto the knife handles through direct contact (primary transfer). She argued against the possibility that it had been transferred via indirect contact through the DNA first making contact with a third party, whose actions had then deposited their DNA on the handle (secondary transfer), or even through further processes of transfer (e.g., tertiary transfer; *R v* Reed (2009)).

The defendants argued that Tomlinson was not justified in making such assertions about the mode of transfer and that the only admissible evidence to which she could testify were the random match probabilities of the DNA evidence (the probability that the DNA could have been deposited from a random member of the population other than the defendants). In giving evidence about transfer in this particular case, Tomlinson was accused by the defence of unduly influencing the way in which the match probabilities were comprehended by juries. The *Reed* appeal sought to challenge 'the admissibility of evaluative evidence of the possible ways in which the DNA was transferred ... on the basis that the scientific basis is insufficiently reliable' (*R v* Reed (2009): para. 114(iii)). The Appeal Court deliberated over the possible explanations that Tomlinson gave regarding how DNA evidence could have been deposited on the knife handles found at the scene. Two issues came under scrutiny: first, whether the underlying science concerning transfer was reliable and, second, whether Tomlinson did or did not give evidence that was in keeping with her status.

The *Reed* trial drew on the Caddy report as guidance, but the court also acknowledged the continuing lack of scientific consensus around LT-DNA profile interpretation. Questions concerning the overall reliability of LT-DNA methods did not, however, directly arise in the *Reed* appeal (*R v Reed* (2009)); instead, it was the circumstances under which a challenge could be made to LT-DNA evidence which came to be considered. The case judgement devoted significant attention to the testimony of the defence witnesses Bruce Budowle and Allan Jamieson. Budowle, an experienced US forensic scientist and defender of conventional DNA profiling methods, testified that the science of DNA transfer had not developed sufficiently to determine the source of DNA material. Nor, according to Budowle, was the science robust enough to determine whether DNA could be identified as a result of primary, secondary or tertiary transfer. Budowle did not regard it permissible for forensic scientists to draw conclusions on the method and timing of DNA transfer. He argued that Tomlinson should therefore not have expressed views regarding the circumstances of the transfer of the material (*R v Reed* (2009)). Budowle also argued that the original LT-DNA profiles had only been interpretable due to chance rather than to the general robustness of the technique.

The court rejected Budowle's assertions for two reasons. First, the court dismissed his claims that experts were not qualified to make inferences about possibilities of transfer. In justifying its argument, the court stated that 'logic dictates' that the possibilities of transfer could be enumerated, given sufficient circumstantial information, and that it was not logical for Budowle to say that an expert could never give such evidence (*R v Reed* (2009): para. 120). The court ruled that it was acceptable for a forensic scientist such as Tomlinson to seek 'reference to her experience and the scientific research that has been undertaken' (particularly one such as Tomlinson who was regarded as being highly experienced in forensic work, including scene of crime operations):

> We consider that the science is sufficiently reliable for it to be within the competence of a forensic science expert to give admissible evidence evaluating the possibilities of *transfer* in DNA cases. (*R v Reed* (2009): para. 122)

The judgement against the other defence witness, Professor Allan Jamieson, whose testimony had been accepted by Judge Weir in *R v Hoey* two years earlier, represented a significant reversal. Although the court accepted he had 'written some peer reviewed papers and carried out academic work in areas of forensic science' (*R v Reed* (2009): para. 105), the court concluded that he had very little practical experience of interpreting low template profiles. It transpired that he conducted no laboratory research of his own on LT-DNA, instead basing his knowledge of DNA analysis on 'papers and discussion with other scientists' (*R v Reed* (2009): para. 106). The court concluded that, despite acquiring a 'degree of experience' of LT-DNA from testifying in cases involving the technique and from discussions with scientists, his expertise did not match that of the practical knowhow acquired by Valerie Tomlinson (*R v Reed* (2009): para. 110). His criticisms of the Caddy report were also attacked for questioning the 'integrity of both the review by Professor Caddy and the providers of processes of Low Template DNA analysis' (*R v Reed* (2009): para. 108).

The issue of determining the biological origins of the DNA profiles and the resulting inferences made by Tomlinson about these origins constituted a key space of disagreement. Defence witnesses argued that the assertions made by Tomlinson were based on subjective past experience rather than statistical method and overstepped the domain of the scientist. Yet the court regarded this experience, despite its less formalized epistemological basis, as relevant and admissible. Here, Tomlinson's practical knowhow was considered epistemically superior to Jamieson's theoretical claims regarding how scientific methods should be validated.

At discussions among legal practitioners which took place in the North of England in 2011, the author detected signs, however, that legal professionals themselves experienced a sense of disenfranchisement regarding the place of expert testimony in the legal process. During these discussions a number of lawyers voiced concerns about precedents established by *R v Reed*. These reflected a perception that expert witnesses had gained more influence at the expense of counsel. One practising barrister opined that when defending, advocates were becoming 'mere mouthpieces' for the expert witness testimony which the defendants saw as more helpful to their case (criminal justice barrister 1 2011). This was perceived as precluding proper legal consideration. Following *Reed*, experts became able to evaluate and enumerate a number of different possibilities concerning the origin of evidence. This was regarded as impinging on the preserve of counsel and risking the erosion of their traditional roles and powers. One interlocutor regarded the adversarial system as coming under a profound existential threat, asserting that there was a 'feeling amongst lawyers that we are moving toward an inquisitorial system' (criminal justice barrister 2 2011).

The passage of LT-DNA through the *Hoey* and *Reed* cases indicates how scientific evidence may engage with and impact upon legal conceptions of admissibility. Such cases, along with others, stimulated debates within scientific communities concerning LT-DNA methods for the production and interpretation of evidence. In addition to the *R v Reed* decision, defenders of LT-DNA cited a case heard in New York, People *v* Megnath (2010), in which LT-DNA had passed a *Frye* admissibility hearing. (The *Frye* standard of evidential assessment, in use in many US states, seeks to determine whether a scientific method has received 'general acceptance' in the relevant scientific community.) The prosecution argued that LT-DNA had been 'generally accepted' in the United Kingdom and New Zealand, and the judge agreed that results from the technique were admissible. The *Megnath* ruling was viewed by some as a significant vindication of LT-DNA in the United States, which had previously demonstrated notable scepticism toward the technique.

Despite hailing the *Megnath* decision, the concept of 'general acceptance' was, however, conceded by LT-DNA developers as problematic from a scientific standpoint, possibly 'beyond definition', and one which exposed considerable differences between science and law (Buckleton 2009: 257). In discussing the issue of reliability, some LT-DNA proponents admitted that profound differences remained between scientists and lawyers over the extent to which deviations from data reproducibility were considered acceptable:

> The two replicates at low template level work will typically be broadly similar but, for example, some alleles present in one replicate may be smaller or not visible in another replicate. This is common knowledge to forensic scientists but was met with deep concern when presented to a group of prosecutors at Auckland, New Zealand, in 2008, thereby exposing the gap between scientific and legal perceptions. (Buckleton 2009: 258)

While scientists working with LT-DNA always anticipated a certain variability in results, this surprised and concerned prosecutors. A 'very considerable gap in view and expectation between forensic scientists and lawyers' was seen to endure (Buckleton 2009: 258). Developers of LT-DNA methods, however, stood by decisions like *Megnath*: 'It is welcome to hear from the judiciary that evidence interpretation does not have to be perfect to be admissible' (Balding and Buckleton 2009: 2).

Referring to American legal methods for assessing scientific admissibility, authors defending LT-DNA methods argued that it was 'misleading to describe reproducibility to be either a *Daubert* requirement or a *Frye* requirement' (Gill and Buckleton 2010: 222; *Daubert v Merrell Dow Pharmaceuticals* (1993) was a Supreme Court ruling that helped to establish tests for the admissibility of expert testimony during federal proceedings. The ruling tasked the trial judge with a 'gatekeeping' role to determine whether claimed scientific evidence is derived from sound scientific method.) '*Variability*', it was argued, '*and indeed uncertainty, is a part of most, if not all, scientific endeavours*' (Gill and Buckleton 2010: 222, emphasis added). Variability and uncertainty were portrayed as inevitable and unavoidable aspects of scientific work which did not necessarily reflect negatively on the evidence. While accepting legal judgements in cases like *Megnath*, proponents of LT-DNA nonetheless expressed concerns about the apparent lack of scientific understanding on the part of lawyers.

## Debates Within Forensic Science International: Genetics

Discussions over LT-DNA also took place between scientists through correspondence published in the journal *Forensic Science International: Genetics* (*FSI:G*). Through this they deliberated over who had ultimate authority concerning decisions about the validity of scientific evidence. During a series of letters, comments and replies published in *FSI:G*, Bruce Budowle and his coauthors, who were critical of LT-DNA, claimed that a 'legal threshold of general acceptance' did not 'equate to scientific reliability' (Budowle and van Daal 2011b: 13) and that '*the proper forum for reliability discussions is the scientific arena*' (Budowle and van Daal 2011b: 13, emphasis added). Proponents of LT-DNA were criticized for seemingly relying on the courts to decide what constituted 'validity, reliability and quality' (Budowle and van Daal 2011b: 13). This kind of epistemic dependency was viewed by Budowle and colleagues as having previously led forensic science to fail to meet normal scientific standards.[3] They claimed that in *Megnath*, the statistical methods used to interpret LT-DNA profiles were erroneous, despite the decision. These critics also viewed the use of the 'general acceptance' criterion to justify adoption of the technique as misleading. While it was argued in *Megnath* that LT-DNA had been 'generally accepted' in the UK and New Zealand, Budowle et al. (2011) claimed that the 'general acceptance' criterion was not the 'exclusive property of the legal community' but based on 'expert scientific opinion' and the *Megnath* decision did not reflect actual 'scientific conclusions' (5). They claimed that no scientific data had been released in either of the latter jurisdictions to provide substantive scientific backing for the validity of LT-DNA.

> LT-DNA developers claimed that interpretation issues could be ameliorated if Bayesian techniques were more widely adopted. If Bayesianism was accepted, these authors suggested, 'nothing else is required, other than to *educate* scientists, judges and lawyers' in the 'uses and practicalities' of such methods. (Gill and Buckleton 2010: 226, emphasis added)

Another issue raised in discussions published in *FSI:G* was the extent to which a discrepancy existed between the theoretical basis of LT-DNA interpretation methods and how LT-DNA profiles were actually interpreted in practice. LT-DNA developers admitted that there existed a need for specialist software to enable their 'probabilistic solutions to be fully implemented' (Gill and Buckleton 2010: 226).[4] They also conceded that adoption of their theoretical solutions had been somewhat forestalled. They regarded this, however, to have stemmed from lack of business interest in uptake rather than strictly technological limitations: 'It is of course disappointing that nearly a decade later, vendors still have not developed commercial solutions based on our statistical thinking' (Gill and Buckleton 2010: 223).

Previously, LT-DNA developers had expressed a view that their theoretical models *could* be used in practice but were hindered by a series of commercial and institutional barriers. For example, the conventions of scientific publications were explained as a hindrance for the open validation of new scientific methods:

> Journal editors are understandably reluctant to publish validation papers. If the technique has been published once and subsequently other laboratories repeat the work and obtain the same or similar results the subsequent papers will be, rightly, branded not novel and hence unworthy of publication. (Buckleton 2009: 257)

This was accepted as normal practice in scientific circles but 'possibly not widely known or understood within the legal community' (Buckleton 2009: 257). In this earlier comment, other institutional factors were cited as precluding open publication of validation protocols:

> Access can be further constrained by intellectual property considerations. In my own organization the placement of a validation report in the Institute website would require permissions and many steps and has never been attempted. (Buckleton 2009: 257).

In the same article, the problem of gaining consensus in organized scientific bodies was also raised:

> One alternative is to have professional bodies or especially commissioned committees endorse certain procedures. … The obvious, but incorrect, implication is that anything not currently endorsed does not make the standard. Obtaining agreement by large committees is difficult and time consuming. Progress can often become stalled on matters of mind numbing detail or on what level of different but parallel methodology is acceptable. Any endorsement tends to set a technique in stone thereby inhibiting progress. (Buckleton 2009: 257).

Despite these issues, LT-DNA evidence subsequently became accepted. Critics expressed concern, however, about the lack of certainty regarding the exact methods used to produce such evidence. 'The forensic science community does not know what the practices of [LT-DNA] laboratories are and whether they are valid and reliable' (Budowle and van Daal 2011a: 15). These critics accused developers of inconsistencies 'between what they recommended and what [was] practiced' (Budowle and van Daal 2011b: 12):

> We now know that the Forensic Science Service (FSS), for example, does not follow the often cited Gill et al. article (written by FSS employees) for statistical assessment of LCN evidence even a decade after its publication. (Budowle and van Daal 2011a: 15)

The same critics also accused forensic scientists in other jurisdictions of engaging in practices 'very different than what is recommended in the scientific literature'

(Budowle and van Daal 2011b: 12). They alleged that some key developers of these 'recommended' interpretation methods had not promoted their own methods to colleagues engaged in casework in New Zealand and Australia.

Other issues debated in the scientific literature raised deeper ontological questions over LT-DNA. Papers published in 2009 and 2010 asserted that an 'underlying confusion' bedevilled LT-DNA. These articles claimed that 'no satisfactory definition' could 'be applied to delineate' between LT-DNA and conventional methods (Gill and Buckleton 2010: 221). The authors of these papers argued that the kind of stochastic interpretation effects, such as contamination or the partial loss of profile elements closely associated with LT-DNA, actually applied to all forms of DNA profiling. They argued that no discrete distinction could be identified between techniques, even though ultrasensitive methods had previously been offered as distinct products by firms such as the FSS. Instead, developers attacked what they now regarded as 'an arbitrary definition of LT-DNA vs. conventional DNA profiling' (Gill and Buckleton 2010: 221). They rejected this definition 'because the *stochastic effects* associated with the analysis of LT-DNA, including analysis by LCN, are undeniably observed with all DNA profiling technologies' (Gill and Buckleton 2010: 221, emphasis in original). In an earlier paper they stated that they had 'abandoned the concept in favour of development of a universal strategy that can be used for all DNA profiles regardless of technique used' (Gill and Buckleton 2009: 555). These authors intended to 'end the socalled LCN "debate" ... *it is a debate about something we cannot define*' (Gill and Buckleton 2010: 226, emphasis added).

This position subsequently elicited a critical response from other quarters:

> Their response has not ended our concerns and we disagree with much of what they attempt to argue to justify avoiding the vagaries of LCN typing. ... LCN typing is not a way of thinking; it is an analytical tool with reproducibility issues that must be considered and properly addressed. (Budowle and van Daal 2011a: 15)

Shortly after these comments were published, a discussant with expertise in forensic genetics described the situation thus:

> It seems the people who invented the technique are now trying to say it's not really a technique at all, and that's what the current thought process actually is ... it does look like they are backtracking in many ways to avoid some of the issues. ... (Seminar discussion 2011)

Hence, different perceptions about what LT-DNA actually was (either a 'tool' or a set of 'conditions') also framed the controversy at this time.

The editors of *FSI:G* stated that they would not publish any more correspondence on these matters following those included in the January 2011 issue. Research did, however, continue to be published on likelihood ratio (LR)-based methods for interpreting complex DNA profiles. *FSI:G* has thus tended to focus on theoretical modelling and experimental data rather than opinions on the status of LT-DNA and related methods. *FSI:G* did, however, publish accounts of a scientific conference held in Italy in 2012, which briefly described presentations by some key figures from all sides of the debate. These accounts suggested that some consensus between the interlocutors emerged from this meeting, although critical voices continued to question the role of the courts:

> [Bruce Budowle] questioned the appropriateness of leaving the issue of 'relevance of the evidence' to the court: jurors and judges may not be technically ready for

this. ... He concluded that reducing complexities to artificially simple concepts cannot be always right, especially when questionable intellectual shortcuts are employed. (Pascalli and Prinz 2012: 776)

## Further legal developments: the acceptance of 'evaluative opinion'

Debates over complex DNA evidence shifted from issues of reliability and the authority of law and science to further focus on the epistemological basis of expert opinion offered in court. Some cases involved DNA evidence produced using methods such as LT-DNA, or methods used to try and separate the DNA profiles of individuals from mixed samples. In January 2013, three cases were considered together by the Appeal Court of England and Wales (*R v Dlugosz, Pickering and MDS* 2013). *R v Dlugosz*, *R v Pickering* and *R v MDS* concerned issues arising from the reporting of DNA evidence in court. In each of these cases, the judge was asked by the Crown to admit low template DNA evidence against the defendant, with DNA derived from a mixed sample to which at least two or three persons had contributed. In each case, 19 or 20 of the components of the appellant's DNA were present in the mixture, but the experts were unable to give a random match probability (*R v Dlugosz, Pickering and MDS* 2013).

All three of these appeals proceeded on the basis that no statistical information, in the form of random match probabilities, could be supplied by expert witnesses. In each of the hearings witnesses had been unable to attribute genetic components of the profiles (known as alleles) to any contributor (*R v Dlugosz, Pickering and MDS* 2013). These cases also involved questions over whether DNA had been deposited by primary, secondary or tertiary transfer. It had been impossible to determine the bodily origin of DNA, such as whether it had originated from sweat or another bodily fluid.

The key objection raised in each of these three cases concerned the acceptance by the original courts of 'evaluative opinion' of expert witnesses about the LT-DNA profiles, where it had been impossible to generate statistical measures. In upholding the decisions, the Appeal Court accepted that witnesses could express evidence in the form of an opinion rather than a quantified expression. The Appeal Court cited the case *R v T* (Chapter 5) as the basis for allowing a court to accept such an evaluative opinion (*R v Dlugosz, Pickering and MDS* 2013). R *v* Reed (2009) and another case R *v* Weller (2010), were also cited as justifications for accepting opinions relating to 'the ways in which DNA could be transferred without there being any statistical database' (*R v Dlugosz, Pickering and MDS* 2013: para. 9).

English law has therefore adopted a seemingly liberal attitude to the reporting of DNA evidence in court. These appeal cases themselves became the focus of scientific work (Gill et al 2014), which criticized the acceptance of evaluative opinions in the absence of statistical data, claiming such opinions reflected the mere 'belief' of reporting scientists. The lack of rigorous hypothesis formulation and testing was regarded as dangerously unscientific (Gill et al. 2014). The *Dlugosz, Pickering* and *MDS* Appeal Court verdicts were also criticized for potentially leading to biased views of DNA evidence, with lay audiences possibly favouring it over potentially more probative nonDNA testimony.

Scientific concerns over bestowing too much authority on the opinions of expert witnesses related to the possibility that such testimony could be misunderstood.[5] It was argued that witnesses might be accused of subsequently misleading courts. In response, research on LRbased methods for the interpretation of complex mixed and LT-DNA profiles continued. Such research reflected continued support for LR methods in scientific communities (Aitken 2012; Biedermann et al. 2012). LR methods have been regarded by advocates as a means of allowing reasoners to utilize the information given by a particular profile as rigorously as possible, while avoiding possible bias on the part of the witness.

While the *Dlugosz, Pickering* and *MDS* verdicts upheld a certain perception of DNA as an evidential gold standard, the scientific community raised concerns that too much authority could be bestowed on DNA ahead of other forms of evidence without due epistemological justification. Fears were expressed that courts could be influenced by the immutable scientific aura attached to DNA in ways which could unduly downplay other potentially more probative evidence. While some justifications of legal decisions about DNA evidence are questionable, it is thus possible to discern how courts helped set certain scientific agendas. Some scientific papers directly referred to court judgements as a motivation for their work (Gill et al. 2014). Hence, while legal judgements raise questions about law's understanding of science, they still play a role in shaping research, even if that research is perceived by scientists as intended to correct perceived legal misunderstandings.

The Appeal Court ruling for *R v MDS* (R v Dlugosz, Pickering and MDS 2013) mentions a probabilistic system for DNA interpretation which was ruled as inadmissible as it had 'not been sufficiently assessed and peer reviewed so that it could be considered to have a sufficient scientific basis to be regarded as part of a body of knowledge and experience recognized as reliable' (*R v Dlugosz, Pickering and MDS* 2013: para. 100).[6] One may question exactly what courts might regard as 'sufficient' scientific assessment which could be open to varying interpretation. Perhaps rather curiously, English courts here placed certain demands on scientific methods, despite accepting less epistemologically formalized evaluative opinion regarding DNA.

LR methods occupy an uncertain place within the criminal justice system, amid a seemingly liberal posture to expert DNA. Earlier social research argued that the objective image of forensic DNA came to be maintained by a combination of technical, legal and administrative means which foreclose areas of challenge (Lynch et al. 2008). This chapter indicates, however, that technical and legal approaches to establishing the credibility of LT-DNA became less systematically coordinated.

## Conclusion

The earlier assertions of contending groups of scientists over LT-DNA can be illuminated if we consider the concept of deficit and surfeit models introduced in Chapter 2. Deficittype discourses can be discerned in developers' assertions that audiences would accept LT-DNA methods once they were sufficiently 'educated'. Other statements by LT-DNA developers, however, suggest other framings. While accepting some key court decisions, LT-DNA developers expressed concerns about lawyers' assumptions regarding scientific practice. The view that variability was normal in scientific research and that lawyers were somehow mistaken in expecting perfectly reproducible data aligns with a surfeit model position.

Still other views expressed by these developers, however, projected another relationship between scientific authority and its audience. Scientists defending their own LT-DNA interpretation methods suggested that these could be regarded as valid, but proving this validity was obstructed by a variety of factors. These included employers' rules preventing the disclosure of data, the sluggish bureaucracy of scientific bodies and the lack of commercial appeal of their methods. The reference to such barriers suggests a framing in which scientific authority is upheld but where exogenous social realities are a hindrance to knowledge transfer. The idea that scientific authority *could* be reinforced were it not for such practicalities suggests a third model of scientific engagement. This could be termed a *social realist* discourse.

The social realist discourse of engagement relates to instances where scientists reflexively locate themselves and their work within a wider set of social practices and constraints. Such a discourse projects a distinction between actuality and possibility. The validity of scientific claims, at least in terms of principles or theories, is upheld by indicating that they *could* be seen to be authoritative if projected 'realities' of life did not get in the way.

Socialrealist discourses are distinguishable from deficittype discourses in that the latter suggest that exogenous constraints to scientific progress can be readily removed once society at large is sufficiently informed. In this way, deficittype discourses are consistent with the notion that society at large becomes 'rationalized' through its engagement with science, a position associated with technological determinism (Beard 1927). In contrast, socialrealist discourses portray societal barriers as obdurate structures that evade circumvention by science alone.

Alternatively, surfeittype discourses express the working realities of scientists which are portrayed as intrinsic to forensic scientific work. These may include issues such as the variability of results, the slow pace of analyses or the labourintensive nature of the work. In contrast, socialrealist discourses refer to a wider zone of extrinsic constraints, which, while impacting upon scientists' claims, do not directly constitute scientific practices. Socialrealist discourses also differ from surfeittype discourses in that the former maintain spaces of possibility for science to maintain a potential hegemony ('*if* it wasn't for societal barriers, our science *could* be shown to be valid'), rather than expressing science as it is. Crucially, in expressing socialrealist discourses, scientists themselves transcend the practicalities perceived as intrinsic to forensic science by surfeittype discourses. Socialrealist discourses depict exogenous interests as affecting the uptake of scientific claims. This may include commercial motivations or bureaucratic procedure. This contrasts with surfeittype discourses which, rather than interests, emphasize expectations, be they skewed on the part of lay audiences who are portrayed as misunderstanding the realities of scientific labour.

Deficittype statements uphold the view that scientists can readily educate the outside world about LT-DNA, which was framed as scientifically valid by its supporters. Surfeittype discourses, on the other hand, may be invoked in engagement with lawyers, such as the acceptance of the *Megnath* verdict, yet at the same time such discourses uphold the authority of science in taking lawyers to task over their conceptions of science. Social-realisttype discourses, however, represent a deeper embedding of science within society at large.

If considered in combination, deficit, surfeit and socialrealist discourses reflect a kind of differential separation/entanglement between science and law and with society at large. It is possible to regard the differential invocation of these discourses as a means by which science positions itself in different ways in relation to wider society. Doing so allows scientific claims to strategically distance themselves from law where appropriate in some cases, while engaging more deeply with law at other times. Socialrealist discourses allow a blurring of the distinction between actuality and possibility. They project an image of nascent forensic scientific innovation facing challenges to its authority from a variety of extrascientific social constraints. Given the variegated terrain of forensic science, it is perhaps not surprising that different discourses intermingle, representing different levels of engagement between science and society at large.

English law and science appear, however, to have diverged on the issue of the epistemological basis of testimony on complex DNA data. The *Reed* decision upheld the English court's capacity to accept evidence on the basis of personal experience. Since then, the *R v T* decision (see Chapter 5) has dissuaded scientists reporting evidence in terms of likelihood ratios. Appeal court decisions have also allowed expert witnesses to express their 'evaluative opinion' on complex DNA profiles rather than in statistical terms. The *Reed* outcome led to concerns being expressed by some lawyers that they risked becoming 'mere mouthpieces' for expert witnesses. Subsequent rulings appear to have increased the capacity for expert witnesses to base their testimony on enumerated possibilities rather than statistical approaches. This, however, could strengthen the position of the expert witness further, relative to that of counsel.

In accepting evaluative opinion and experiential testimony, English law reasserted its authority to hear forensic evidence in any way it sees fit. This suggests that deficit discourses might relate to law as well, reflecting an attitude that law has absolute authority and that nonlegal actors merely need to be educated in its ways. While this challenges the authority of science, the reference to lawyers becoming 'mere mouthpieces' reflects concerns that recent rulings also potentially undermine them. These concerns could suggest a kind of legal surfeit discourse, whereby individual lawyers might conceivably maintain that legal practice is too uniquely nuanced to allow scientific witnesses to dominate proceedings.

A move to reassert legal authority may hold other implications. Law's reassertion to rule over forensic evidence could risk marginalizing statistical methods associated with the interpretation of forensic evidence. Many in the scientific community were uncomfortable with the prospect of expressing opinions rather than quantified evidence, with some expressing concern over the risks that courts may misinterpret and read too much into such testimony.

Introducing three forms of engagement discourses (deficit, surfeit, socialrealist) illuminates the 'co-production' and reproduction of law–science relations in response to emerging and contested claims to forensic authority (Jasanoff 2004). It has indicated how law, in asserting its own authority, might find some internal resistance, with some lawyers perceiving it to be becoming increasingly dependent on scientific expert witnesses at their expense. This is despite scientists themselves having expressed discomfort with the ways in which they may have to testify and the potential risks and consequences. This suggests that law–science co-production exhibits other, possibly counterintuitive, effects to which researchers should be aware.

In order to build a finergrained understanding of law–science co-production, it is worthwhile to focus on a series of other themes, concerning how new forensic technologies shape who becomes subject to the forensic gaze, those who decide who gets subjected to that gaze, and the implications such engagements hold for ethics and social justice. These are discussed in more detail in the next chapter.

## Notes

1 Weir's judgment stated: 'There has been no international agreement on validation and a conference held in the Azores in September 2005 had ended with agreement only that more work in that area was needed. ... This lack of agreement on LCN was in marked contrast to the normal SGM+ test for DNA for which there were internationallyagreed validation guidelines and definitions approved by the Scientific Working Group on DNA Analysis Methods (SWGDAM)' (R *v* Hoey (2007): para. 62).
2 The Caddy report accepted that forensic science providers had established 'guidelines' for interpretation but that work was 'continuing' and it was the responsibility of the Forensic Science Regulator to 'bring about some standardization in interpretation amongst all providers' (Caddy et al. 2008: 1).
3 'In contrast Buckleton and Gill imply that acceptance of science by the courts suggests validity, reliability and quality, an issue that has plagued the forensic science disciplines far too long and has been highlighted by the recent National Academy of Sciences report on the forensic sciences' (Budowle and van Daal 2011b: 12).
4 They also wrote: 'LCN or LT-DNA is not a method or technique, it is a way of thinking' (Gill and Buckleton 2010: 226).

5 There are also issues concerning the use of quantitative numerical expressions versus verbal forms of reporting.
6 Probabilistic algorithms to help interpret complex DNA profiles have been commercially produced. These have, however, raised legal disputes, particularly in the United States. Some cases addressed the issue of whether algorithms alone could be regarded as autonomous witnesses or simply as assistive tools (*People v Wakefield* 2019; *People v HK* 2020). Efforts to scrutinize algorithms and their source code to assess admissibility have been complicated by claims to commercial confidentiality on the part of algorithm providers (Kwong 2017; Bright et al. 2020; *State of New Jersey vs Pickett* 2021).

## Bibliography

Aitken, C. (2012) 'An introduction to a debate', *Law, Probability and Risk*, 11 (4): 225–228.

Aronson, J.D. (2007) *Genetic Witness: Science, Law, and Controversy in the Making of DNA Profiling*. New Brunswick, NJ and London: Rutgers University Press.

Bal, R. (2005) 'How to kill with a ballpoint pen: credibility in Dutch forensic science', *Science, Technology and Human Values*, 30 (1): 52–75.

Balding, D.J. and Buckleton, J. (2009) 'Interpreting low template DNA profiles', *Forensic Science International: Genetics*, 4 (1): 1–10.

Beard, C.A. (1927) 'Time, technology and the creative spirit in political science', *American Political Science Review*, 21 (1): 1–11.

Biedermann, A., Taroni, F. and Champod, C. (2012) 'How to assign a likelihood ratio in a footwear mark case: an analysis and discussion in the light of R *v* T', *Law, Probability and Risk* 11 (4): 259–277.

Bright, J.-A., Kelly, H., Kerr, Z., McGovern, C., Taylor, D. and Buckleton, J. (2020) 'The interpretation of DNA profiles: an historical perspective', *Journal of the Royal Society of New Zealand*, 50 (2): 211–225.

British Broadcasting Corporation. (2005) 'Outback Handcuffs "Contaminated"', BBC News, 2 November; online at: http://news.bbc.co.uk/1/hi/world/asiapacific/4398428.stm (accessed 12 August 2015).

British Broadcasting Corporation. (2007) 'Verdict Raises DNA Evidence Doubt', BBC News, 20 December; online at: http://news.bbc.co.uk/1/hi/northern_ireland/7154189.stm (accessed 20 December 2007).

Buckleton, J. (2009) 'Validation issues around DNA typing of low level DNA', *Forensic Science International: Genetics*, 3 (4): 255–260.

Buckleton, J. and Gill, P. (2004) 'Low copy number', in J. Buckleton, C.M. Triggs and S.J. Walsh (eds), *Forensic DNA Evidence Interpretation*. Boca Raton, FL: CRC Press, pp. 275–299.

Budowle, B., Eisenberg, A.J. and van Daal, A. (2011) 'Response to comment on "Low Copy Number Typing Has Yet to Achieve 'General Acceptance' (Budowle et al., 2009 *Forensic Sci. Int.: Genetics* Supplement Series 2: 551–552)", by Caragine, T. and Prinz, M.', *Forensic Science International: Genetics*, 5 (1): 5–7.

Budowle, B. and van Daal, A. (2011a) 'Comment on "A Universal Strategy to Interpret DNA Profiles That Does Not Require a Definition of Low Copy Number by Peter Gill and John Buckleton, 2010, *Forensic Sci. Int. Genetics* 4, 221–227"', *Forensic Science International: Genetics*, 5 (1): 15.

Budowle, B. and van Daal, A. (2011b) 'Reply to Comments by Buckleton and Gill on "Low Copy Number Typing Has Yet to Achieve 'General Acceptance' by Budowle, B. et al., 2009, *Forensic Sci. Int.: Genet.* Suppl. Series 2, pp. 551–552"', *Forensic Science International: Genetics*, 5 (1): 12–14.

Caddy, B.G., Taylor, G.R. and Linacre, A.M.T. (2008) *A Review of the Science of Low Template DNA Analysis*. London: Home Office.

Clayton, T. (1998) 'Analysis and interpretation of mixed forensic stains using DNA STR profiling', *Forensic Science International*, 91 (1): 55–70.

*Daubert v Merrell Dow Pharmaceuticals, Inc.* (1993) 509 U.S. 579 (U.S.).

Edmond, G. (2000) 'Judicial representations of scientific evidence', *Modern Law Review*, 63 (2): 216–251.

Findlay, I., Taylor, A., Quirke, P., Frazier, R. and Urquhart, A. (1997) 'DNA fingerprinting from single cells', *Nature*, 389: 555–556.

Forensic Science Service. (2005) *Forensic Science Service Fact Sheet 6: DNA Low Copy Number*. Birmingham: Forensic Science Service.

Gilder, J., Koppl, R., Kornfield, I., Krane, D., Mueller, L. and Thompson, W. (2009) 'Comments on the review of low copy number testing', *International Journal of Legal Medicine*, 123 (6): 535–536.

Gill, P., Bleka, O. and Egeland, T. (2014) 'Does an English appeal court ruling increase the risks of miscarriages of justice when complex DNA profiles are searched against the National DNA Database?', *Forensic Science International: Genetics*, 14: 167–175.

Gill, P. and Buckleton, J. (2004) 'Biological basis for DNA evidence', in J. Buckleton, C.M. Triggs and S.J. Walsh (eds), *Forensic DNA Evidence Interpretation*. Boca Raton, FL: CRC Press, pp. 1–26.

Gill, P. and Buckleton, J. (2009) 'Low copy number typing – where next?', *Forensic Science International: Genetics Supplement Series*, 2 (1): 553–555.

Gill, P. and Buckleton, J. (2010) 'A universal strategy to interpret DNA profiles that does not require a definition of lowcopynumber', *Forensic Science International: Genetics*, 4 (4): 221–227.

Jamieson, A. and Bader, S. (2008) *Press Release on Behalf of the Forensic Institute, Glasgow, Regarding the Caddy Review of Low Template DNA*. Glasgow: Forensic Institute.

Jasanoff, S. (1998) 'The eye of everyman: witnessing DNA in the Simpson trial', *Social Studies of Science*, 28 (5–6): 713–740.

Jasanoff, S. (2004) 'The idiom of coproduction', in S. Jasanoff (ed.), *States of Knowledge: The Co-Production of Science and Social Order*. London: Routledge, pp. 1–12.

Jasanoff, S. (2008) 'Making order: law and science in action', in E.J. Hackett, O. Amsterdamska, J. Wajcman and M. Lynch (eds), *Handbook of Science and Technology Studies*, 3rd ed. Cambridge, MA: MIT Press, pp. 761–786.

Kwong, K. (2017) 'The algorithm says you did it: The use of black box algorithms to analyze complex DNA evidence', *Harvard Journal of Law & Technology*, 31 (1): 275–301.

Lynch, M. (1998) 'The discursive production of uncertainty: the O.J. "Dream Team" and the sociology of knowledge machine', *Social Studies of Science*, 28 (5–6): 829–868.

Lynch, M., Cole, S.A., McNally, R. and Jordan, K. (2008) *Truth Machine: The Contentious History of DNA Profiling*. Chicago: University of Chicago Press.

Lynch, M. and McNally, R. (2003) '"Science", "common sense", and DNA evidence: a legal controversy about the public understanding of science', *Public Understanding of Science*, 12 (1): 83–103.

Pascalli, V.P. and Prinz, M. (2012) 'Highlights of the conference "The Hidden Side of DNA Profiles: Artifacts, Errors and Uncertain Evidence"', *Forensic Science International: Genetics*, 6 (6): 775–777.

*People v HK*. (2020) NY Slip Op 50709 (69 Misc 3d 774).

*People v Megnath*. (2010) NY Slip Op 20037 (27 Misc 3d 405).

*People v Wakefield*. (2019) NY Slip Op 06143 (175 A.D. 3d 158).

*R v Dlugosz, Pickering and MDS*. (2013) Judgement, Court of Appeal (Criminal Division), *Regina v Dlugosz, Pickering and MDS* [2013] EWCA Case No: 2011/04122/C2, 2012/03728/B1, 2012/02955/D4, 30 January.

*R v Hoey*. (2007) Judgement, Crown Court Sitting in Northern Ireland. *Regina v Sean Hoey*. NICC 49. 20 December.

*R v Reed*. (2009) Judgment, Court of Appeal (Criminal Division). *Regina v Reed, Reed and Garmson* [2009] EWCA Crim 2698. 21 December.

*R v Weller*. (2010) Judgement, Court of Appeal (Criminal Division). *Regina v Weller* [2010] EWCA Crim 1085. 4 March.

*State of New Jersey vs Pickett*. (2021) 466 NJ Super. 270 (246 A.3d 279).

Wynne, B. (1989) 'Establishing the rules of laws: constructing expert authority', in B. Wynne and R. Smith (eds), *Expert Evidence: Interpreting Science in the Law*. London: Routledge, pp. 23–55.

# 7 Forensic DNA technology
## Social and ethical issues

### The National DNA Database

The investigative utility of forensic DNA has been harnessed through national DNA databases. One of the first such forensic databases was the National DNA Database of England and Wales (NDNAD). Formally launched in 1995, the NDNAD was, at its peak, the largest of its kind by proportion of population. The NDNAD has, however, been marked by a significant degree of ethical and legal controversy. In outlining a brief history of the NDNAD, this section highlights these controversies and the circumstances which have shaped legislation governing DNA sampling and retention.

The emergence of the NDNAD has been characterized as a 'history of multiple and continuous changes to the ways in which the police can legitimately take, store and use DNA samples' (Williams et al. 2004: 41). The NDNAD thus owes its existence to legislative developments as much as it does to technological progress (see Williams et al. [2004] for a more detailed overview). A number of parliamentary acts, most of them amendments to the 1983 Police and Criminal Evidence Act (PACE), helped to bring the NDNAD into being. These are summarized in Table 7.1.

Legislative changes made over time concerned rules governing who the police were allowed to sample, the length of time that police could retain samples and the powers given to law enforcement bodies to search the database in order to detect possible

*Table 7.1* Legislation Governing Police Powers to Sample and Retain DNA in England and Wales – 1994–2003.

| Parliamentary Act | Change to Police Powers |
| --- | --- |
| Criminal Justice and Public Order Act (CJPOA) 1994 | Redefined mouth samples as 'non-intimate' and gave police the right to take non-intimate samples without consent in connection with the investigation of any recordable offence. |
| The Criminal Procedure and Investigations Act (1996) (section 64) | Widened the power of the police to speculatively search samples and profiles taken from arrestees. |
| Criminal Justice and Police Act (CJPA) 2001 | Police could retain the samples and profiles of persons arrested in connection with a recordable offence, regardless of whether they were subsequently acquitted. |
| Criminal Justice Act 2003 | Granted the police powers to sample and retain, without consent, individuals arrested but not subsequently charged or convicted in connection with a recordable offence. |

DOI: 10.4324/9781003126379-7

matches between unknown crime scene DNA and known profiles of individuals included on the NDNAD. The 2001 Criminal Justice and Police Act (CJPA) is particularly notable in that it allowed police in England, Wales and Northern Ireland to indefinitely retain DNA samples and fingerprints from anyone arrested of a recordable offence, even if they were subsequently released without charge or found not guilty. The DNA sampling regime was expanded further by the 2003 Criminal Justice Act (CJA). While the CJPA allowed police to retain biological material, the CJA went one step further in obliging the police to upload DNA samples from arrestees onto the NDNAD, regardless of whether those persons were charged of any subsequent offence. The NDNAD therefore became populated with a significant proportion of persons who, in the eyes of the law, were innocent.

The population of the NDNAD was boosted by an expansion plan initiated by the Labour government between 2000 and 2005 aimed at increasing the number of samples collected and the number of DNA matches. The government's initial intention was to capture the profiles of 'the whole "active criminal population", convicted or not, and to ensure the collection of DNA from 'all viable crime scenes' (Williams et al. 2004: 54).

This initiative prompted much ethical reflection (Nuffield Council on Bioethics 2007; Human Genetics Commission [HGC] 2009; McCartney et al. 2010). In the case of convicted criminals, there are arguably grounds for retention on a database, because conviction – and the punishment which follows – is commonly regarded as justifying a greater level of interference with the right to privacy. It is accepted that conviction may lead to imprisonment. If the right to privacy is diminished in those cases, why not sample DNA? But what about those whose DNA is retained but who haven't been convicted of any offence? If their right to privacy hasn't been justifiably diminished, why should their DNA be retained in the same way? Does their continued presence on the database contradict the right to be considered innocent until proved guilty – what status do these individuals have (Lynch and McNally 2009)? Justifying the retention of unconvicted individuals on the NDNAD suggests a tacit assumption that these people may pose a future threat of reoffending or risk being investigated in connection with a future offence. This raises further questions concerning what risks such individuals may pose to society.

A person must be under suspicion in the first place before they are arrested. The decision to arrest is a key threshold moment in terms of determining whether a person ends up on the NDNAD (HGC 2009). What constitutes the grounds for suspicion may not, however, always be very clear. The decision to arrest may be made in the heat of the moment and so may not always be an entirely rational decision.

At its peak in 2012, the NDNAD contained the profiles of over six million individuals, representing more than 10 per cent of the total population of England and Wales. A significant proportion (approximately 8 per cent) of profiles originated from persons aged 10–17 at the time of arrest, although that figure was claimed to be an underestimate (Wallace 2008).

Concerns have also long been expressed over the disproportionate representation of certain groups, such as young males from ethnic minorities, on the NDNAD. Estimates suggested that AfroCaribbean men were four times more likely than white men to have their DNA profiles stored on the NDNAD (HGC 2009). Other sources of inequality were raised over the inclusion of vulnerable persons on the NDNAD. In a 2009 report, the HGC raised the issue of the high likelihood of people with mental health problems being arrested and sampled (HGC 2009; see also Wallace 2008).

It was argued that the UK's policy created grey areas where people never convicted of an offence still found themselves stigmatized due to their continued inclusion on the

NDNAD or risked discrimination. This led some to call for a universal DNA Database to include the whole population of England and Wales (British Broadcasting Corporation 2007). Other arguments for a universal database were based on the potential to trace missing persons or identify human remains (HGC 2009). Studies reported that some persons who complained of police harassment welcomed possible inclusion on a universal database if it meant they could be easily exonerated (HGC 2009). Some critics, however, argued that universal DNA databases would not prevent discrimination. In an earlier critique, Troy Duster asserted that as long as arrests and policing remained discriminatory, as has been alleged in many jurisdictions, universal databases would not serve their intended purpose (Duster 2004). A DNA match alone does not definitively prove guilt but simply links a person to the scene where a crime may, or may not, have occurred. DNA evidence in isolation may not, however, establish exactly what activities occurred at the scene, who did what and whether those activities constituted a crime. (Lawless 2009). Arguably, such questions may be overlooked if police are motivated to incriminate someone.

Two cases were, however, to lead to some reforms to the NDNAD regime in the form of the 2012 Protection of Freedoms Act. The next section describes the *S & Marper* cases and subsequent developments regarding DNA sampling and retention legislation.

## S & Marper

In 2008, the European Court of Human Rights (ECtHR) heard the cases of *S & Marper*, two residents of Sheffield, South Yorkshire, who had their profiles sampled and loaded onto the NDNAD. 'S' had been arrested at the age of 11 in connection with an alleged robbery but was later acquitted. Marper's DNA profile had been taken when he was charged with harassment of his partner with whom he was eventually reconciled and charges subsequently not pressed. Both S and Marper appealed to the ECtHR to have their DNA removed from the NDNAD on the grounds that their inclusion breached Article 8 of the European Convention on Human Rights. The court ruled in their favour. The UK Government subsequently passed the 2012 Protection of Freedoms Act (PoFA), which led to significant changes to police powers to sample and retain biological material (See Table 7.2).

PoFA states that adult (over 18) criminals convicted of any offence may have their DNA and fingerprints retained indefinitely, with indefinite inclusion for those under 18 years convicted of serious 'qualifying' offences of a sexual, violent or terrorist nature. Under-18s convicted of relatively less serious 'non-qualifying' offences have their data retained for a period of five years, plus the length of any custodial sentence which arises. Anyone, regardless of age, who is arrested and charged with a qualifying offence but not subsequently convicted has their data retained for three years, to which a district judge can order a twoyear extension. Those persons arrested but not subsequently charged with a qualifying offence can have their data retained on databases in certain circumstances for up to three years. This requires a chief police officer to appeal to the UK Biometrics Commissioner, who then makes a decision regarding retention (if granted, this period can be extended by a further two years by order of a district judge). This is only possible, however, if an arrestee has not been convicted of any previous offence; otherwise, the data of previously convicted individuals are retained indefinitely. Regardless of age, persons arrested and/or charged in connection with a non-qualifying offence but who are subsequently not convicted and have never previously been in contact with the police have their data automatically deleted if an NDNAD search does not reveal any matches.

### 2012 Protection of Freedoms Act – DNA and fingerprint retention

| Types of offence | Age | Convicted | Charged | Arrested |
|---|---|---|---|---|
| 'Qualifying' Offences<br>- Violent crimes<br>- Sexual offences<br>- Terrorism<br>- Burglary | Under 18 | Indefinite | 3 years + possible 2 yr extension by District Judge | 3 yrs if police appeal to **Biometrics Commissioner** possible 2yrs extra |
| | 18 or over | Indefinite | | |
| | | | | Indefinite if prev. conviction |
| Other Offences | Under 18 | 5yrs+ custodial sentance<br>Indefinite if: >5yr sentence 2nd conviction | DNA searched against unknown crime scene samples – if no match DNA is then deleted | |
| | 18 or over | Indefinite | | |

*Table 7.2* DNA Retention Rules Under the 2012 Protection of Freedoms Act.

Annual reports by UK Biometrics Commissioners (UKBCs) and other studies have, however, highlighted a series of challenges in implementing PoFA. These have included limitations to the Police National Computer system regarding the need for manual data entry to drive the 'automatic' deletion of profiles from the NDNAD, which is now allowed by PoFA in certain cases. 'Erroneous retention of biometric data' has been reported (Amankwaa and McCartney, 2019: 121). Limited engagement with the PoFA system on the part of police forces was also identified as another challenge, with forces making a markedly small number of applications for retention of biometric data (Amankwaa and McCartney 2019).

DNA databasing policy and practice is now characterized by greater complexity, particularly in terms of assessing the risks posed by individuals to society. One issue that impacts upon questions of retention and inclusion on DNA databases relates to the utility of such data. To what extent can we attribute DNA as having a meaningful impact on the detection rate for particular crimes relative to other forms of evidence, and how does DNA impact upon police practices? How is it possible to measure the impact of solving one case in terms of impact on the wider landscape of criminal offending? Is the resolution of certain crimes more 'valuable' relative to other forms of crime? A small number of quantitative studies have addressed the effect of DNA databasing on offending (see, for example, the work of Roman et al. 2008; Doleac 2012). Measuring the impact of forensic DNA is, however, problematic. DNA evidence may play varying roles in criminal investigations, and forensic scientists often stress the need to account for the wider framework of case circumstances when interpreting DNA profiles. This highlights the need to also understand how DNA is used by police, rather than just measuring the impact of its use.

Other innovations in forensic DNA technology and databasing have emerged. DNA familial searching sought to exploit the NDNAD further. Forensic genealogy and DNA phenotyping also utilize DNA data sets. The following sections introduce these examples to highlight the legal, social and ethical issues such innovations raise.

## Familial searching

Familial searching involves comparing an unknown DNA profile recovered from a crime scene with known DNA database profiles to determine whether the unknown DNA source may be related to someone on the database. Revealing such a link may help the police to identify fresh leads and to possibly identify new persons of interest. The technique exploits the inheritance of DNA from an individual's parents and the likelihood that an individual shares considerable amounts of DNA with siblings. Putative familial search matches are typically reported using a statistical framework which evaluates the extent to which two profiles might be related. It takes into account the probability that certain individuals might share particular DNA elements (alleles).

Familial searching has been used in cases in which no obvious suspects could be identified or in cold cases which may have lain unresolved for several years. The identification of leads and new suspects through familial search can be aided further by other information, such as a suspect's locality, age or appearance, which may help to increase the likelihood that a suspect identified through familial search may be the perpetrator.

In 1973, three 16-year-olds were raped, strangled and left in wooded areas near Neath, South Wales. The same unknown DNA profile was found at each scene. The offences remained unsolved for nearly 30 years before the case was reopened. Five hundred nominal suspects were investigated and the DNA of 353 persons of interest were typed but no matches with the perpetrator were found. Suspect no. 200 was Joseph Kappen, from whom no DNA sample had been taken due to his death 12 years earlier.

In 2001, an FSS scientist manually searched the NDNAD looking for an allelesharing pattern typical of a parent–child relationship. He identified Paul Kappen, who was seven years old at the time of the murders. Paul Kappen was Joseph's son. Paul had been arrested in connection with car theft and had his DNA loaded onto the NDNAD. The search identified a possible parent–child match and police considered that there might be some family connection with Paul Kappen and the murderer. The police found out that Paul's father was Joseph Kappen. They persuaded Paul's mother (Joseph's wife) and Joseph's daughter (Paul's sister) to volunteer samples. From this combination of profiles they were able to piece together a DNA profile which they deduced was Joseph Kappen's and which also matched the DNA sample recovered from the three victims. The police then sought permission to exhume Joseph Kappen's body and took DNA from bone and teeth tissue. They found it matched with the profile which they had pieced together from Kappen's family and which also matched the unknown profile from the three crime scenes.

The familial search method has raised concerns over how it might challenge ideas people may hold about privacy, family relationships and kinship (Suter 2010). It has been argued that implicating family members in an investigation where a relative might be involved could have significant consequences. Haimes (2006) suggested that technologies of forensic *identification* may exert a profound impact on matters of *identity* for individuals and families. Via familial searching, an individual can become a 'genetic informant', who may feel responsible for consequences of a familial search. The position of the genetic informant on the database may bring unwanted intrusion. Any subsequent scrutiny into a family's life could lead to the suspect becoming ostracized. Families may feel collectively labelled as 'criminal types' (Haimes 2006; Murphy 2010). Familial search may reveal new genetic links which might expose instances of adultery or incest. These hitherto assumed genetic links could challenge longstanding social relationships. Through familial searching, individuals could in theory find that they are not genetically related to those they assumed to be family. Major revelations about previously unknown associations could, in some cases, lead individuals to question, and even redefine, who they and their families are. Families will have to deal with these possible consequences long after the police investigation is over, regardless of the outcome of the latter.

Familial searching has also been criticized for potentially perpetuating erroneous assumptions about criminality and heredity and discriminatory attitudes about ethnicity and crime (Murphy 2010). It has been argued that familial DNA searching creates a sub-class of individuals related to suspects or convicted offenders and that this may have a greater impact on minority and disadvantaged groups in society, who may be disproportionally over-represented in criminal DNA databases (Murphy 2010).

*Forensic genealogy*

Other methods have emerged which exploit genetic databases and heredity. In recent years, commercial DNA genealogy databases, primarily created as a means for publics to trace their family trees, have been used to pursue criminal investigations (O'Leary 2018; Phillips 2018; Kennett 2019; Ram et al. 2019; Wickenheiser 2019). Contemporary genealogy databases compare sequences across thousands of specific points within individual genomes found on chromosomes, known as single-nucleotide polymorphisms (SNPs). The extent to which individuals may share the same SNP sequences can indicate how closely individuals are related (Biometrics and Forensics Ethics Group [BFEG] 2020). Forensic genealogy may be assisted by male DNA profiles showing close association with surnames in patriarchal societies. Other information, including online searching of databases such as voter registration records, may reveal where a person has lived or worked. After a match is found, researchers use a variety of resources to produce family trees. Common resources include census records, newspaper archives, public 'people search' databases, social media data and pre-existing public family trees. It may be possible to identify an unknown individual from a distant relative match given knowledge of their biological sex, location within 100 miles and age within five years. Erlich et al. (2018) claimed that a database representing only 2 per cent of a specific ethnically defined population (e.g., 'Caucasian') may be sufficient to allow comparison of a suspect's DNA, which may reveal a link between a third cousin or closer relative.

Like familial searching, forensic applications of genealogy have tended to follow after failure to match an unknown profile with a DNA database of known individuals. Investigators have uploaded unknown DNA profiles from crime scenes of potential suspects to commercial databases. If a partial match with possible genetic relatives is identified, other data resources are used to construct a putative family tree which might identify a possible named suspect. A DNA profile from the suspect may be collected, either knowingly or surreptitiously, and compared with the unknown recovered profile to determine a possible match.

Unsuccessful attempts in earlier investigations (Kennett 2019) did not impede police enthusiasm in the United States, and genealogical analysis has since come to be associated with some high-profile cases. In 2015 genealogical analysis was reported as providing a lead to the arrest of Bryan Patrick Miller for Arizona's Canal Killer murders (Phillips 2018; Ram et al. 2019). The Buckskin Girl case (referring to a murder victim's jacket), which had remained unsolved for 37 years, was also resolved through genealogical analysis.

Analysts claimed an identification via family links on GEDMatch, a public genealogy service (Kennett 2019).

One of the most high-profile forensic uses of genealogy concerns the Golden State Killer (GSK) case (O'Leary 2018; Kennett 2019; Ram et al. 2019; Wickenheiser 2019). The GSK was linked to a string of rapes, murders and burglaries committed in California between 1976 and 1986. A DNA profile of the GSK had been obtained from a rape kit. The profile was uploaded to GEDMatch, which identified 10–20 distant relatives, possibly great-great-great-grandparents (Katsanis 2020), who appeared to share genetic material with the rape kit profile.

Police investigators, working with genealogist Barbara Rae-Venter, constructed a family tree based on this information, which implicated two men. One of these was exculpated following a DNA test. The other, Joseph James DeAngelo, was identified as the main suspect. In April 2018, a DNA sample was surreptitiously collected from the door of DeAngelo's car and another was collected from a tissue from his external refuse bin. Both of DeAngelo's DNA profiles matched with crime scene samples linked with the GSK.

Commercial genetic genealogy services have attracted considerable public participation in recent years. By 2018, 26 million individuals in the United States were thought to have had analyzed their DNA via these services (Regalado 2019). A group of employees of the company Parabon Nanolabs which developed genealogical methods claimed that the arrest of the GSK increased awareness and led to more participants registering with GEDMatch (Greytak et al. 2019). A survey of public opinion conducted by Guerrini et al. (2018) claimed significant public support for police searches of genealogy websites, for companies to disclose customer information to police and for police to submit fake profiles to commercial services or under a false name. This survey returned considerable public support for such practices when connected with the investigation of violent crime, crimes against children and missing persons cases, although only 39 per cent of respondents supported use for non-violent crimes.

The GSK case raised the issue of public participation in forensic genealogical investigations. Although participation reportedly increased following the case, GEDMatch also experienced demand among some users to delete their genetic data (O'Leary 2018). Greytak et al. (2019), however, claimed that GEDMatch provided sufficient information to make customers aware that some of their data may be used by police prior to analysis, and similar messages were communicated in their terms of service. Television advertising has encouraged publics to upload their DNA to genealogical databases to help catch criminals (Kennett 2019). Such a call has a potential global reach. One appeal encouraged people in New Zealand to submit data to investigate crimes elsewhere (Kennett 2019). A US congresswoman made a request to the provider 23AndMe to assist in the reunification of Mexican families (Syndercombe Court 2018).

Much debate has focused on the extent to which customers consent to the use of their data for certain purposes. Commercial genealogy providers present terms of service to users, although it is questionable whether this constitutes a form of informed consent, particularly if they may be changed post hoc (Cleary 2019; Katsanis 2020). One case involving the provider Familytree allegedly allowed law enforcement to access data without notifying customers (Ram and Roberts 2019). It transpired that Familytree had collaborated with the FBI for some time (BFEG 2020). Other providers have adopted different attitudes regarding police co-operation (Kennett 2019; Lund 2020). US law is relatively unclear over the extent to which individuals are protected from police searches of commercial databases (Ram et al. 2019). Under US law, there may be scope for commercial providers to resist subpoenas to release data to law enforcement, but this has not always been the case in practice. In November 2019 a Florida judge ruled that GEDMatch had to comply with a request for their entire data to be searched, to which they acquiesced within 24 hours (Katsanis 2020). Terms and conditions of use are also potentially subject to change through takeovers. In December 2019 GEDMatch was taken over by the forensics company Verogen (BFEG 2020). GEDMatch is partnered with Parabon Nanolabs, which monitors GEDMatch data on a weekly basis to assist casework (Katsanis 2020). There are thus concerns that law enforcement agencies may hold a power discrepancy over individual users (Cleary 2019). Using publicly available genealogy data sources for law enforcement raises questions over 'function creep', namely, the use of technology for purposes other than what was originally envisaged (Koops 2021). Possible function creep further complicates the matter of informed consent, arguably raising uncertainty over how an individual's data may be used.

The rights of relatives of users of genealogy services have attracted judicial concern (Williams and Wienroth 2014; Syndercombe Court 2018; Scudder et al. 2019). It has been questioned whether familial search and genealogy threatens the Equal Protection Clause of the 14th Amendment to the US Constitution, guaranteeing impartial treatment of all citizens (Murphy 2010). Forensic genealogy arguably extends investigations further and further from suspects and offenders (Scudder et al. 2019), to the extent that it might even justify universal DNA databases. One alternative option may be to specify how distant a familial relationship can be considered an 'actionable lead' (Scudder et al. 2019: 208).

Other practicalities present a challenge to the application of genealogy. The UK Forensic Science Regulator has raised concerns about scientific standards (BFEG 2018), and it has been reported that many commercial methodologies may not have been validated for forensic use (Kennett 2019). Validation may involve consideration of many processes (Wickenheiser 2019). Concerns have also been raised about overly simplistic police understandings of the science behind genealogical testing and how it might influence the course of investigations (Wickenheiser 2019). Other issues include the possible lack of suitable accreditation among genealogical researchers and the ability of police to discern competent from incompetent experts (Kennett 2019). The investigative process may be time-consuming, perhaps acting as a limiting factor influencing what cases it might be used for. The GSK investigation took four months (Wickenheiser 2019).

Another issue concerns exceptionality, namely, how to justify which cases should be investigated via genealogical methods (Granja and Machado 2019). In April 2018 GEDMatch changed their site policy to allow the uploading of deceased person's samples and crime scene samples involved in suspected violent crimes, defined as 'homicide or sexual assault' (Cleary 2019). In 2019 forensic genealogy was used in the so-called Sioux Falls Baby and Julie Valentine cases to identify and charge two women with murder following the abandonment of newborn babies in 1981 and 1990, respectively (Cleary 2019). This raised questions over whether the historical circumstances which led to the abandonment were overlooked (Molteni 2019; Zhang 2019). Scudder et al. (2019) reported that genealogy was involved in a case which simply involved the theft of loose change from a vehicle in Colorado. It has been debated whether genealogy should be used in other circumstances; for example, to investigate missing persons (Kennett 2019). Scudder et al. (2019) proposed regulations for using genealogy which entail detailing the types of offences for which it could be permitted. This, however, raises a potential ethical dilemma in that the system may overlook persons who commit relatively minor crimes before moving on to commit more serious ones.

The Golden State Killer case also raised legal and ethical concerns over the surreptitious sampling of suspect DNA. This practice has been challenged over whether it transgresses the 'abandonment principle' of the 4th Amendment to the US Constitution. The question is whether surreptitious sampling of DNA constitutes abandoned property, which investigators are allowed to use in the pursuit of a criminal case (Lund 2020).

Another issue concerns whether genealogy threatens the right of spatial anonymity, namely, the right not to have one's whereabouts traced by others (Katsanis 2020). Genealogy may present jurisdictional challenges in that it may identify relatives living in other countries (BFEG 2020). Differences in the law exist across US states (Wickenheiser 2019) and between different parts of the world. For example, due to data protection laws, European Union–based users are allowed to opt out of police investigations, in contrast to the United States (Ram and Roberts 2019).

Genealogy has so far largely been used in the United States, although methods have been used to develop leads in a case in Sweden (Tillmar et al. 2020) and have been tested in a UK setting (Thomson et al. 2019). It was reported in 2018 that UK police had received queries about the possible use of genealogical testing (BFEG 2018). A report prepared by members of BFEG stated that police use of genealogy in the UK 'would need to be clearly established with reference to Article 8 of the European Convention of Human Rights and the Human Rights Act 1998' (BFEG 2020: 6). BFEG also recommended that use of forensic genealogy for law enforcement should only be used if other existing methods were considered 'no longer adequate or effective' (BFEG 2020: 6), were based on clear evidence and were verified by an independent body. Informed consent was considered to be a potentially insufficient legal basis in the purview of the 2018 Data Protection Act, the EU Law Enforcement Directive and case law related to Article 8 of the European Convention of Human Rights (BFEG 2020: 6).

## Forensic DNA phenotyping

Phenotypes are genetically inherited physical characteristics. DNA phenotyping refers to methods which claim to infer the physical appearance of individuals from genetic data. Earlier forensic applications of phenotyping involved the analysis of characteristics such as eye colour. Phenotyping research has since focused on more complex potential relations between genetics, appearance and ancestry (Kayser 2015; Phillips 2015). Contemporary phenotyping research, aided by improvements in data analysis, compares the DNA of populations of individuals to attempt to identify linked patterns of appearance. DNA is sampled from large populations of individuals of known appearance (Parabon Nanolabs 2021). Data mining techniques seek to identify shared patterns in the DNA of people within these populations and attempt to establish probabilistic relationships between DNA patterns in these populations and appearance. If such relationships are identified, the DNA of unknown individuals' DNA is compared and phenotyped. The accuracy of phenotyping methods is tested by predicting phenotypes of new subjects with a known phenotype and comparing predicted with actual phenotypes.

Forensic applications of phenotyping have involved predicting the appearance of an individual from DNA samples left at suspected crime scenes. Early methods to discern 'external visible characteristics' (EVCs; Toom 2012) were used in the investigation of the rape and murder of 16-year-old Marianne Vaatstra, who was found dead near her home town of Zwaagwesteinde in the Netherlands (Jong and M'charek 2018). DNA analysis in this case pointed to the likelihood of the perpetrator being of Northern European appearance, which, it was claimed, alleviated local tensions (Jong and M'charek 2018). Vaatstra's body had been found nearby a temporary shelter for asylum seekers from the Middle East and North Africa (Sankar 2010).

Forensic DNA phenotyping (FDP) has been employed when known individuals, such as family, friends, partners or colleagues, have been excluded as possible suspects. FDP groups together individuals of similar appearance (e.g., male, brown eyes, European ancestry, etc.). These individuals may become targeted as subjects of interest for further investigation. In the Netherlands, police have organized so-called DNA dragnets, where those sharing a particular appearance were requested to provide DNA (Toom 2012). Phenotyping has raised concerns that it leads to a reversal of the onus of proof and a possible erosion of the presumption of innocence (HGC 2009).

The legislative basis of phenotyping, and law enforcement use of DNA sequences which code for genes, is unclear in many jurisdictions and is not internationally harmonized (Wienroth 2018; Samuel and Prainsack 2019). The Netherlands passed legislation in 2003 which regulates the determination of EVCs of unknown suspects by genetic methods. Germany amended federal legislation to allow more extensive genetic analysis for forensic purposes (Amelung and Machado 2021). This allows for the inference of eye, hair, skin colour and age. Many jurisdictions, such as England and Wales, however, have yet to fully consider specific legislation (Wienroth 2018).

Some scientists supportive of FDP have claimed it to be at least in theory a more epistemologically robust form of identification compared to human eyewitness testimony (Kayser 2015). They argue that EVCs are visible to all and can be reported in more precise, conditional probabilistic terms. Kayser and Schneider (2009) also claimed that police will only evaluate the predicted information in the context of other intelligence within a given case. FDP has been regarded as a means of corroborating and supporting eyewitness evidence, which in turn might lead to efficiencies in investigative resources (Scudder et al. 2018).

FDP has attracted wider interest in some cases. One example surrounded a case in Germany. On 16 October 2016, a student was found raped and murdered in the university town of Freiburg. Around this time there were calls for including FDP into German law. On 3 December 2016, a suspect was arrested, a young refugee from Afghanistan. Lipphardt (2017) reported that following the rape-murder, media coverage of FDP became 'overtly positive', particularly in Freiburg itself (Lipphardt 2017). The first support for FDP came from a flyer campaign by local right-wing political groups. Local police representatives and politicians lobbied for the use of FDP in November 2016, followed by wider regional and national media campaigns a month later. Lipphardt (2017) reported that supporters of FDP claimed the law needed to be updated to reflect technological progress. Supportive arguments in these campaigns also claimed that the success rate of such technology was high, that FDP only studied visible traits and did not entail racial profiling and that groups lobbying for FDP claimed there were no data protection issues.

Pressure to allow forensic phenotyping in Germany was countered by opposing concerns from academic communities that scientific issues and complexities regarding FDP data had been overlooked. These critical voices claimed the technology had been portrayed simplistically and overly positively by media and politicians (Lipphardt et al. 2016; Lipphardt 2017; Jong and M'charek 2018). Linked to these criticisms were concerns about the manner in which DNA methods, including FDP, might render vulnerable populations such as Roma or Sinti as suspect groups (Lipphardt and Surdu 2020). These groups previously received unwarranted attention from German police who misinterpreted DNA data when investigating a murder in the town of Heilbronn (Lipphardt et al. 2016).

Social scientists have raised further ethical and scientific issues regarding FDP (Smith and Urbas 2011; M'charek et al. 2012; Toom et al. 2016), arguing that there are considerable difficulties in defining specific population and ethnic groups. In raising the issue of 'defining populations – both at the level of scientific research, and the application of EVCs in criminal investigation' – these authors suggested that the civil rights of entire populations are at stake (M'charek et al. 2012: e17). An increasing amount of forensic genetics research has sought to explore possible links between specific DNA patterns and certain ethnic groups. In doing so, it has been argued that this general approach exposes the risks of assuming too much knowledge of ethnicity, derived from genetic research which is itself based on a priori, sociocultural assumptions regarding ethnic classification (Ossorio and Duster 2005). The use of FDP to identify putative 'suspect' populations, and the pressure on individuals identified within those populations to submit DNA to exonerate themselves, has raised concerns about the discriminatory targeting of certain populations in addition to concerns about presumptions of innocence being challenged (Toom 2012; Toom et al. 2016; Scudder et al. 2018). In the 1990s, the Metropolitan Police misinterpreted ancestry and skin pigmentation tests during an investigation into a serial sex attacker, known as Operation Minstead. Police wrongly inferred the suspect was of Caribbean origin and sought 'voluntary' DNA samples from thousands of men. Those who did not comply allegedly faced police intimidation (Skinner 2020).

Much ethical discussion around FDP thus relates to concerns about how this technology may problematically construct conceptions of race and relations between individuals and collectives (M'charek and Wade 2020). Studies have articulated concerns over whether technologies such as FDP essentialize relations between genetic and social categorization (Roberts and Rollins 2020; Skinner 2020). Skinner (2020) pointed to terms such as 'race', 'ethnicity', etc., as reflecting a slippage between objective/subjective and social/biological accounts.

> Assertions also assume that markers of race and ethnicity are obvious and unproblematic and in the process gloss over questions of categorization: why pick particular race categories, how should people be placed in or out of those categories, and what operational and social implications attach to these choices.
>
> (Skinner 2020: 340)

Such perceptions raise concerns about forensic scientists constructing racial categorizations which may be invalid, discriminatory and prejudicial. Critics of phenotypic profiling and related research claim that ethnic classifiers (e.g., 'white' 'Caucasian', etc.) are inevitably cultural labels and do not reflect underlying genetic reality (Ossorio and Duster 2005). Certain terms such as 'Afro-Caribbean' or 'Caucasian', formerly used as 'ethnic appearance' classifiers in England and Wales, are social conventions, not scientifically established categories. Such labels are not essential features of DNA profiles and thus make visible the risk of FDP reinforcing a tautologous relationship between culturally assumed labels and claims to ethnic linkages with DNA.

Parabon Nanolabs, a company which has received support from the US Department of Defence, produced a method known as Snapshot which it claims can produce facial images of persons from unknown DNA profiles. Snapshot has attracted much interest from law enforcement communities (Samuel and Prainsack 2019; Wienroth 2020), and Parabon Nanolabs has claimed numerous successes (Murphy 2018; Parabon Nanolabs 2021). In 2015, Snapshot attracted media attention when it was used to investigate the deaths of Candra Alston and her threeyear-old daughter in Columbia, South Carolina, USA (Parabon Nanolabs 2015). Investigating this suspected double murder had been hindered by the lack of clues and eyewitness information. City of Columbia police went public with an image purporting to resemble a 'person of interest'.

The use of FDP has been critiqued over the accuracy of images and the validity and reliability of the underlying science (Gannon 2017; Samuel and Prainsack 2019; Wienroth

2018). The resulting image generated by Snapshot in the Alston case resembles that of a fairly young AfroAmerican male (Parabon Nanolabs 2015). It is, however, generic and arguably not far removed from that found in a computer game. The lack of verisimilitude raised concerns over the risk of possible confirmation bias and misidentification in areas where racial sensitivities may exist (expert discussion 2015).

FDP raises the issue of whether it can be used reliably as evidence or whether it is better suited for intelligence purposes, providing information which is 'indicative rather than substantive' (Wienroth 2018: 143), narrowing down the pool of suspects in an investigation and prioritizing leads. This also concerns whether such data should be released publicly or limited to police use. Intelligence may have a lower threshold of reliability if it is merely used to guide an investigation, where other, more robust evidence may be subsequently found (notwithstanding the possibility of racially discriminatory police practices; Duster 2004).

Another issue specific to FDP concerns the limits in terms of what kind of genetically inherited traits should be used for investigative purposes. DNA phenotyping may not just potentially involve predicting physical appearance but could also be used to ascertain health conditions. This raises issues concerning 'the right of people not to know what their DNA tells about propensities for diseases or other propensities, data protection and privacy … the risk of stigmatization and discrimination, and the vision of a slippery slope leading, ultimately, to eugenics' (Koops and Schellekens 2008: 160; see also Perepechina 2013; Toom et al. 2016).

There is, however, a paucity of formalized ethical guidance concerning this application of phenotyping. Ethical guidelines do exist for the use of genetic testing for health purposes, but they largely remain within a conventional medical purview. Genetic traits may indicate current or possible future health conditions. Conventional medical ethics normally emphasizes the right of the individual to know potential future health conditions or to live without that knowledge. In theory, DNA phenotyping could be used ultimately to identify those with health traits which could be useful for identification purposes. Phenotyping which could be used to detect genes linked with health conditions from an unknown sample could conceivably lead to suspects being tested for the presence of the same genetic markers. Those health traits may not have been previously known to the person under suspicion. While currently more theoretical than practical, such an issue raises the question as to what kind of phenotypes might be considered ethically acceptable to rely on for investigative purposes in the future. While health traits could be strongly probative, they raise issues of the right to know.

### Co-producing forensic DNA phenotyping

As the previous discussion has indicated, social research has challenged certain aspects of FDP. These studies caution against an overly simplistic view of FDP, questioning scientific assumptions and raising related ethical issues. Additional empirical studies conducted by social scientists engaging with forensic geneticists suggest that these scientists and other stakeholders frame human bodies and phenotyping technologies in fluid and variable ways (Granja et al. 2020). Social research has challenged the status of FDP as a unified, stable scientific approach and has examined how scientifically coherent assumptions about FDP rest on a variety of practices (Wienroth 2018; Hopman and M'charek 2020). More significant still, these studies reveal complex, contingent and fluid entanglements between notions of the collective and the individual and a fragile balancing of scientific, ethical and law enforcement imperatives.

In their ethnographic study of a phenotyping laboratory, Hopman and M'charek (2020) described the construction of a phenotyped facial image. In 'providing insight into how race is done' (Hopman and M'charek 2020: 459) they identified three distinct practices through which relations between collectives and individuals are constructed: firstly, a probabilistic characterization of an individual's putative membership of a collective based on categories of skin pigmentation; second, the metrical attribution of an individual to a group by 'associating facial morphology to ancestry' (Hopman and M'charek 2020: 459); and, finally, a geographical construction of a collective through assumptions of a shared locational ancestry to facilitate identification of an individual.

Authors have explored the social and ethical heterogeneity of FDP in other ways (Samuel and Prainsack 2019; Granja et al. 2020). Studies have involved a range of stakeholders as respondents, including forensic scientists, police officers, lawyers, government representatives and social scientists. These respondents varied in how they linked thresholds of reliability. validity and probabilistic measures of accuracy, with investigative utility and the relative seriousness of the crime being investigated via FDP. Some respondents were also found to draw boundaries between their standpoints and those of other stakeholders. Granja et al. (2020) introduced the concept of '(de)materialization' to describe the fluid and variable ways forensic geneticists frame human bodies and technology. Forensic geneticists drew boundaries between two forms of 'materializing criminal bodies', namely, eyewitness and biological testimony, but they acknowledged scientific uncertainty and controversies over FDP, not just in purely technical terms but through also expressing concerns over how FDP might reinforce structural forms of discrimination. Through maintaining the conditionality and contingency of FDP, these respondents sought to retain control over their area of expertise. Granja et al. (2020) described how forensic geneticists variously used the notion of epistemic risk (see Chapter 5) to distance science from acceptable and unacceptable applications in law enforcement, bestowing this responsibility to the latter. Scientists drew distinctions between their perceptions of limitations, risks and affordances of FDP on one hand and police interpretation of data on the other. Scientists delegated responsibility to the latter to learn new conditional, statistical vocabularies of data interpretation. Elsewhere, Wienroth (2020) found that scientists contested claims about phenotyping in terms of an ethic of transparency, which they associated with public-domain scientists, versus the seemingly questionable and opaque claims of commercial entities such as Parabon Nanolabs (Wienroth 2020).

Other heterogeneities have been discerned which allude to how FDP has constructed an authoritative status in the face of critical responses. Wienroth (2018) discussed three different forms of 'anticipatory practices' which pre-empt such challenges. Promissory practices entail discursive expectations which frame FDP as beneficial, or at least ethically neutral, and inevitable. Epistemic practices shape the ontological and epistemological basis of FDP, such as the assumption that phenotypes can be inferred from genotypes, justifications for categorizing data and the probabilistic basis of FDP analysis. Finally, operational practices embed technologies into law enforcement alongside other forms of investigative information (Wienroth 2018). Wienroth also noted how 'anticipatory governance' of FDP variously entails international organizations, standard setting and training and, in doing so, also pointed to the underlying complexity required to maintain the stability of FDP.

## Conclusion

This chapter has sought to convey the probative force attributed to DNA in law enforcement contexts. DNA data have been collected, organized and analyzed in various ways. These practices and technologies shape and are shaped by a combination of scientific, technical, legal, policing, ethical and policy imperatives. The technological achievement of the NDNAD has been shaped by a series of laws which have granted police changing powers to sample and retain genetic material from individuals who may be innocent. Familial search represents a further attempted iteration of the utility of NDNAD but which has raised additional ethical concerns. Law enforcement has gone further in utilizing collections of DNA data via forensic genealogy. DNA phenotyping represents another means of exploiting the collective potential of genetic data, albeit one which has also raised much social and ethical critique. Sociological research has highlighted how DNA methods like phenotyping are co-produced via the practices and standpoints of different actors such as scientists and police.

DNA databasing, familial search, forensic genealogy and phenotyping have been framed in different ways. Some voices frame them positively, as powerful tools for justice. Others express caution about the scope of their utility, while others still have expressed ethical concerns over risks to social justice. This volume considers the social and policy significance of this technology further in the final chapter. Other biometric technologies have been the subject of a similar series of framings. Chapter 8 moves on to discuss issues concerning facial recognition.

## Bibliography

Amankwaa, A.O. and McCartney, C. (2019) 'The UK National DNA Database: implementation of the Protection of Freedoms Act 2012', *Forensic Science International*, 284: 117–128.

Amelung, N. and Machado, H. (2021) 'Governing expectations of forensic innovations in society: the case of FDP in Germany', *New Genetics and Society*, first published online 20 January 2021. doi:10.1080/14636778.2020.1868987.

Biometrics and Forensics Ethics Group. (2018) *Meeting Minutes*, 3 December 2018 at the Home Office London.

Biometrics and Forensics Ethics Group. (2020) *Should We Be Making Use of Genetic Genealogy to Assist in Solving Crime? A Report on the Feasibility of Such Methods in the UK*. Biometrics and Forensics Ethics Group. London: Home Office.

British Broadcasting Corporation. (2007) 'All UK Must Be on UK Database', BBC News, 25 September; online at http://news.bbc.co.uk/1/hi/uk/6979138.stm (accessed 27 September 2013).

Cleary, J. (2019) 'Ethical dilemmas and data sharing in genetic genealogy', Poster presented at Personal Genomes: Accessing, Sharing and Interpretation. Wellcome Genome Campus, Cambridge, UK, 11–12 April 2019.

Doleac, J. (2012) *The Effects of DNA Databases on Crime*, Batten Working Paper 2013–001 December.

Duster, T. (2004) 'Selective arrests, an ever-expanding DNA forensic database, and the specter of an early twenty-first-century equivalent of phrenology', in D. Lazer (ed.), *The Technology of Justice: DNA and the Criminal Justice System*. Cambridge, MA: Harvard University Press, pp. 315–334.

Erlich, Y., Shor, T., Carmi, S. and Pe'er, I. (2018) 'Re-identification of genomic data using long range familial searches', *bioRxiv*, 350231.

Gannon, M. (2017) 'Amazing DNA Tool Gives Cops a New Way to Crack Cold Cases: DNA Phenotyping Can Produce a Sketch of the Suspect. But Is It Ready for Primetime?' NBCnews, 12 July 2017; online at https:// http://www.nbcnews.com/mach/science/amazing-dna-tool-gives-cops-new-way-crack-coldcases-ncna781946 (accessed 27 August 2021).

Granja, R. and Machado, H. (2019) 'Ethical controversies of familial searching: the views of stakeholders in the United Kingdom and Poland', *Science, Technology & Human Values*, 44 (6): 1068–1092.

Granja, R., Machado, H. and Queiros, F. (2020) 'The (de)materialization of criminal bodies in forensic DNA phenotyping', *Body & Society*, 27 (1): 60–84.

Greytak, E.M., Moore, C. and Armentrout, S.L. (2019) 'Genetic genealogy for cold case and active investigations', *Forensic Science International*, 299: 103–113.

Guerrini, C.J., Robinson, J.O., Petersen, D. and McGuire, A.L. (2018) 'Should police have access to genetic genealogy databases? Capturing the Golden State Killer and other criminals using a controversial new forensic technique', *PLOS Biology*, 16 (10): e2006906.

Haimes, E. (2006) 'Social and ethical issues in the use of familial searching in forensic 19 investigations: insights from family and kinship studies', *Journal of Law, Medicine and Ethics*, 34 (2): 263–276.

Hopman, R. (2020) 'Opening up forensic DNA phenotyping: The logics of accuracy, commonality and valuing', *New Genetics and Society*, 39 (4): 424–440.

Hopman, R. and M'charek, A. (2020) 'Facing the unknown suspect: Forensic DNA phenotyping and the oscillation between the individual and the collective', *BioSocieties*, 15: 438–462.

Human Genetics Commission. (2009) *Nothing to Hide, Nothing to Fear? Balancing Individual Rights and the Public Interest in the Governance and Use of the National DNA Database*. London: Human Genetics Commission.

Jong, L. and M'charek, A. (2018) 'The high-profile case as 'fire object': following the Marianne Vaatstra murder case through the media', *Crime Media Culture*, 14 (3): 347–363.

Katsanis, S.H. (2020) 'Pedigrees and perpetrators: uses of DNA and genealogy in forensic investigations', *Annual Review of Genomics and Human Genetics*, 21: 535–564.

Kayser, M. (2015) 'Forensic DNA phenotyping: predicting human appearance from crime scene material for investigative purposes', *Forensic Science International*, 18: 33–48.

Kayser, M. and Schneider, P.M. (2009) 'DNA-based prediction of human externally visible characteristics in forensics: motivations, scientific challenges, and ethical considerations', *Forensic Science International: Genetics*, 3: 154–161.

Kennett, D. (2019) 'Using genetic genealogy databases in missing persons cases and to develop suspect leads in violent crimes', *Forensic Science International*, 301: 107–117.

Koops, B.-J. (2021) 'The concept of function creep', *Law, Innovation and Technology*, 13 (1): 29–56.

Koops, B.-J. and Schellekens, M. (2008) 'Forensic DNA phenotyping: regulatory issues', *Columbia Science & Technology Law Review*, 9: 158–202.

Lawless, C. (2009) *Helping with Inquiries: Theory and Practice in Forensic Science*. Phd thesis, Durham University.

Lipphardt, V. (2017) 'Adapting the law to the technology? Germany's current debate on DNA Phenotyping', ESRC Seminar Series on Genetics, Security and Justice: Crossing, Contesting and Comparing Boundaries, Newcastle-upon-Tyne, 24 March 2017; online at: http://www.ncl.ac.uk/media/wwwnclacuk/policyethicsandlifesciences/files/Lipphardt_slides.pdf (accessed 31 August 2020).

Lipphardt, V., Lipphardt, A., Buchanan, N., Surdu, M., Toom, V., Wienroth, M., Mupepele, A.C., Bradbury, C. and Lemke, T. (2016) 'Open Letter on Critical Approaches to Forensic DNA Phenotyping (FDP) and Bio-geographical Ancestry (BGA)', open letter published online 8 Dec 2016; online at: https://www.academia.edu/32678436/OPEN_LETTER_ON_CRITICAL_APPROACHES_TO_FORENSIC_DNA_PHENOTYPING_FDP_AND_BIOGEOGRAPHICAL_ANCESTRY_BGA_originally_published_Dec_08_2016 (accessed 27 August 2021).

Lipphardt, V. and Surdu, M. (2020) 'DNA data from Roma in forensic genetic studies and databases: risks and challenges', Unpublished draft submitted to *American Journal of Bioethics*; online at: https://www.researchgate.net/publication/345808962_DNA_Data_From_Roma_In_Forensic_Genetic_Studies_And_Databases_Risks_And_Challenges (accessed 27 October 2021).

Lund, S. (2020) 'Ethical implications of forensic genealogy in criminal cases', *The Journal of Entrepreneurship & The Law*, 13 (2): 185–208.

Lynch, M. and McNally, R. (2009) 'Forensic DNA databases and biolegality: the co-production of law, surveillance technology and suspect bodies', in P. Atkinson, P. Glasner and M. Lock (eds), *Handbook of Genetics and Society: Mapping the New Genomic Era*. Abingdon: Routledge, pp. 283–301.

Machado, H. and Granja, R. (2020) *Forensic Genetics in the Governance of Crime*. Singapore: Palgrave Macmillan.

McCartney, C., Wilson, T.J. and Williams, R. (2010) *The Future Use of Forensic Bioinformation*. London: Nuffield Foundation.

M'charek, A., Toom, V. and Prainsack, B. (2012) 'Bracketing off population does not advance ethical reflection on EVCs: a reply to Kayser and Schneider', *Forensic Science International: Genetics*, 6: e16–e17.

M'charek, A. and Wade, P. (2020) 'Doing the individual and the collective in forensic genetics: governance, race and resitution', *BioSocieties*, 15 (3): 317–328.

Molteni, M. (2019) 'DNA crime-solving is still new, yet it may have gone too far', *Wired*, 14 March 2019; online at: https://www.wired.com/story/dnacrime-solving-is-still-new-yet-it-may-have-gone-too-far/ (accessed 27 August 2021).

Murphy, E. (2010) 'Relative doubt: familial searches of DNA databases', *Michigan Law Review*, 109 (3): 291–348.

Murphy, E. (2018) 'Forensic DNA typing', *Annual Review of Criminology*, 1: 497–515.

Nuffield Council on Bioethics. (2007) *The Forensic Use of Bioinformation: Ethical Issues*. London: Nuffield Council on Bioethics.

O'Leary, D.E. (2018) 'DNA mining and genealogical information systems: not just for finding family ethnicity', *Intelligent Systems in Accounting, Finance and Management*, 25: 190–196.

Ossorio, P. and Duster, T. (2005) 'Race and genetics: controversies in biomedical, behavourial and forensic sciences', *American Psychologist*, 60 (1): 115–128.

Parabon Nanolabs. (2015) 'SnapshotTM Puts a Face on Four-Year-Old Case', online at http://parabon-nanolabs.com/nanolabs/news-events/2015/01/snapshot-puts-face-on-four-year-old-cold-case.html (accessed 19 October 2015).

Parabon Nanolabs. (2021) 'The Snapshot DNA Phenotyping Service', online at: https://snapshot.parabon-nanolabs.com/phenotyping (accessed 17 August 2021).

Perepechina, I.O. (2013) 'Legislative framework and value of the forensic DNA examination of health-related information for crime investigation', *Forensic Science International Genetics Supplement Series*, 4: e360–e361.

Phillips, C. (2015) 'Forensic genetic analysis of bio-geographical ancestry', *Forensic Science International: Genetics*, 18: 49–65.

Phillips, C. (2018) 'The Golden State Killer investigation and the nascent field of forensic genealogy', *Forensic Science International*, 36: 186–188.

Ram, N., Guerrini, C.J. and McGuire, A.L. (2019) 'Genealogy databases and the future of criminal investigation', *Science*, 360 (96393): 1078–1079.

Ram, N. and Roberts, J.L. (2019) 'Forensic genealogy and the power of defaults', *Nature Biotechnology*, 37: 707–708.

Regalado, A. (2019) 'More than 26 million people have taken an at-home ancestry test', *MIT Technology Review*. 2 November 2019; online at: https://www.technologyreview.com/2019/02/11/103446/more-than-26-million-people-have-taken-an-at-home-ancestry-test/ (accessed 23 August 2020).

Roberts, D.E. and Rollins, O. (2020) 'Why sociology matters to race and biosocial science', *Annual Review of Sociology*, 46: 195–214.

Roman, J.K., Reid, S., Reid, J., Chalfin, A., Adams, W. and Knight, C. (2008) *The DNA Field Experiment: Cost-Effectiveness Analysis of the Use of DNA on the Investigation of High-Volume Crimes*. Washington, DC: Urban Institute of Justice Policy Center.

Samuel, G. and Prainsack, B. (2019) 'Forensic DNA phenotyping in Europe: views "on the ground" from those who have a professional stake in the technology', *New Genetics & Society*, 38 (2): 119–141.

Sankar, P. 2010. 'Forensic DNA phenotyping: reinforcing race in law enforcement', in I. Whitmarsh and D.S. Jones (eds), *What's the Use of Race?* Cambridge, MA: MIT Press, pp. 49–62.

Scudder, N., McNevin, D., Kelty, S.F., Walsh, S.J. and Robertson, J. (2018) 'Forensic DNA phenotyping: developing a model privacy assessment', *Forensic Science International: Genetics*, 34: 222–230.

Scudder, N., McNevin, D., Kelty, S.F., Funk, C., Walsh, S.J. and Robertson, J. (2019) 'Policy and regulatory implications of the new frontier of forensic genomics: Direct-to-consumer genetic data and genealogy records', *Current Issues in Criminal Justice*, 31 (2): 194–216.

Skinner, D. (2020) 'Forensic genetics and the prediction of race: what is the problem?', *BioSocieties*, 15 (3): 329–349.

Smith, M. and Urbas, G. (2011) 'Regulating new forms of forensic DNA profiling under Australian legislation: familial matching and DNA phenotyping', Australasian Institute of Judicial Administration Conference, Sydney, 7–9 September 2011.

Suter, S.M. (2010) 'All in the family: privacy and DNA familial searching', *Harvard Journal of Law and Technology*, 23 (2): 310–399.

Syndercombe Court, D. (2018) 'Forensic genealogy: some serious concerns', *Forensic Science International: Genetics*, 36: 203–204.

Thomson, J., Clayton, T., Cleary, J., Gleeson, M., Kennett, D., Leonard, M. and Rutherford, D. (2019) 'The effectiveness of forensic genealogy techniques in the United Kingdom – an experimental assessment', *Forensic Science International: Genetics Supplement Series* 7: 765–767.

Tillmar, A., Sjölünd, P., Lundqvist, B., Klippmark, T., Älgenäs, C. and Green, H. (2020) 'Whole-genome sequencing of human remains to enable genealogy DNA database searches – a case report', *Forensic Science International: Genetics*, 46: 102233.

Toom, V. (2012) 'Bodies of science and law: forensic DNA profiling, biological bodies, 6 and biopower', *Journal of Law and Society*, 39 (1): 150–166.

Toom, V., Wienroth, M., M'Charek, A., et al. (2016) 'Approaching ethical, legal and social issues of emerging forensic DNA phenotyping (FDP) technologies comprehensively: Reply to "Forensic DNA Phenotyping: Predicting Human Appearance from Crime Scene Material for Investigative Purposes" by Manfred Kayser', *Forensic Science International: Genetics*, 22: E1–E4.

Wallace, H. (2008) *Prejudice, Stigma and DNA Databases*, paper for the Council for Responsible Genetics, online at: http://www.councilforresponsiblegenetics.org/page-Documents/PDAFXSTDPX.pdf (accessed 26 September 2013).

Wickenheiser, R.A. (2019) 'Forensic genealogy, bioethics and the Golden State Killer case', *Forensic Science International Synergy*, 1: 114–125.

Wienroth, M. (2018) 'Governing anticipatory technology practices. forensic DNA phenotyping and the forensic genetics community in Europe', *New Genetics & Society*, 37 (2): 137–152.

Wienroth, M. (2020) 'Socio-technical disagreements as ethical fora: Parabon Nanolabs forensic DNA Snapshot$^{TM}$ service at the intersection of discourses around robust science, technology validation, and commerce', *BioSocieties*, 15 (1): 28–45.

Williams, R., Johnson, P. and Martin, P. (2004) *Genetic Information and Crime Investigation: Social, Ethical and Public Policy Aspects of the Establishment, Expansion and Police Use of the National DNA Database*. Project Report, Durham.

Williams, R. and Wienroth, M. (2014) 'Identity, mass fatality and forensic genetics', *New Genetics and Society*, 33 (3): 257–276.

Zhang, S. (2019) 'An abandoned baby's DNA condemns his mother', *The Atlantic*, 13 March 2019; online at: https://www.theatlantic.com/science/archive/2019/03/38-years-later-dna-leads-to-teenager-who-abandoned-her-babyin-a-ditch/584683/ (27 August 2021).

# 8 Facial recognition

## Introduction: rationale and use

Facial recognition (FR) technology has been deployed by law enforcement to monitor public spaces. FR is now used in numerous countries (Big Brother Watch 2018; Richardson 2021), although some jurisdictions, such as Scotland and New Zealand, have exhibited significant caution towards this technology. FR has been banned in some cities such as San Francisco (Scottish Parliament 2020). Facial data was, however, cited as a key element of the UK Government's 2018 Biometrics Strategy, and FR has been trialled and used by some police forces in England and Wales. In January 2020, the Metropolitan Police Service announced it would commence regular operational use of FR (British Broadcasting Corporation 2020).

Facial matching compares an individual's image with a database of other images, such as the collection of custody photographs (sometimes known as 'mugshots') stored on the UK-wide Police National Database (PND). In 2018, it was revealed that some UK police forces had retained approximately nineteen million custody images onto the database, without seeking legal permission (Big Brother Watch 2018). FR can be used in different ways. Retrospective facial recognition may enable police to recognize persons of interest from CCTV or other such footage (Metropolitan Police Service 2021). Methods involving live or automated facial recognition technology scan the faces of individuals in crowds or public spaces in real time, comparing them with an image database or 'watchlist' of persons known to the police who may be suspects or considered known troublemakers. These watchlists may be constructed at least partially from custody image data (Davies et al. 2018) or from other sources, possibly images taken in non-controlled environments. Algorithms are used to assess matches between persons and watchlist data.

The use of FR technology for policing purposes has been justified in various ways: for claimed benefits of detection, deterrence, crime displacement and disruption. Fussey and Murray (2019) argued that these reflect clear differences in purposes, 'requiring distinct necessity calculations' (11), and indicate how decisions to use FR are highly contextualized.

A number of police forces in England and Wales have deployed FR. Leicestershire Police used FR at a music festival in 2015. In 2017 South Wales Police (SWP) deployed FR at a series of major sporting fixtures and music concerts, including the UEFA Champions League Final and rugby internationals. SWP also deployed FR at a protest against an arms trade convention in Cardiff, which raised concerns over whether such use could dissuade the public from exercising their right to freedom of expression or legitimate protest (Big Brother Watch 2018).

FR technology has also been used by other authorities and within the private sector to identify known shoplifters, people engaged in antisocial behaviour in stores or others deemed to be acting suspiciously, in addition to anonymously tracking the movements of

DOI: 10.4324/9781003126379-8

customers for marketing purposes (fieldwork 2019; Centre for Data Ethics and Innovation [CDEI] 2020). FR was used by a property firm overseeing redevelopment in the Kings Cross area of London and is used by Glasgow City Council (Big Brother Watch 2018; Scottish Parliament 2020).

As recounted in Chapter 4, FR has been subject to a number of UK parliamentary inquiries. These accused the UK Government and police of inactivity over ethical and individual rights issues relating to the acquisition and collection of facial data. The 2019 House of Commons Science and Technology Select Committee inquiry heard claims from the group Big Brother Watch that the custody image database had increased from 19 million to 23 million in the course of a year and that 10 million of these had been made searchable by FR systems (House of Commons Science and Technology Select Committee 2019). The Information Commissioner's Office, responsible for overseeing data protection legislation (see *Bridges v South Wales Police*), claimed that individuals were likely to be unaware of their rights to have facial data deleted. At this point, promised improvements to the deletion system had not yet occurred.

Between 2019 and 2020, the Policing Sub-committee of the Scottish Parliament conducted its own inquiry into FR. Police Scotland had intended to introduce FR by the end of 2026 (Scottish Police Authority 2017). Police Scotland had claimed the equality and human rights impact of FR was 'likely to be positive in nature' (Scottish Police Authority 2018: 1). The Policing Sub-committee took a markedly different view, concluding that 'there would be no justifiable basis for Police Scotland to invest in this technology.' (Scottish Parliament 2020: 1). The sub-committee also claimed that FR would be 'a radical departure from Police Scotland's fundamental principle of policing by consent' (Scottish Parliament 2020: 1) and that there was an imperative on the part of politicians to establish whether there was public support for police use of FR. In response to any future consideration of FR, the sub-committee emphasized the need for full and transparent assessment of its necessity and accuracy and to fully understand the potential impact on communities, including full consideration of data protection and human rights requirements. In addition, the sub-committee raised concerns about access to images held possibly illegally on the UK Police Database.

FR has also raised concerns at the supranational level. In April 2021 the European Commission (EC) proposed an artificial intelligence (AI) bill which sought to restrict FR but did not ban it outright (EC 2021; Heikkila 2021). Previous concerns have been expressed elsewhere about the European Union's investment in biometrics and the level of public consultation (Gunnarsdottir and Rommetweit 2017).

In England and Wales, it has been claimed that FR was introduced without any formal legal basis (Big Brother Watch 2018; House of Commons Science and Technology Select Committee 2019). Data protection legislation has been identified as the only significant piece of current UK legislation that 'sets limitations on the use of [FR] in this context, and there is no exact interpretation of the conditions it sets' (CDEI 2020). In 2019, the House of Commons Science and Technology Select Committee expressed concern over the 'lack of a clear legislative framework for this technology' (14). It has been claimed that a number of pieces of legislation engage with FR, including the 1998 Human Rights Act, the 2000 Freedom of Information Act, the 2012 Protection of Freedoms Act, the 2018 Data Protection Act and the 2000 Regulation of Investigatory Powers Act (Surveillance Camera Commissioner [SCC] 2019). However, in response to a written parliamentary question from Layla Moran MP, Nick Hurd, the UK Minister of State for Policing, stated, 'There is no legislation regulating the use of CCTV cameras with FR' (Big Brother Watch 2018: 9). In 2018 the then Surveillance Camera Commissioner additionally raised the issue of the lack of a clear statutory footing for FR.

Others have called for a more focused legal framework for FR and have been critical of the Home Office's claim that sufficient legal justification already exists (see, for example, Purshouse and Campbell 2019). While police are required by law to produce a data protection impact assessment (DPIA) before using FR, they are not required to publish it (Purshouse and Campbell 2019). Neither are there any stipulated criteria for watchlist inclusion within the current regulatory framework. A Private Members Bill originating from the House of Lords, titled 'The Automated Facial Recognition Technology (Moratorium and Review) Bill', was introduced in February 2020. As of August 2021, however, this remained at the earliest stages of parliamentary process (UK Parliament 2021).

The Information Commissioner's Office (ICO) has previously submitted and published statements concerning facial data (ICO 2019a, 2019b). In written evidence to the House of Commons Science and Technology Select Committee, the ICO stated that biometric data 'is afforded an additional level of protection', through Part 3 of the 2018 Data Protection Act, which applies to the processing of personal data 'in the context of law enforcement' (ICO 2019b). In the same written submission to the 2019 Commons inquiry, the ICO expressed concern over the ongoing retention of custody images of individuals not subsequently convicted of an offence (ICO 2019b). A custody image review held in 2017 led to such individuals being allowed to request deletion of these images. The ICO stated, however, that 'it is unclear how those individuals would know that they could make a request and we are aware that there have not been a significant number of requests, indicating a lack of awareness' (ICO 2019a: 1). Retention of such images, the ICO claimed, had 'no clear basis in law' (ICO 2019a: 1). The failure to implement an automated deletion system was viewed as breaching the 2018 Data Protection Act (House of Commons Science and Technology Select Committee 2019).

Separately, the Information Commissioner issued an opinion on the use of live facial recognition by law enforcement in October 2019. This document claimed that data protection law 'applies to the whole process ... from consideration about the necessity and proportionality for deployment, the compilation of watchlists, the processing of the biometric data through to the retention and deletion of that data', whether 'for a trial or routine operational deployment' (ICO 2019a: 2). The Information Commissioner further opined that the use of such technology constitutes 'sensitive processing' under the terms of the 2018 Data Protection Act 'as it involves the processing of biometric data for the purpose of uniquely identifying an individual' and that this category applies to all facial images captured and analysed by software (ICO 2019b: 2). The Commissioner expressed a view to work towards a binding code of practice, possibly building upon that of the Surveillance Camera Code (see *Bridges v South Wales Police*) but with 'a clear and specific focus on law enforcement use of [live facial recognition] and other biometric technology', applicable to both current and future technology (ICO 2019b: 3). Without such a code, the Commissioner opined that 'we are likely to continue to see inconsistency across police forces and other law enforcement organisations in terms of necessity and proportionality determinations relating to the processing of personal data' (ICO 2019a: 10).

The ICO has statutory powers and an enforcement capacity and has played a key role in defining the legal status of biometric systems. While the ICO has drawn attention to issues relating to the retention of facial data, this has been in a responsive mode and it remains to be seen precisely how the ICO might go about addressing possible data protection breaches regarding biometric data use by law enforcement. The ICO's opinion on facial recognition has not stopped it being deployed in England and Wales.

The then SCC published a guidance document on police use of automated facial recognition systems with surveillance cameras in March 2019. (Since then, this role has been combined with the Biometrics Commissioner role to create the UK Biometrics and

Surveillance Camera Commissioner, UKBSCC). In this document it was stated that the SCC 'does not give legal advice and nothing within this document should be construed or otherwise interpreted as amounting to such' (SCC 2019: 3, emphasis added). In this document the SCC stated that 'any use of facial recognition or other biometric characteristic recognition systems needs to be clearly justified and proportionate in meeting the stated purpose and be suitably validated' (SCC 2019: 6). The SCC delegated this validation to the Forensic Science Regulator's Codes of Practice and Conduct, which was non-statutory at the time. With regard to ethical guidance, the SCC delegated to a notable extent to the Biometrics and Forensics Ethics Group (BFEG; SCC 2019).

Possessing no statutory powers, the SCC was limited to encouraging voluntary adoption of the code by other operators of surveillance camera systems. While the Forensic Science Regulator now has statutory powers to address possible non-compliance of areas it regards within their remit, it remains to be seen to what extent the Regulator may view FR as falling within its code of practice. The now-merged UK Biometrics and Surveillance Camera Commissioner role still currently lacks its own statutory powers to address FR, representing a potentially significant legal and regulatory lacuna.

Before the merging of roles, the SCC published opinions on issues such as the Appeal to the *Bridges* case (SCC 2020). The civil rights groups Liberty supported the case of *Bridges v South Wales Police*, which challenged the use of FR by SWP. The High Court in Cardiff rejected Bridges' claim that the technology was unlawfully used against him, but a subsequent hearing in the Appeal Court ruled in Bridges' favour.

## Bridges v South Wales Police

The *Bridges* case involved a claim made by Edward Bridges against South Wales Police regarding the latter's 'AFR Locate' system. AFR Locate was deployed in December 2017 at a busy shopping area in Queen Street, Cardiff, and in March 2018 at the Defence Procurement, Research, Technology and Exportability Exhibition held at the Motorpoint Arena, also in Cardiff. Bridges claimed to have been present and to have been caught on camera on both occasions. In the latter case Bridges was attending a protest against the event. Bridges claimed that SWP's use of AFR Locate contravened rights granted under the European Convention on Human Rights (ECHR) regarding Article 8, which provides for rights to respect private and family life. Bridges also claimed that the use of FR contravened data protection legislation and the 2010 Equality Act.

In the original case, heard in the Cardiff High Court of Justice in September 2019, Bridges' claim was rejected. Within their judgement the court ruled that the use of AFR Locate was not disproportionate under the terms of the ECHR and that SWP had satisfied data protection legislation. The original court ruling also rejected the claim that the use of AFR Locate was discriminatory under the terms of the Equality Act. The High Court's ruling was, however, overturned on appeal. In the latter hearing, the Appeal Court found SWP's use of AFR Locate to be unlawful and in contravention of human rights. The Appeal Court found 'fundamental deficiencies' in the legal framework for using FR and that SWP gave undue discretion to individual police officers to decide who should be placed on watchlists (Hunton Privacy Blog 2020). The Appeal Court also found deficiencies in SWP's DPIA, ruling that the DPIA failed to fully assess the risks to rights and freedoms of data subjects under the terms of the 2018 Data Protection Act. Finally, the Appeal Court found that SWP had 'not gathered sufficient evidence' to assess possible bias in AFR Locate (Bridges v Chief Constable of South Wales Police 2020). SWP had deleted individuals who did not match their watchlists, which led the Appeal Court to conclude they had no basis on which to analyze possible bias. Nor were SWP aware of the data set on which AFR Locate had been trained and thus 'could not establish whether there had been a demographic imbalance in the relevant training data' (Hunton Privacy Blog 2020). The Appeal Court concluded that SWP could not therefore assess whether the system was biased prior to use. The Appeal Court stated that:

> We would hope that, as AFR is a novel and controversial technology, all police forces that intend to use it in the future would wish to satisfy themselves that everything reasonable which could be done had been done in order to make sure that the software used does not have a racial or gender bias. (Bridges v Chief Constable of South Wales Police 2020)

The Bridges appeal thus marked a notable intervention. At time of writing it remains to be seen how police use of FR will develop, but the judgement reflects certain ongoing concerns. These relate to police transparency in terms of how FR data are assessed and evaluated and how they may establish whether or not FR may be regarded as discriminatory in operational contexts. Matters of rights and freedoms also continue to be raised.

## Proportionality and the chilling effect

As with other biometrics, the issue of proportionality has framed much of the debate concerning facial recognition technology in the UK. This has focused on the balance between public safety and individual privacy (BFEG 2019). Debates around proportionality and FR are linked to operational and technical variables. These include whether FR technology is used in a real-time or retrospective fashion, the accuracy and reliability of this technology, how effective it is or to what extent it can be regarded as deterrent, who is using it (e.g., police or private actors), for what purposes it is used (e.g., to address minor nuisance behaviour or serious crimes) and in precisely what locations it may be deployed. For example, it could be argued that persons paying to attend a sporting event or concert are entitled to their safety, which might justify FR in those contexts. Using FR out in streets where publics may freely wander may, however, be more difficult to justify. The possibility has been raised that FR deployment might exercise a chilling effect, discouraging people from exercising their freedom of assembly and right to protest.

The argument that awareness of being watched influences how we behave has a long and well-worn history in social science. Students of surveillance studies will no doubt be familiar with Jeremy Bentham's notion of the panopticon which was subsequently taken up by Michel Foucault in *Discipline and Punish* (Foucault 1973). The argument for individual privacy in public spaces has, however, been put forward. It has been argued that privacy in public is vital for making and maintaining social relationships (Rachels 1975). Public privacy has been regarded as vital for allowing people to maintain different social spheres and social boundaries between professional, family and personal lives. An awareness of prior anonymity enables people to decide when and how and with whom they share aspects of themselves. Public privacy has also been claimed to be an important factor in activities such as political protests (Gavison 1980; Nissenbaum 2010; Aston 2017). Political demonstrations are dependent on social networks and social capital to plan and organize them (Feldman 2002; Aston 2017). Aston (2017), however, reported protestors feeling unable to share social links with others on demonstrations if they knew they were under surveillance, for fear of incriminating others.

Aston (2017) also argued that UK courts have adopted an unreasonably narrow view of privacy in relation to public surveillance. Courts have relied upon the 'reasonable expectation of privacy' criterion and concluded that there is no such reasonable expectation when being observed or photographed by others (Aston 2017: 13). Elsewhere the European Court of Human Rights has found that Article 8 rights under the terms of the Convention ('the right to respect for private and family life, home and correspondence') apply when information has 'been obtained and retained in a permanent or systematic manner, even if such information is taken from the public domain' (Aston 2017: 13). While UK courts have acknowledged the privacy impact of the long-term storage of data such as facial information, it has been argued that both the Court of Appeal and the Supreme Court have failed to adequately challenge and problematize police surveillance of demonstrators (Aston 2017).

## FR: fit for purpose?

Much concern has been expressed over the accuracy and reliability of FR technology. While estimates of error rates differ, even the more conservative reports have suggested a potentially significantly high rate of false positive matches (Big Brother Watch 2018; Fussey and Murray 2019). Certain social groups such as women and Black, Asian and minority ethnic (BAME) individuals have been regarded as more likely to be falsely identified due to bias being introduced into the algorithms used to compare images (BFEG 2019).

Numerous facial data sets used to train algorithms have been found to be considerably skewed towards much higher proportions of White and/or male individuals (Buolamwini and Gebru 2018; Gebru 2020). The instability inherent in racial/ethnic classifications, as discussed in Chapter 7, has been recognized as significantly problematic for FR as well. As Buolamwini and Gebru (2018) observed, in the United States the term 'Black' can refer to many skin hues, which may affect the reliability of algorithms. Racial and ethnic categories differ across geographic regions and may vary within one location over time (Buolamwini and Gebru 2018).

The IT community has displayed growing awareness of issues around bias in machine learning and their social justice impacts (Gebru 2020; Jo and Gebru 2020). The composition of data sets and historical archives has gained increased salience given their use for researching and developing machine learning. These data sets may, however, reflect historical and structural inequities or reflect specific preoccupations or biases of those who collected the data. Jo and Gebru (2020) suggested that more interventionist forms of data collection and archiving, involving more inclusive, consensual and participatory practices, might alleviate bias or inaccuracy in subsequent machine learning outcomes. While it is conceivable that the reliability of algorithms may improve considerably in the near future, increased accuracy of FR may not necessarily be considered a panacea against entrenched racism. Quinton (2015) argued that racism may endure if race as a category is given predominance in police work (Quinton 2015). Issues may also lie within the technology industry. Critics have questioned the level of diversity within the workforces of tech companies and the lack of voice given to those subject to inequitable and discriminatory technologies (Gebru 2020).

In addition to issues over bias against BAME communities and women, concerns have been raised over some other suggested uses of FR. Technology producers have made ambitious claims that FR can be used to anticipate behaviours or even infer sexuality. A study carried out by researchers from Stanford University claimed that their FR system could identify LGBTQ individuals more effectively than humans (Wang and Kosinski 2018). This work was strongly criticized by two leading US LGBTQ groups (Levin

2017; Wang 2018). One of the researchers, Michal Kosinski, defended the research by claiming that it upheld LGBTQ rights by supporting a biological basis for sexual orientation. This itself is, however, arguably controversial in the light of debates over to what extent sexuality has a biological or social basis. Another controversial piece of research carried out at Shanghai's Jiaotong University claimed to be able to use FR to predict criminality in individuals (Wu and Zhang 2016).

Automated gender recognition (AGR) refers to algorithms which use FR and other methods to classify an individual's gender. AGR has found increasing application in technology, security and marketing (Hamidi et al. 2018). Technology producers, however, appear to be still grappling with the complexity of gender in both individual and socio-cultural terms (Repo 2015). It is questionable whether this technology recognizes that gender presentation varies across time and space (Gebru 2020). Hamidi et al. (2018) studied the responses of individuals identifying as transgender, including those employed within the tech industry. This study reported 'overwhelmingly negative' and sceptical responses towards AGR (Hamidi et al. 2018: 10). These respondents also described the harm of being misgendered through such technology and threats to their privacy. Hamidi et al. proposed interventions such as allowing those subject to AGR to opt out, to let them define their own gender identity, and for greater awareness of gender diversity in the design of AGR systems.

Both previous Surveillance Camera Commissioners and the UK Biometrics Commissioners have expressed the view that FR systems should be appropriately tested (OBC 2019; SCC 2019). Designing tests, however, requires careful consideration, as technical and ethical issues arose in FR trials conducted in England and Wales. SWP and the Metropolitan Police Service (MPS) trialled FR through actual police operations. It was argued that testing FR in this way broke the principle of informed consent and blurred the distinction between technical testing and operational use (Fussey and Murray 2019). During the MPS trial, research objectives appear to have been conflated with police objectives, leading to members of the public being seriously inconvenienced, with evidence of possible discrimination (Big Brother Watch 2018; Fussey and Murray 2019). Mixing the testing of FR with operational deployment appears to have created some significant ethical issues concerning consent, legitimacy and trust. The apparent conflation of objectives obscures an important distinction between an individual's right to withhold consent to participate in research and their consent to the use of technology in police operations (Fussey and Murray 2019). From the point of view of research ethics, avoiding cameras may indicate an individual's right to withhold consent to participate in a trial or to uphold their right to privacy. Such behaviour may, however, be seen quite differently from a policing point of view, possibly raising suspicion.

Questions of informed consent also relate to how clearly the public may be notified by police forces deploying FR technology and the kind of time frame in which publics may be able to exercise consent. The use of FR in public spaces additionally raises uncertainties over the agency of individuals to exercise different choices, such as taking different routes to avoid cameras and how police might interpret such behaviour (Big Brother Watch 2018; Fussey and Murray 2019).

BFEG members have issued ethical guidelines for the use of facial recognition (BFEG 2019, 2021). This identified a series of issues that may affect the performance of live FR. These included data and training of the algorithms, generation of outputs, the role of human operators and deployments in live operational contexts (BFEG 2019). Output generation may be affected by several factors, such as watchlist image quality (pixel size, lighting, background and custody images versus social media, etc.) and those of captured images; watchlist size; the environmental conditions ('principally, but not limited to, lighting and camera position where the image is captured'); 'thresholds that are set to determine a match, which may determine the number of false and correct matches'; 'whether a "match" instigates a near realtime response or not'; and 'whether the response includes a human who decides to take further action or to overrule the machine-generated biometric match' (BFEG 2019: 2).

The way in which operators and users of FR interact with this technology has been raised as another significant issue (Davies et al. 2018; Fussey and Murray 2019). Software outputs are not necessarily self-evident. Human operators have to interpret and act upon this information. Police have to decide first whether to accept a possible match or override one, which may determine whether or not they intervene through, for example, a possible arrest or other such intervention. Concerns here relate to errors or bias on the part of both technology and operators. It has been argued that inaccurate algorithmic outputs can perpetuate biased policing attitudes. Big Brother Watch cited one example whereby a teenage boy of colour was stopped and handcuffed by police following FR analysis (Big Brother Watch 2018). Another potential risk relates to operators over-trusting FR systems and not exercising critical judgement when a match is called (BFEG 2019). Alternatively, operators could ignore outputs if a system generates too many false matches. Match probability thresholds may be set in ways which might risk too many false positives. It is unclear to what extent forces using FR are following BFEG's guidelines and principles.

The debate over police deployment of FR in England and Wales also raised concerns about the consistency of decision-making processes. The MPS were found to use multiple and conflicting types of decision-making practices (Fussey and Murray 2019). Multiple adjudicators based in a control room conferred on possible matches, which sometimes led to differences of opinion. When a possible match was communicated to street-level officers, communications issues sometimes arose over whether this represented an instruction to intervene or merely to maintain observation. In other cases street-based officers were equipped with handheld devices which could alert them to a possible match. It was reported that in these latter instances, street-based teams took a decision to intervene even though control room–based teams had decided otherwise.

Davies et al.'s (2018) study highlighted significant learning curves concerning the operational use of FR by South Wales Police. Davies et al. (2018) found that 'multiple organizational reforms and innovations were required' (8) before FR operated to a satisfactory level. Training was identified as an issue during the SWP deployment. The amount of formal training given to initial operators appears to have been brief, and many subsequent operators used FR without any formal training. A host of technical and practical issues only became apparent following operational deployment.

Determining whether an individual should be placed on a watchlist constitutes a significant threshold moment. Fussey and Murray (2019) found that in England and Wales, persons were flagged by FR for serious offences that had already been dealt with through the criminal justice system. Some of these persons were, however, still wanted in relation to minor offences and were arrested accordingly. It was questionable, however, whether these lesser offences would have been sufficient to justify inclusion on the previous watchlist. Davies et al.'s (2018) study of SWP's use of FR recommended that decisions around watchlist size and composition should be 'made public for the purposes of public accountability' (43).

Inconsistency of decision making and communications issues, together with concerns over the practicality of using FR, thus indicate the range of operational and technical challenges presented by this technology. These in turn have been linked with ethical issues such as the risk of misidentification and discrimination and the composition of watchlists.

Like DNA, measuring the policing effectiveness of facial data has been found to be methodologically challenging. The original business case made by SWP in their application for Home Office funding to justify their FR project emphasized resource efficiencies within the police, rather than any public benefit (Davies et al. 2018). The stated purposes for using FR by police have been highly diffuse, fluid and contextualized, including claimed purposes of detection, deterrence, disruption and displacement, which further problematizes the issue of assessing criminal justice impact (Fussey and Murray 2019). The expectations concerning FR are highly emergent, in terms of ideas about its function, how it is used operationally (involving significant learning curves), its accuracy and what ethical impacts it may exert.

## Public–private collaborations

In 2021 BFEG predicted that public and private bodies could increasingly collaborate on facial recognition in the near future (BFEG 2021). According to Liberty, who assisted BFEG, public bodies like the police may work with private organisations in numerous ways (BFEG 2021). Police could provide private operators of FR with watchlists, which might include suspects or missing persons to be used in spaces such as shopping centres. Second, private actors may generate their own watchlists, leading to matches which necessitate police intervention. Finally, private companies may sell FR systems to police forces or sub-contract or outsource parts of the system for provision by third parties.

BFEG raised a number of ethical concerns, such as the possibility that private providers of FR could use data collected during public–private collaborations for other purposes. This might entail using data to develop algorithmic systems or be repurposed for use by third parties (BFEG 2021). While some FR systems such as Amazon's Rekognition allow users to control how data are shared, the potential to repurpose data raises rights around privacy and data protection. BFEG anticipated that FR could be combined with other forms of data, such as social media or immigration data, for possible risk-based analysis and behavioural inference of individuals. Cloud computing could increase the possibilities of combining data from public and private sources (BFEG 2021).

Greater public engagement has been urged concerning the use of FR (Scottish Parliament 2020). Surveys of public opinion towards FR have been relatively few and far between, although data have begun to emerge in recent years. A 2019 study by the London Policing Ethics Panel studied public opinion to the MPS use of Live FR. This involved a weighted sample of 1092 London-based respondents, in which a sub-set of 50 respondents were invited to take part in follow-up telephone interviews (London Policing Ethics Panel 2019). This survey found that, overall, more than half of the respondents thought that police use of FR to identify people could be acceptable, but these views varied considerably depending on the seriousness of the offences for which police might pursue identification. This survey found 81–83 per cent support for serious crime but only 55 per cent for minor crime and less than 50 per cent for 'nuisance behaviour' (London Policing Ethics Panel 2019). Half the respondents thought that Live FR would make them feel safer, but just over a third were concerned about the impact on their privacy and whether police would be collecting data on innocent people (London Policing Ethics Panel 2019). Almost half of those surveyed thought that FR would lead to data being collected 'more often about some groups than others' (London Policing Ethics Panel 2019: 21). In general, younger respondents were less accepting than older people, while respondents who identified as Asian or Black were less accepting than White groups (London Policing Ethics Panel 2019).

The London Policing Ethics Panel survey also addressed the issue of the chilling effect. This survey claimed that, overall, less than one in five respondents thought that it might dissuade them from attending events, but again there was significant variation across sociodemographic groups. 38 per cent of 16- to 24-years-olds compared to 10 per cent of those aged 55 or over reported they were more likely not to attend events if FR were to be used, and the proportion reporting from Asian, Black and mixed groups was also higher. This survey did, however, draw upon interview data to claim that some of those respondents said they would feel safer at public events if FR were to be used. Yet only 56 per cent of respondents thought police would use personal data 'in accordance with the law' (London Policing Ethics Panel 2019: 7). Trust in police appeared to be a key factor identified in this survey, with those who had a high level of trust in the police more supportive of using FR. Trust in police was regarded as a general indicator of trust in all technologies (London Policing Ethics Panel 2019).

The London Policing Ethics Panel concluded that FR should be 'limited to managing serious offences' and that FR watch lists 'should only include images from people wanted for serious offences or presenting serious threat of harm' (London Policing Ethics Panel 2019: 10). The panel made a number of recommendations, much of which reflected wider concerns about FR, including that its use should demonstrably offer 'more than marginal benefit to the public, sufficient to compensate for the potential distrust it may invoke' (London Policing Ethics Panel 2019: 10: 11), the need to demonstrably avoid gender and racial bias in operations and a range of recommendations for oversight ranging from operational to strategic levels.

Another 2019 survey was conducted by YouGov on behalf of the Ada Lovelace Institute (Ada Lovelace Institute 2019). This study concluded that public awareness of FR was high but knowledge of it was low, which the authors claimed warranted a more informed debate. The survey found a notable fear of the normalization of surveillance, and there was no unconditional support for police deployment of FR. Public support was instead conditional 'upon limitations and subject to appropriate safeguards' (Ada Lovelace Institute 2019: i). This survey identified ethical concerns relating to accuracy, validity, bias and discrimination, transparency, privacy and trust and data security (Ada Lovelace Institute 2019). The results of this survey also indicated a degree of support for the ability to consent to or opt out of FR. Forty-six per cent of respondents supported this idea, compared to 28 per cent who disagreed (Ada Lovelace Institute 2019). The survey results suggested that respondents feared the 'normalization of surveillance' (Ada Lovelace Institute 2019: 8) but would accept FR if there was a clear public benefit. In this survey, 70 per cent of respondents thought that FR should be used by police in criminal investigations, and 54 per cent thought it should be used to unlock smartphones, while 50 per cent thought FR could be used in airports to replace passports. Respondents supported the use of safeguards for police use. A notably low level of trust was discerned regarding the use of FR by commercial organizations; for example, if used by shops to track customers (77 per cent opposed) or used by human resources departments to use FR to recruit workers for entry-level jobs (76 per cent opposed). Forty per cent of respondents agreed with the assertion that the use of FR in schools should be outlawed, compared with 30 per cent who disagreed (Ada Lovelace Institute 2019).

The Ada Lovelace Survey recruited 4109 participants. While BAME respondents were regarded as under-represented, it was noted that there was a 'higher level of discomfort' with police use of FR among these groups (Ada Lovelace Institute 2019: 16). Separate research by Areeq Chowdhury (2020) situated facial recognition within the context of racialized practices of law enforcement, such as the disproportionate use of stop and search. In a series of workshops, focus groups and roundtable exercises, Chowdhury's respondents often drew links between FR and police discrimination. Possible future improvements to the accuracy of FR systems were regarded as futile if it meant privacy rights were infringed and if police assumptions against certain sections of society continued to be biased (Chowdhury 2020). Some respondents also called for greater transparency and demonstrable diversity among technology producers.

Even from the limited data on public opinion, it is apparent that there is some support for police use of FR, but this may be conditional on the precise circumstances of its use (e.g., for certain more serious offences over others), and that police use needs to be regulated. While the potential chilling effect of FR needs more research in terms of public opinion, a certain heightened lack of trust in FR is discernible, particularly among BAME populations, and there is a notable level of suspicion regarding the use of FR by commercial companies. Public engagement regarding FR may need to take into account a possible knowledge deficit on the part of publics, as suggested by the Ada Lovelace Institute report.

## Conclusion

Through exploring facial recognition technology, this chapter has raised a number of operational, social and ethical issues. These range from concerns about the accuracy of this technology, how it is used and how it may impact individuals and groups. FR presents significant issues about privacy rights and discrimination, but it is unclear how far current legislation in England and Wales safeguards individual rights. The algorithms used in these systems have also raised concerns about how they are understood by operators. The potentially increased access of FR to both public and private operators raises numerous possibilities but also additional ethical risks. These relate to the potential for facial data to be combined with other data forms, such as social media, which could facilitate forms of behavioural analysis. The possibility has been mooted that FR could also be combined with DNA phenotyping in the future (fieldwork 2019) or that FR could be used to try and predict an individual's DNA data (Sero et al. 2019).

Like DNA phenotyping, these developments can and should be addressed with a critical eye to how they may construct notions of race but may also reflect and perpetuate institutional discrimination and prejudice (Skinner 2020a, 2020b). David Skinner has argued that biometric technologies help reconstruct race as a 'multi-valent assemblage of corporeal, digital and informational elements' (Skinner 2020a: 346), albeit an elusive entity which requires us to trace it in operational, scientific, technical, political and ethical terms. Thinking in terms of assemblages and networks is useful to conceptualize FR as a means of reconfiguring relations between different actors and data flows (Latour 1999). We see this in the ways FR may open up new possibilities for public–private collaboration and data combination, for example. This re-networking also has consequences for how individual subjects are enrolled into networks and (re)constituted, variously as 'responsible citizens, problematic travellers, compliant suspects' (Skinner 2020b: 94–95) or 'risky individuals'. More significant still, the way in which FR and other biometric systems circulate among spaces, connecting and enrolling actors and data, has consequences for how categories of race and gender are shaped and understood, with attendant ethical and social justice implications.

Recent literature on facial technology and AI exhibits a growing preoccupation with the place of concepts such as 'ethics' and 'fairness' (Sloane 2018). While the ethics of automated systems and AI is a recognized concern, it is unclear exactly what substance is being attached to ethical concepts. As Sloane (2018) pointed out, 'Ethics and values are social phenomena, something people *do* (with or without machines) rather than abstract concepts that can be coded into AI' (emphasis in original). Ethics and values are thus enacted, and this points to a possible role for social science in identifying the practices and dynamics which shape and reflect such enactments. Sociologically informed, empirical studies of ethical decision making around the construction and use of FR may be fruitful (Haimes 2002). Yet the increasing tendency for FR to embed actors, data and objects into networks complicates the matter. How may we understand how ethics is constructed across what may be complex assemblages? How do ethics hold across such networks, if this is it all possible?

Social research should not, however, shirk from this challenge. Thinking more carefully about the differing standpoints of those who become embedded in FR – whether as producer, operator, decision maker or subject – may be one possible route to conceptualizing and addressing the social impact of this technology. This could involve focussing on how different standpoints contest and negotiate FR, with particular focus on ethical deliberations. Whose voices and views predominate, should they and how may they be challenged?

## Bibliography

Ada Lovelace Institute. (2019) *Beyond Face Value: Public Attitudes to Facial Recognition Technology*. London: Nuffield Foundation.

Aston, V. (2017) 'State surveillance of protest and the rights to privacy and freedom of assembly: A comparison of judicial and protestor perspectives', *European Journal of Law and Technology*, 8 (1): 1–19.

Big Brother Watch. (2018) *Face Off: The Lawless Growth of Facial Recognition in UK Policing*. London: Big Brother Watch.

Biometrics Commissioner. (2019) 'Automated Facial Recognition: Biometrics Commissioner Response to Court Judgment on South Wales Police's use of Automated Facial Recognition Technology', 10 September 2019; online at: https://www.gov.uk/government/news/automated-facial-recognition (accessed 1 November 2019).

Biometrics and Forensics Ethics Group. (2019) *Ethical Issues Arising from the Police Use of Live Facial Recognition Technology*. London: Home Office.

Biometrics and Forensics Ethics Group. (2021) *Briefing Note on the Ethical Issues Arising from the Public-Private Collaboration in the Use of Live Facial Recognition Technology*. London: Home Office.

*Bridges, R (on application of) v Chief Constable of South Wales Police*. [2020] EWHC 2341 (Admin).

British Broadcasting Corporation. (2020) 'Met Police to Deploy Facial Recognition Cameras', 30 January 2020; online at: https://www.bbc.co.uk/news/uk-51237665 (accessed 17 August 2021).

Buolamwini, J. and Gebru, T. (2018) 'Gender shades: Intersectional accuracy disparities in commercial gender classification', *Proceedings of Machine Learning Research*, 81: 1–15.

Centre for Data Ethics and Innovation. (2020) *Snapshot Series: Facial Recognition Technology*. London: UK Government.

Chowdhury, A. (2020) *Unmasking Facial Recognition: An Exploration of the Racial Bias Implications of Facial Recognition Surveillance in the United Kingdom*. London: Webroots Democracy.

Davies, B., Innes, M. and Dawson, A. (2018) *An Evaluation of South Wales Police's Use of Automated Facial Recognition*. Universities' Police Science Institute & Crime & Security Research Institute, University of Cardiff.

European Commission. (2021) *Proposal for a Regulation of the European Parliament and of the Council: Laying Down Harmonized Rules on Artificial Intelligence (Artificial Intelligence Act) and Amending Certain Union Legislative Acts*, COM (2021) 206 final. 21 April 2021; online at: https://eur-lex.europa.eu/resource.html?uri=cellar:e0649735-a372-11eb-9585-01aa75ed71a1.0001.02/DOC_1&format=PDF (accessed 27 October 2021).

Feldman, D. (2002) *Civil Liberties and Human Rights in England and Wales*, 2nd ed. Oxford: Oxford University Press.

Foucault, M. (1973) *Discipline and Punish*. London: Penguin.

Fussey, P. and Murray, D. (2019) *Independent Report on the London Metropolitan Police Service's Trial of Live Facial Recognition Technology*. Human Rights Centre, University of Essex.

Gavison, R. (1980) 'Privacy and the limits of law', *Yale Law Journal*, 89 (3): 421–471.

Gebru, T. (2020) 'Race and gender', in M.D. Dubber, F. Pasquale and S. Das (eds), *The Oxford Handbook of Ethics of AI*. New York: Oxford University Press, pp. 253–270.

Gunnarsdottir, K. and Rommetveit, K. (2017) 'The biometric imaginary: (dis)trust in a policy vacuum', *Public Understanding of Science*, 26 (2): 195–211.

Haimes, E. (2002) 'What can the social sciences contribute to the study of ethics? Theoretical, empirical and substantive considerations', *Bioethics*, 16 (2): 89–113.

Hamidi, F., Scheuerman, K.M. and Branham, S.M. (2018) 'Gender recognition or gender reductionism? The social implications of automatic gender recognition systems', Paper presented at the Computer Human Interaction 2018 Conference, 21–26 April 2018, Montreal.

Heikkila, M. (2021) 'Europe's AI rules open door to mass use of facial recognition, critics warn', *Politico*, 7 June 2021; online at: https://www.politico.eu/article/eu-ai-artifrulesicial-intelligence-facial-recognition/ (accessed 18 August 2021).

Home Office. (2019) *Written Evidence Submitted by Baroness Williams of Trafford, Minister of State for Countering Extremism, Home Office*. Submitted to House of Commons Science and Technology Select Committee: *The Work of the Biometrics Commissioner and the Forensic Science Regulator*, 19th Report of Session 2017–2019.

House of Commons Science and Technology Select Committee. (2015) *Current and Future Uses of Biometric Data and Technologies: Sixth Report of Session 2014–15*. London: Her Majesty's Stationery Office.

House of Commons Science and Technology Select Committee. (2018) *Biometric Strategy and Forensic Services: Fifth Report of Session 2017–19*. London: Her Majesty's Stationery Office.

House of Commons Science and Technology Select Committee. (2019) *The Work of the Biometrics Commissioner and the Forensic Science Regulator: Nineteenth Report of Session 2017–19*. London: Her Majesty's Stationery Office.

Hunton Privacy Blog. (2020) 'UK Court of Appeal Finds Automated Facial Recognition Technology Unlawful in Bridges v South Wales Police', 12 August 2020; online at: https://www.huntonprivacyblog.com/2020/08/12/uk-court-of-appeal-finds-automated-facial-recognition-technology-unlawful-in-bridges-v-south-wales-police/ (accessed 4 August 2021).

Information Commissioner's Office. (2019a) *Information Commissioner's Opinion: The Use of Live Facial Recognition Technology by Law Enforcement in Public Places*. Wilmslow: Information Commissioner's Office.

Information Commissioner's Office. (2019b) *Written Evidence Submitted by Steve Wood, Deputy Commissioner for Policy, Information Commissioner's Office (WBC0008)*. Submitted to House of Commons Science and Technology Committee: *The Work of the Biometrics Commissioner and the Forensic Science Regulator*, 19th Report of Session 2017–2019.

Jo, E.S. and Gebru, T. (2020) 'Lessons from archives: strategies for collecting sociocultural data in machine learning', in *Conference on Fairness, Accountability, and Transparency (FAT* '20), January 27–30, 2020, Barcelona, Spain*. New York: ACM, pp. 306–316. doi:10.1145/3351095.3372829.

Latour, B. (1999) *Pandora's Hope: Essays on the Reality of Science Studies*. Cambridge, MA: Harvard University Press.

Levin, S. (2017) 'LGBT groups denounce "dangerous" AI that uses your face to guess sexuality', *The Guardian*, 9 September 2017; online at: http://www.theguardian.com/world/2017/sep/08/ai-gay-gaydar-algorithm-facialrecognition-criticism-stanford (accessed 17 August 2017).

London Policing Ethics Panel. (2019) *Final Report on Facial Recognition*. London: London Policing Ethics Panel.

Metropolitan Police Service. (2021) 'Live Facial Recognition'; online at: https://www.met.police.uk/advice/advice-and-information/facial-recognition/live-facial-recognition/ (accessed 16 August 2021).

Nissenbaum, H. (2010) *Privacy in Context: Technology, Policy and the Integrity of Social Life*. Stanford, CA: Stanford University Press.

Office of the Biometrics Commissioner. (2019) *Commissioner for the Retention and Use of Biometric Material: Annual Report 2018*. London: Her Majesty's Stationery Office.

Purshouse, J. and Campbell, L. (2019) 'Privacy, crime control and police use of automated facial recognition technology', *Criminal Law Review*, 3: 188–204.

Quinton, P. (2015) 'Race disproportionality and officer decision-making', in R. Delsol and M. Shiner (eds), *Stop and Search: The Anatomy of a Police Power*. Basingstoke, UK: Palgrave, pp. 57–78.

Rachels, J. (1975) 'Why privacy is important', *Philosophy and Public Affairs*, 4 (4): 323–333.

Repo, J. (2015) *The Biopolitics of Gender*. Oxford: Oxford University Press.

Richardson, R. (2021) *Facial Recognition in the Public Sector: The Policy Landscape*. Washington, DC: The German Marshall Fund of the United States.

Scottish Parliament. (2020) *Facial Recognition: How Police in Scotland Makes Use of This Technology*. Edinburgh: Scottish Parliament, Justice Sub-committee on Policing.

Scottish Police Authority. (2017) *Our 10 Year Strategy for Policing in Scotland*. Edinburgh: Scottish Police Authority.

Scottish Police Authority. (2018) 'Equality and Human Rights Impact Assessment (EqHRIA) Summary of Results', 9 March 2018; online at: https://www.scotland.police.uk/assets/pdf/459397/2026-eqhria-summary-ofresults?view=Standard (accessed 17 August 2021).

Sero, D., Zaidi, A., Li, J., White, J.D., et al. (2019) 'Facial recognition from DNA using face-to-DNA classifiers', *Nature Communications*, 10: 1–12.

Skinner, D. (2020a) 'Forensic genetics and the prediction of race: what is the problem?', *BioSocieties*, 15 (3): 329–349.

Skinner, D. (2020b) 'Race, racism and identification in the era of technosecurity', *Science as Culture*, 29 (1): 77–99.

Sloane, M. (2018) 'Making artificial intelligence socially just: why the current focus on ethics is not enough', LSE British Policy and Politics Blog, 6 July 2018; online at: http://blogs.lse.ac.uk/politicsandpolicy/artificial-intelligence-and-society-ethics/ (accessed 4 August 2021).

Surveillance Camera Commissioner. (2019) *The Police Use of Automated Facial Recognition Technology with Surveillance Camera Systems*. London: Home Office.

Surveillance Camera Commissioner. (2020) 'Surveillance Camera Commissioner's Statement: Court of Appeal Judgment (R) Bridges v South Wales Police – Automated Facial Recognition', 11 August 2020; online at: https://www.gov.uk/government/speeches/surveillance-camera-commissioners-statement-court-of-appeal-judgment-r-bridges-v-south-wales-police-automated-facial-recognition (accessed 4 August 2021).

UK Parliament. (2021) 'The Automated Facial Recognition Technology (Moratorium and Review) Bill', 5 May 2021; online at: https://bills.parliament.uk/bills/2610 (accessed 28 August 2021).

Wang, J. (2018) *What's in Your Face? Discrimination in Facial Recognition Technology*. MA thesis, Georgetown University.

Wang, Y. and Kosinski M. (2018) 'Deep neural networks are more accurate than humans at detecting sexual orientation from facial images', *Journal of Personality & Social Psychology*, 114 (2): 246–257.

Wu, X. and Zhang, X. (2016) 'Automated inference on criminality using face images', *arXiv*, 13 November 2016; https://arxiv.org/pdf/1611.04135v1.pdf (accessed 4 August 2021).

# 9 Digital forensics

## Introduction: a short history of digital forensics (DF)

Crime scene examination increasingly involves mapping the online transactions of persons of interest or victims, alongside more established forms of forensic evidence such as DNA or fingerprints. DF entails the recovery of files from computerized devices of interest to criminal investigations. Such data have increasing utility to assist investigation of a wide range of possible offences, by no means limited to so-called cybercrimes. In 2018 it was claimed that at least 70 per cent of criminal investigations in the UK involved a digital element and that the figure could be as high as 90 per cent if DF was used in the broadest terms to encompass CCTV, cyber-attacks or the use of communications or social media data. A representative of the Metropolitan Police Service (MPS) estimated that over 90 per cent of murders and complex rape cases involved a digital element (House of Lords Science and Technology Committee 2018).

DF work typically entails accessing a device in read-only mode and using tools to create copies or 'images' of files. DF practitioners are expected to maintain the integrity of any recovered hardware such as hard drives (Caviglione et al. 2017). In addition to the practices of extracting and interpreting data, DF has to concern itself with integrating these data into an investigation alongside other information sources and wider intelligence analysis which may entail managing large amounts of data and knowledge of criminal activity (Ribaux et al. 2020).

The history of DF parallels that of information technology in general. DF initially emerged in the wake of criminal applications of computing which themselves have evolved over time (Wall 2007; Bossler et al. 2015). Until the home computing boom of the early 1980s, computers were mainly used by large businesses, universities, research agencies and government (Pollitt 2010). Auditing of data processing in these organizations ensured the efficiency and accuracy of computing systems, which were expensive to run. This also provided a means of identifying possible irregularities. One such notable early example of digital investigation was recounted by Clifford Stoll in his book *The Cuckoo's Egg* (Stoll 1989). Stoll managed computers at California's Lawrence Berkeley National Laboratory. The presence of a $0.75 accounting irregularity led Stoll to discover that an unauthorized individual had used nine seconds of computing time. *The Cuckoo's Egg* charts how Stoll's investigations uncovered a hacker based in West Germany, who sought to penetrate high-security US government systems and sell the results to the Soviet KGB (Stoll 1989).

The emergence of home microcomputers in the 1980s opened up opportunities to hack systems, although this initially facilitated relatively low-level fraud (Bossler et al. 2015). During the 1980s through to the mid-1990s, forensic activity in relation to computer crime was limited to a relatively small number of individuals (Pollitt 2010).

DOI: 10.4324/9781003126379-9

While this period saw some early initiatives from US government agencies, DF investigations were still largely carried out by individuals who taught themselves and who often used their own equipment without any formal oversight (Pollitt 2010). Academic interest in DF was also largely non-existent at this point.

The mid-1990s, however, led to a wholesale increase in interest and activity in DF driven by the emergence of the internet, which opened up a plethora of new criminal opportunities. In addition to hacking and fraud, illegal pornography and exploitation facilitated by computer networks became a significant area of concern.

The period 1999–2007 has nonetheless been regarded as a 'Golden Age' for digital forensics by one leading commentator (Garfinkel 2010). During this time, while cybercrime was acknowledged as an emerging threat, investigations were rendered relatively straightforward by a number of factors, such as the relative ubiquity of Microsoft Windows, the existence of relatively few file formats of forensic relevance, widespread hardware standards, and the easy availability of good-quality DF tools (Garfinkel 2010). Examinations largely involved single computer systems, which meant DF work was relatively less complicated.

As technology evolved, however, so did the threats. The ability to bring down entire systems through direct denial of service (DDoS) attacks and ransomware and to target individuals through phishing quickly became major priorities for organizations, governments and law enforcement. As the 20th century moved into the 21st, mobile phones became increasingly indispensable, particularly following the advent of the smartphone and the multitude of applications which followed. The use of extensive cryptographic systems and digital rights management in these devices presented significant barriers to recovering evidence (Caviglione et al. 2017). Other devices such as video game consoles and e-book readers also posed problems for DF practitioners through the systems contained within them to protect intellectual property (Garfinkel 2010).

Awareness increased among law enforcement of the scope and scale of digital transactions and their utility for a wider variety of criminal investigations. Over time it became standard UK casework practice to pursue the 'digital profile' of victims and suspects. This involved investigating data such as social media, store card or online banking activity. During fieldwork conducted in 2014, a UK National Crime Agency (NCA) representative described this as the emergence of a 'whole new operating model'.

In the mid-2010s the majority of digital forensics work was performed by police forces inhouse, although external providers were used in the event of excessive workloads. It was perceived by external providers that the tendency towards inhousing prevented an understanding of what kind of digital forensic methods were used within police forces. Questions were asked about the independence of practitioners performing digital forensics work (NCA representative, fieldwork 2014). Those who performed data extractions were potentially also directly involved with the investigations, which raised concerns about bias, or certain data being selectively emphasized while the significance of other data was overlooked. These issues were perceived to be linked to infrastructure and resourcing issues and police pressures. As one practitioner stated: 'We say [to the police] we charge you for your forensic needs, but the police say we provide you with the infrastructure in which you do your work' (digital forensics practitioner 2014).

During this time, DF practitioners increasingly concerned themselves with anticipating the use and misuse of new technology and the challenges of extracting and interpreting data:

> The key questions are: How do we get data out of it [a device]? How do we make sense of that data? How do we manage that data? Each new app creates a small new problem in one of those questions. (Digital forensics practitioner 2014)

The increasing diversity of common digital devices with online connectivity, or the so-called Internet of Things (IoT), compounded these issues, particularly given the increasing variety of such devices available for publics to own. This led to an increasing variety of file formats encountered by digital forensics practitioners. They often found themselves lacking the means of converting these files into formats which allowed them to be viewed and analyzed. Investigators struggled to keep up with the range of new devices, which begat new file formats. Digital forensics investigation requires 'codecs', programs or devices that are able to convert one file format into another. One investigator stated the problem succinctly as:

> I've got this problem – I've got this crime to investigate but I haven't got the codec – so I can't investigate. (Digital forensics practitioner 2014)

Increasing numbers of codecs were required to meet the needs of specific investigations. There was little commercial incentive, however, to develop codecs on a casebycase basis. One particular codec would only be specific to a certain case and may not have been useable in subsequent investigations. The absence of a specific codec, however, prevented a particular investigation going ahead which might have related to a serious crime. Discussions with experts indicated that the latter felt that the police often did not understand the challenges digital forensic practitioners faced at this time (digital forensics practitioner 2014).

In even technologically and economically advanced jurisdictions, DF has historically largely been the preserve of small numbers of individuals. This model has, however, been increasingly recognized as unworkable in the face of the plethora of devices available to individuals, the opportunities they present to perpetrators and the demand of recovering investigative intelligence or evidence from vast quantities of data. As we shall see later in this chapter, much discussion has thus concerned itself with how DF can be organized and configured to face these challenges. As the role of digital evidence has become more prominent, DF as a practice has also attracted increasing attention, encompassing reflection on matters of best practice and professionalization.

## DF professionalization vs practice

Some commentaries which have reflected on the nature of DF work, past, present and future, have at times drawn directly upon sociology of professions perspectives (Losavio et al. 2016; Seigfried-Spellar et al. 2017). In a paper published in 2016, Losavio et al. distinguished between DF as an occupation and DF as a profession. According to them, DF can be regarded as having become close to occupation status, if not having achieved it, but may not yet be considered a profession. They distinguish occupations from more menial 'jobs' by suggesting the former entails a 'greater commitment by the entrant as [they] may have to possess some minimum competency that requires skills, knowledge, or training developed via certification or other credentialing process', requiring 'a long-term commitment by the entrant to the work being performed and a modicum of substantive interest in it' (Losavio et al. 2016: 146–147). Here, occupations are associated with formal systems of training and accreditation and the formation of national associations to provide a unified public voice. Losavio et al., in contrast, framed a 'profession' as an elite status requiring substantial university education to develop 'specialized knowledge and skills' involving 'relatively autonomous client-centred work' (Losavio et al. 2016: 147). Drawing upon a specific source (Volti 2011), these authors argued that DF, at least in the United States, must address three areas to enable it to become recognized as a profession. The first is to address gender balance and the second the social status of DF practitioner's clientele.

Regarding the latter, Losavio et al. claimed that the professional status of DF is impeded as practitioners, at least in the United States, largely serve law enforcement officers, who themselves are not regarded as having acquired professional status (these authors, however, largely restricted themselves to the US context, and further work could focus on whether DF practitioners might have a higher position in other jurisdictions; for example, if they directly work with legal counsel or judges). The third criterion for professionalism suggested by Losavio et al. is the ability to convince publics, and the DF practitioner community themselves, that DF is a profession. The authors claimed that a lack of awareness of DF may impede such perceptions.

It is instructive to compare these stipulative assertions with UK-based social research which has employed ethnographic methods to study the experiences of DF practitioners (Wilson-Kovacs 2020; Rappert et al. 2021; Wilson-Kovacs et al. 2021). Some of this work has addressed the initial stages of DF examination. The proliferation of devices, increased storage capacity and the widening array of file formats and functionalities have led some police forces to adopt a triage approach to digital analysis. Triage has commonly been employed in acute medical situations and disaster response as a preliminary means of prioritizing treatment according to the urgency of individual needs (Wilson-Kovacs 2020). In policing, the triage concept has previously been used in some forensic responses to volume crime to pre-assess the information value of evidence recovered from crime scenes in order to reduce time wastage (Julian and Kelty 2015; Reedy 2020; Ribaux et al. 2020).

Wilson-Kovacs (2020) described how DF triage involves 'ranking apprehended digital items in terms of their importance to a case and likelihood that they contain the data required' (Wilson-Kovacs 2020: 78). Specialized software scans devices and automatically identifies potential evidence, such as the existence of obscene or illegal images. Triage acts as a first step in DF investigations and should only require personnel to possess rudimentary technical knowledge. In theory it should allow DF investigators to manage time and use limited equipment in the most efficient way. Wilson-Kovacs' ethnographic study of DF triage, however, identified notable limitations. The effectiveness of automated scanning in terms of recovering evidence was affected by a number of variables, including device type, the alleged offence, availability of specific software packages and technical proficiency of personnel (Wilson-Kovacs 2020. Elsewhere issues have been reported in terms of itemizing device data, recovering data created and stored across a specific time frame, or recovering data which may have been subsequently deleted; Biometrics and Forensics Ethics Group [BFEG] 2020.)

Wilson-Kovacs (2020) found that a lack of communication between police officers and DFs about the limitations of triage, and limited technical awareness, was linked with risking the biased 'cherry-picking' of evidence and the failure to fully evaluate and interpret evidence according to recognized standards and guidelines. This in turn was found to have an interdependent adverse impact on the clarity and coherence of investigative strategies (lack of police knowledge and training in cybercrime and computing skills has been identified as an issue across a number of jurisdictions; De Paoli et al. 2020).

DF triage was thus found to exhibit a notable difference between an explicitly formalized portrayal of rationalization and resource efficiency and its enactment in operational environments. Rappert et al. (2021) found that DF triage in practice was marked by sometimes lengthy discussions between police officers and DF practitioners in prioritizing specific items. These additional deliberations at times contradicted formal policy and procedures. Rather than facilitating resource efficiency, these interactions, exacerbated by inadequate prior information sharing, and perceived differences between police and practitioners in the course of fluid investigative understandings, created extra work undetectable to formal management channels.

DF practitioners have thus been found to experience significant organizational and technical pressures, involving notable challenges to managing and negotiating expectations of police colleagues, who themselves experience operational demands. DF work also imposes other significant emotional and psychological stresses. Over 80 per cent of DF work is estimated to involve indecent images of children (Wilson-Kovacs et al. 2021). While triage is intended as a resource management tool to ease the burden on DF practitioners, the social research which exists to date suggests that the latter may still have to balance an imperative to educate police colleagues and clarify the nature of their work on one hand, with responding to new incoming case information on the other. This may impact upon priorities and reflect fluid investigative strategies, all while working under time and other resource constraints. This questions the extent to which DF work can be reduced to unproblematically enacted linear procedures and protocols. Social research suggests that DF entails a notable degree of individual agency in terms of the discretionary deployment of technical skills combined with personal skills in terms of understanding, communication, judgement, tact, flexibility and time management. This in turn reflects a sense in which DF practice can be regarded as entailing a sense of professionalism over routine technical work. This professional identity, in relation to particularly challenging aspects of the role, may also be maintained via espousing a sense of independence and duty and through DF practitioners being organizationally distanced from police and casework verdicts. The lack of media archetypes for DF workers may also enable some protection from public expectations (Wilson-Kovacs et al. 2021).

Ethics has been proposed as an important element of the professionalization of DF. A number of organizations linked to DF have addressed ethics, albeit with a notable degree of variance in terms of specific considerations including professional diligence, competency, qualifications, practice, testimony, conflict of interest, reporting, financial stakes, responsibility to client, lawful compliance in matters of privacy and disclosure rights (Sharevski 2015; Ferguson et al. 2020; Reedy 2020).

Developing a universally agreed code of ethics, as addressed by Seigfried-Spellar et al. (2017), has been proposed as a longer-term aim. Matters of ethics nonetheless present more immediate issues given current police reliance on DF. One such issue example concerns digital device triage systems, often known as 'cyber kiosks' (Scottish Parliament 2019). Cyber kiosks resemble personal computers and are designed to image or extract data stored on various digital devices such as mobile phones or tablet computers to enable that data to be analyzed by police. Cyber kiosks allow investigators to bypass security measures such as passwords or encryption to access data stored on electronic devices or information stored on cloud-based server accounts. Such information may include biometric data such as photographs and fingerprint or voice data. Police Scotland purchased 41 such devices intending to use them from Autumn 2018 onwards. A number of concerns, however, were raised with the Policing Sub-committee of the Scottish Parliament's Justice Committee. An inquiry conducted by the sub-committee heard concerns about the legality and ethical basis of their use by Police Scotland. Cyber kiosks were used to search the mobile phones of suspects, witnesses and victims without making these individuals aware that they would be used as part of a police trial, nor were they given the option of providing or withdrawing consent. No human rights, equality or community impact assessments were conducted for cyber kiosks, nor was any public information campaign run. The sub-committee heard that cyber kiosks could acquire potentially highly sensitive personal data, however, including that from third parties. The sub-committee recommended that cyber kiosks should not be used until 'clarity on the legal framework is established' (Scottish Parliament 2019: 25).

Recovering data from complainants' and witnesses' devices raises a series of ethical issues in relation to consent and other matters. Striking a balance between the privacy of victims and witnesses and securing justice has been recognized as a key challenge (BFEG 2020). Ensuring that sensitive data are collected in a proportionate, focussed and legal manner has been regarded as key, together with clear guidelines on the length of time it may be stored. In addition, clarity over the potential utility of collecting a complainant's data has been regarded as important in terms of 'firm belief' that evidence stored on a complainant's device could advance an investigation, together with a clear sense of what investigative purposes that evidence could serve (BFEG 2020: 5). Such ethical decision making may, however, be less than straightforward given the highly contextualized nature of policing which may entail responding to varied, fluid and unfolding situations under significant time pressure.

Anticipating the possible presence of data which may be informative in the context of a particular incident may not necessarily be clear. Malicious upload of data or spoof images which might erroneously incriminate an individual are other examples of ethical and technical challenges faced by DF practitioners (BFEG 2020).

While the literature on the occupational or professional identity of DF and ethics remains relatively limited at time of writing, the preceding discussion should suffice to indicate a number of issues. First, technical limitations can affect the consistency of evidential recovery. Second, there appear to be issues concerning how DF is perceived by police clients and the level of technical awareness on the part of the latter. Third, DF outcomes in casework are highly contextualized and, fourth, there exists a gap between formalized management protocols for DF and how digital evidence is understood and used in the context of actual casework. This in turn raises further questions when conceptualizing professionalization. To what extent can a code of ethics be representative of the operational realities of DF work? Similarly, what role should, or can, training or accreditation play in shaping DF practice given the pressures and contingencies identified by social researchers (Wilson-Kovacs 2020; Rappert et al. 2021)? These pieces of research suggest that DF work in frontline policing is not an altogether technical exercise but that it also requires a significant social and ethical sensibility on the part of practitioners to educate clients, manage expectations and respond to changing circumstances. The question remains as to what extent this can be captured and accommodated for in exercises such as accreditation and training programmes and codes of ethics.

Other key formalizations include scientific and technical standards. As the next section demonstrates, these have also been the subject of discussion. These deliberations have been accompanied by comparisons with the organizational and epistemic character of other forensic practices.

## DF and scientific standards

DF literature has reflected on precisely what constitutes the scientific aspects of DF practice (see, for example, Pollitt et al. 2018). This has partly concerned to what extent DF can be regarded as analogous or distinct to other forms of forensic science, sometimes framed in comparison as so-called 'trace' or 'wet' forensics (House of Lords Science and Technology Committee 2018; Pollitt et al. 2018). This has fed into debates regarding whether the regime of standards for trace forensics is compatible with digital forensics. ISO17020 and ISO17025 have been promoted as standards in trace forensics. Briefly, ISO17025 is used to govern testing laboratories, whereas ISO17020 is a set of standards which applies to organizations undertaking inspections. These standards have been promoted in UK forensic settings and have been regarded by some as providing an effective broad means of addressing organizational systems and processes, and overall quality management in laboratories (Stokes, cited in House of Lords Science and Technology Committee 2018). They entail auditing systems and involve blind proficiency testing.

While ISO17020 and ISO17025 have been widely promoted in trace forensics, their compatibility and appropriateness as means of regulating DF practice have been disputed and debated (England 2018; Marshall and Paige 2018; Page et al. 2019; Tully et al. 2020). The ISO17020 and ISO17025 regimes have been regarded as highly costly to DF practitioners, particularly to those who may operate as small private businesses (Collie, cited in House of Lords Science and Technology Committee 2018). These businesses were regarded as playing a particularly important role in assisting defendants. The Lords inquiry heard concerns that the removal of such firms due to standardization costs could risk miscarriages of justice (House of Lords Science and Technology Committee 2019).

DF overlaps with forms of biometric analysis such as voice recordings, videos, photographs and facial analysis in addition to other data forms. Activities such as file extraction, making forensic copies of evidence and running presumptive tests such as checking for child pornography on devices have been suggested as areas quality assurance and accreditation regimes could readily address (Tully et al. 2020).

Concerns remain about the quality of DF casework (Reedy 2020). Recognized quality issues include inaccurate or insufficient recording of information, including chain of custody; shortcomings in security and backup procedures; missing or insufficiently detailed procedures and lack of full compliance with procedures; validation issues; lack of proof of competence; using unvalidated storage devices; and lack of awareness of permissions for data extraction (fieldwork 2019; Casey and Souvignet 2020).

DF has been viewed by some as entailing a different investigatory process. It was claimed in the 2019 Lords inquiry that a range of ISO standards exist which are more specifically focused on DF. ISO 27037, for example, is titled 'Guidelines for Identification, Collection, Acquisition and Preservation of Digital Evidence' (House of Lords Science and Technology Committee 2019). Rather than running an experiment such as a DNA profiling exercise which can be isolated from other processes and can be subject to laboratory conditions, DF has been characterized as involving complex technologies where it is difficult to think in terms of separate tests. Given that digital technology involves a vast and ever-increasing series of component types, device types, file formats, etc., it has been regarded as near-impossible to establish that pre-developed tests could be used in DF – instead, DF practitioners may have to work in a sometimes improvised fashion. Technology producers may have more knowledge about the performance of a particular device, software, file or component but may not be in a position to share that with a specific DF practitioner or investigatory team.

Other activities, such as the interpretation and evaluation of digital evidence, are regarded as more complex and may not so easily fit into an accreditation framework (Sommer, cited in House of Lords Science and Technology Committee 2018). Much debate has also addressed whether the kind of paradigms used to interpret non-digital trace evidence can also be used for digital data (Ribaux et al. 2020). Some influential authors have proposed that DF should be framed through formalized reasoning processes similar to those used for analysis of trace evidence (Pollitt et al. 2018; Casey 2020). They claim that DF is susceptible to the same kinds of potential cognitive bias found in other kinds of forensic analyses, and similar kinds of epistemological and probabilistic approaches proposed for other evidential analysis (see Chapter 5) have been suggested for digital data. Another international standard, ISO 21043, is currently under preparation, which is intended to involve a likelihood ratio (LR) approach possibly similar to that utilized in CAI (Casey 2020). How to standardize digital evidence interpretation and evaluative opinion thus remains the subject of debate.

Efforts to standardize DF methods are also compounded by the variety of uses for digital evidence (Casey 2020). DF has found numerous use contexts, not limited to police but also to military, intelligence and protection of critical infrastructures (Reedy 2020). This stretches beyond criminal and civil law to encompass cyber-attack investigations, forensic intelligence activities, counter-terrorism operations, accident reconstructions and international conflicts (Casey 2020). These different contexts frame digital evidence within different procedures, which might hinder effective transfer of information across domains and risk misinterpretation.

DF remains dependent on commercial tools and vendor training, which may not fully reflect the operational contexts in which DF is required and may not necessarily be fit for purpose. DF teams may not even have the agency to source equipment if IT services are the responsibility of a separate department (Reedy 2020). Even if laboratories are able to invest in new technology, this may present challenges in terms of needing new quality control processes (Casey et al. 2019) or require new forms of expertise which may be difficult to source or beyond the capacity or resources of laboratories.

As with other areas of forensic practice, there is the issue of to whom standards should apply. Despite the significance of DF to criminal investigation, serious concerns were raised in the 2018–19 House of Lords inquiry (Chapter 4) over the level of police understanding. While it was claimed that at least some police had access to relatively sophisticated DF tools and had familiarity with social media, doubts were expressed over whether police officers had the skills to critically interpret and evaluate resulting evidence. A lack of training was regarded as compounding the issue:

> They are being given these rather whizzy magic tools that do everything, and a regular police officer, as good as he may be, is not a digital forensic analyst. They are pushing some buttons, getting some output and, quite frequently, it is being looked over by the officer in charge of the case, who has no more training in this, and probably less, than him. They will jump to conclusions about what that means because they are being pressured to do so, and they do not have the resources or the training to be able to make the right inferences from those results. (Collie, cited in House of Lords Science and Technology Committee 2018: 3)

Aside from standards, DF faces other challenges. Case management in investigations and trials has been reported as being severely complicated by the potentially vast amount of data recoverable from devices and the demands of the courts. One witness to the 2018–19 Lords inquiry reported instances whereby they had been requested to analyze new evidence at extremely short notice with a lack of awareness on the part of criminal justice actors over how long this would take (Sommer, cited in House of Lords Science and Technology Committee 2018). Defence lawyers were accused by another witness of lacking awareness of the significance of digital evidence and the organization to request timely disclosure (Collie, cited in House of Lords Science and Technology Committee 2018). This was also seen as risking the presentation of clear defence arguments. Courts were thus seen to place unreasonable demands on DF investigators. An instance was reported in which a judge at short notice demanded that all data from a password-protected iPad be downloaded. This task was reported as taking 20 police officers working a whole weekend to recover and work through the data (Stokes, cited in House of Lords Science and Technology Committee 2018).

Serious cases may involve up to 44,000 social media messages from a single device, to quote one example given to the Lords inquiry (House of Lords Science and Technology Committee 2018). The analysis of chat logs and social media messages presents challenges in terms of understanding slang or forms of argot such as emojis or other graphical modes of expression. The use of foreign languages could also considerably complicate analysis. The interpretation of such messages could conceivably be contested between counsel in court.

Machine learning and artificial intelligence have been recognized as possibly assisting with the analysis of potentially vast amounts of data. The term 'digital transformation' has been used to describe the increasing dependence on ever more sophisticated technologies, including artificial intelligence, to conduct routine work (Casey and Souvignet 2020). Yet caution has been expressed about the limits of AI and machine learning. Similar to their possible applications to other forms of forensic information such as DNA or facial data, risks have been perceived in terms of the potential for automated systems to develop bias in their analysis. There is much concern over how such systems might be trained and by whom:

> If the wrong people teach them they will learn the wrong things. (Stokes, cited in House of Lords Science and Technology Committee 2018: 10)

Further questions concern how these systems relate to the evolving technical and legal architecture within which practitioners, their clients and their targets, together with other stakeholders such as victims and the law, are embedded. As we shall see in the next section, much commentary has focused on how the organization of DF may need to change. This section charts a discernible transition, from DF as a 'cottage industry' (National Police Chief's Council [NPCC] 2020), whereby practitioners work individually and on a responsive and piecemeal basis, to the concept of 'digital forensics as a service' (DFaaS), which entails a more strategic, centralized and sophisticated practice, drawing upon advances such as cloud computing.

## Digital forensics as a service

As with other forensic practices, DF encompasses a wide variety of stakeholders (Casey et al. 2019). The notion of the networking of forensic data, in the sense of providing greater access to a wider community of users and greater interoperability, has been identified as a potential force multiplier for more efficient forms of criminal investigation. It has been argued that such networking facilitates much swifter data analysis concerning investigative questions of location, identity, chronology and relationships (Casey et al. 2019; Ribaux et al. 2020).

A preoccupation with networking through devolution of technical access has, however, raised the issue of how communication across stakeholders can be maintained and to avoid duplication of tasks. The historical provision of DF in the UK has been labelled a 'cottage industry' in the NPCC's *Digital Forensic Science Strategy* published in 2020. Here, the term framed DF as having tended to involve numerous individuals or small companies working in a fragmented way (NPCC 2020). Within UK policing, DF is still regarded by the NPCC as 'disjointed' (NPCC 2020: 19), with 40 digital forensic units (DFUs) serving 43 forces. The NPCC described a situation whereby collaboration between forces was limited and in which individual DFUs had evolved in variable, non-standardized ways with notable differences in methods and use of hardware and software. This has been regarded by the NPCC as highly inefficient, with significant duplication of effort (NPCC 2020). The NPCC's strategy seeks to standardize methods and to create common, centralized support services utilizing cloud computing and to work with the private sector.

The challenges to DF in terms of the volume and variety of data and devices and the increasing role of digital evidence have been addressed elsewhere. Members of the

Netherlands Forensic Institute developed the concept of DFaaS in an attempt to improve communication and collaboration between police, DF practitioners and other clients (van Baar et al. 2014; van Beek et al. 2020). This involved the development of a central platform and configurable tools to manage data recovered from devices in investigations. DFaaS allows data and metadata to be stored, formatted and collated in a central system and for these data to be readily queried, filtered and aggregated. From this centralized system, information can be made accessible to DF practitioners, police and legal professionals. DFaaS has been regarded as crucial to realizing the NPCC digital strategy in England and Wales (Casey 2020).

The NFI's DFaaS system is known as 'Hansken', and it has been claimed to have been used in over 1,000 cases as of 2020, including investigations which have involved over 1,000 devices, instances involving 100 terabytes of raw data to process and periods where 100 cases were being investigated concurrently (van Beek et al 2020). Authors have claimed that in a complex case involving the seizure of Canadian email servers by Dutch prosecutors, Hansken withstood legal scrutiny concerns over quality control, involving questions such as ensuring accurate data entry and editing. Hansken has not involved any specific new technologies but instead has entailed adapting existing third-party products. Around 35 people are employed to maintain Hansken, including roles such as IT developers, forensic specialists, system architects and engineers and those employed to test the system. Development and testing are able to take place on different parts of the system concurrently. Authors reported that the user base for Hansken can be readily expanded and allows automation of some functions. Other DFaaS-type systems have been developed elsewhere, reflecting increasing interest in reconfiguring DF into more centralized and shareable platforms. For example, Peritus is a Brazilian DF tool designed specifically to handle multimedia data which has been able to link together the heterogeneous state and federal law enforcement networks (Cunha et al. 2020).

Implementing DFaaS does face challenges. van Beek et al (2020) reported that they found it difficult to make a clear business case in terms of clearly identifying benefits in terms of budget, time and labour. This was due to the difficulty in identifying hidden costs which pre-centralization were distributed over different organizations, teams and individuals. While providing new opportunities to progress casework, it took time for users to become familiarized with the new working methods. Challenges also became apparent in terms of reconciling different agencies to work together in new ways and the bureaucracy involved in developing a system within a government context.

The emergence of DFaaS exemplifies the increased ambition being brought to bear on DF and the potential to move rapidly on from the cottage industry model. Yet such systems also present marked complexity in terms of the ways in which they may re-configure sociotechnical relations, which include political boundaries and jurisdictional concerns. DFaaS may promise greater efficiency and advanced ways of addressing the ever-increasing challenges presented to DF practitioners, but they also present their own issues in terms of obdurate organizational and practitioner cultures.

Other emerging DF methods present opportunities for investigators but equally raise issues around privacy and jurisdictionality. Netfox, for example, is a network forensics tool which allows investigators to gather IP addresses or log files that may contain within them private data such as passwords, usernames and credit card numbers (Pluskal et al. 2020). Such data acquisition is a highly sensitive and controversial matter and is subject to very different laws in different jurisdictions, such as North American and European territories.

In addition, the capacity of perpetrators to stay one step ahead of such advances continues to occupy the minds of the DF community. While cloud computing presents opportunities for DF, it also presents new possibilities for criminal activity which might transcend jurisdictional boundaries. DF also faces potential emerging challenges such as the notion of 'crime as a service', readily available and generic 'business models' (Caviglione et al. 2017) which allow access to tools, programming frameworks and other services to allow cybercrimes to be committed. One such example is Tox, a ransomware construction kit which can be customized and distributed. DF in general faces challenges from the use of anti-forensic measures which may block, hinder or corrupt evidence acquisition and analysis. These can hide or alter digital evidence to render it inadmissible (Bhat et al. 2021).

On the other hand, technology may continue to provide an ever wider range of data that could be analyzed and disseminated through centralized platforms. These opportunities may, however, pose further technical issues. For example, the IoT may continue to pose such challenges and opportunities (Caviglione et al. 2017; Stoyanova et al. 2020). IoT systems problematize the recovery of data, in that it may only be stored for a limited amount of time on IoT devices, or in partial form if the device has limited energy sources, as in the case of solar-powered IoT. On the other hand, IoT devices for the home, such as alarm systems, surveillance cameras, smart doorbells or smoke/carbon monoxide detectors, are equipped with sensors which may autonomously generate data or in response to human action such as movement or opening doors (Servida and Casey 2019). Such data may be of forensic interest in the event of investigating when a door was opened or an alarm disabled or to determine the approximate time a fire started. Data stored on Amazon's Alexa and Echo systems have been implicated in criminal investigations (Cuthbertson 2018; Burke 2019).

## Conclusion

Digital forensics is now recognized as a key source of information for criminal investigation, as vital, if not now more so, than DNA or fingerprint evidence. This chapter has, however, shown that DF in England and Wales faces a number of challenges. Many of these are largely technical in character. Electronic devices continue to proliferate in number and type, as do the file formats in which data are stored. Concerns remain about the capacity of police forces and external providers to deal with potentially vast quantities of data. The 'cottage industry' model, with 43 forces and external providers working on DF casework on a piecemeal and fragmented basis, has been regarded as inappropriate in this context and given near-future scenarios. DF tools have recognized limitations and have performed inconsistently in casework (BFEG 2020; Wilson-Kovacs 2020). In time-pressured situations, resource and technical constraints risk the selective extraction of evidence. Even with more capable technology, evidence may be subject to questionable interpretation in the light of concerns over police understandings and expectations. AI may not be a panacea to bias and partiality if such systems are not properly trained and tested. The question of how to validate and standardize DF tools and practices has, however, been open to question. This concerns whether standards used for other forensic practices are readily applicable to DF or if more bespoke regimes need to be developed. This possibly points to more profound questions concerning the epistemic character of DF. Is it commensurate with the notion of isolated laboratory testing, such as DNA analysis, or is it a more complex and responsive activity which entangles itself with other forensic practices?

Other issues, perhaps more social in nature, problematize DF further. Some of these reflect a possible tension between idealized depictions of DF as a profession and the experiences of DF practitioners in police environments. Some have drawn upon the sociology of professions to project a sense of direction through which DF may gain greater recognition and standing within criminal justice. Ethnographic studies have indicated that realizing such assertions rests on managing police expectations, itself not straightforward given the pressures both police and DF practitioners find themselves under, variable levels of police understandings of digital evidence and the potentially fluid and non-linear nature of criminal investigation in which the perceived significance of evidence may fluctuate as events unfold. Ethical decision making may also be less than clear-cut in the heat of the moment. While still limited in scope, qualitative sociological research has indicated the difficulties in capturing the professional identity of DF practice through formalized, externally imposed regimes.

Finally, this chapter outlined how actors, data and devices could be reconfigured into renewed sociotechnical networks via the concept of DFaaS and centralizing visions such as those presented in the NPCC's strategy. The NPCC strategy represents an ambitious national imaginary to re-shape England and Wales' DF capability to reflect future assumed policing priorities. The glimpse of DF presented in this chapter, however, suggests some possible challenges which may stand in the way of such a vision. Notably, this includes the question of how various actors will be embedded and recruited into such a network. Police and DF practitioners may need time to collectively familiarize themselves with new ways of working and communicating. It remains to be seen precisely how 43 police forces, with differing resources and priorities, will work together, particularly if they are not mandated to do so. The question of how legal professionals and the courts will comprehend and engage with DFaaS needs to be addressed, given that managing their expectations has sometimes been highly challenging. The possible use of automation in such a framework, and the potential risks, is another issue. Validating such a complex network may be challenging if international standards only provide partial coverage.

This list of issues highlights how realizing a renewed vision for DF in England and Wales may not be a straightforward matter of applying technical and economic rationality. What can be discerned from this chapter is that externally projected visions for DF may not fully align with the standpoint of those who become embedded within the networks which such imaginaries may help bring into being. Nor might technical interventions necessarily work as planned. While DF could be said to be a response to technological evolution, it is not a wholly technical practice but a sociotechnical phenomenon which has to serve wider criminal justice interests. We should not lose sight that, regardless of its configuration, DF is situated within even more diverse, heterogeneous and, above all, unpredictable environs.

## Bibliography

Bhat, W.A., AlZahrani, A., and Wani, M.A. (2021) 'Can computer forensic tools be trusted in digital investigations?', *Science & Justice*, 61: 198–203.

Biometrics and Forensics Ethics Group. (2020) *Notes of 14th Meeting*, 3 December 2020; online at: https://assets.publishing.service.gov.uk/government/uploads/system/uploads/attachment_data/file/966986/BFEG_dec_2020_minutes_-_final.pdf (3 August 2021).

Bossler, A.M., Seigfried-Spellar, K.C. and Holt, T.J. (2015) *Cybercrime and Digital Forensics: An Introduction*. London: Routledge.

Burke, M. (2019) 'Amazon's Alexa may have witnessed alleged Florida murder, authorities say', NBC News, 2 November 2019; online at: https://www.nbcnews.com/news/us-news/amazon-s-alexa-may-have-witnessed-alleged-florida-murder-authorities-n1075621 (accessed 23 August 2021).

Casey, E. (2020) 'Standardization of forming and expressing preliminary evaluative opinions on digital evidence', *Forensic Science International: Digital Investigation*, 32: 200888.

Casey, E., Ribaux, O. and Roux, C. (2019) 'The Kodak syndrome: risks and opportunities created by decentralization of forensic capabilities', *Journal of Forensic Sciences*, 64 (1): 127–136.

Casey, E. and Souvignet, T.R. (2020) 'Digital transformation risk management in forensic science laboratories', *Forensic Science International: Digital Investigation*, 316: 110486.

Caviglione, L., Mazurcyck, W. and Wendzel, S. (2017) 'The future of digital forensics: challenges and the road ahead', *IEEE Security and Privacy Magazine*, November: 12–17.

Cunha, D.O., Silva, E.A., Lambert, J. de A. and Ribeiro, R.O. (2020) 'Peritus framework: towards multimedia evidence analysis uniformization in Brazilian distributed forensic model', *Forensic Science International: Digital Investigation*, 35 (1): 301089.

Cuthbertson, A. (2018) 'Amazon ordered to give Alexa evidence in double murder case', *The Independent*, 14 November 2018; online at: https://www.independent.co.uk/life-style/gadgets-and-tech/news/amazon-echo-alexa-evidence-murder-case-a8633551.html (accessed 23 August 2021).

De Paoli, S., Johnstone, J., Coull, N., et al. (2020) 'A qualitative exploratory study of the knowledge, forensic, and legal challenges from the perspective of police cybercrime specialists', *Policing*. First published 29 July 2020. doi:10.1093/police/paaa027.

England, G. (2018). *Written Evidence to the House of Lords Inquiry into Forensic Science*; online at: http://data.parliament.uk/writtenevidence/committeeevidence.svc/evidencedocument/science-and-technology-committee-lords/forensic-science/written/89891.html (12 November 2019).

Ferguson, I., Renaud, K., Irons, A. and Wilford, S. (2020) 'PRECEPT: a framework for ethical digital forensics', *Journal of Intellectual Capital*, 21 (2): 257–290.

Garfinkel, S.L. (2010) 'Digital forensics: the next 10 years', *Digital Investigation*, 7: S64–S73.

Horsman, G. and Errickson, D. (2019) 'When finding nothing may be evidence of something: anti-forensics and digital tool marks', *Science & Justice*, 59: 565–572.

House of Lords Science and Technology Committee. (2018) *Corrected Oral Evidence: Forensic Science*. Evidence session No. 12, 27 November 2018.

House of Lords Science and Technology Committee. (2019) *Forensic Science and the Criminal Justice System: A Blueprint for Change*. London: House of Lords, 3rd Report of Session 2017–19. London: Her Majesty's Stationery Office.

Julian, R. and Kelty, S.F. (2015) 'Forensic science as "risky business": identifying key risk factors in the forensic process from crime scene to court', *Journal of Criminological Research*, 1 (4): 195–206.

Losavio, M., Seigfried-Spellar, K.C. and Sloan, J.J. (2016) 'Why digital forensics is not a profession and how it can become one', *Criminal Justice Systems*, 29 (2): 143–162.

Marshall, A.M. and Paige, R. (2018) 'Requirement in digital forensics method definition; observations from a UK study', *Digital Investigation*, 27: 23e29. doi:10.1016/j.diin.2018.09.004.

National Police Chief's Council. (2020) *Digital Forensic Science Strategy*. London: National Police Chief's Council.

Page, H., Horsman, G., Sarna, A. and Foster, J. (2019) 'A review of quality procedures in the UK forensic sciences: what can the field of digital forensics learn?', *Science and Justice*, 59: 83–92. doi:10.1016/j.scijus.2018.09.006.

Pluskal, J., Breitinger, F. and Rysavy, O. (2020) 'Netfox detective: a novel open-source network forensics analysis tool', *Forensic Science International: Digital Investigation*, 35 (1): 301019.

Pollitt, M. (2010) 'A history of digital forensics', in K.-P. Chow and S. Shenoi (eds), *Advances in Digital Forensics IV*. Berlin: Springer, pp. 3–15.

Pollitt, M., Casey, E., Jaquet-Chiffelle, D.-O. and Gladyshev, P. (2018) *A Framework for Harmonizing Forensic Science Practices and Digital/Multimedia Evidence*. Organization of Scientific Area Committees Technical Series 0002. Gaithersburg, MD: National Institute of Standards and Technology.

Rappert, B., Wheat, H. and Wilson-Kovacs, D. (2021) 'Rationing bytes: managing demand for forensic digital examinations', *Policing and Society*, 31 (1): 52–65.

Reedy, P. (2020) *Strategic Leadership in Digital Evidence: What Executives Need to Know*. Elsevier: London.

Ribaux, O., Delémont, O., Baechler, S., Roux, C. and Crispino, F. (2020) 'Digital transformations in forensic science and their impact on policing', in J.J. Nolan, F. Crispino and T. Parsons (eds), *Policing in an Age of Reform*. London: Palgrave MacMillan, pp. 173–191.

Scottish Parliament. (2019) *Report on Police Scotland's Proposal to Introduce the Use of Digital Device Triage Systems (Cyber Kiosks)*, 1st Report (Session 5). Scottish Parliament Justice Sub-committee on Policing. Edinburgh: Scottish Parliament.

Seigfried-Spellar, K.C., Rogers, M. and Crimmins, D. (2017) 'Development of a professional code of ethics in digital forensics', Paper presented at the Annual ADSFL Conference on Digital Forensics, Security and Law, 16 May 2017, Daytona Beach, FL.

Servida, F. and Casey, E. (2019) 'IoT forensic challenges and opportunities for digital traces', *Digital Investigation*, 28: 522–529.

Sharevski, F. (2013) 'Digital forensic investigation in cloud computing environment: impact on privacy', Systematic Approaches to Digital Forensic Engineering, Eighth International Workshop, 21–22 November, Hong Kong.

Sharevski, F. (2015) 'Rules of Professional Responsibility in Digital Forensics: A Comparative Analysis', *Journal of Digital Forensics, Security and Law*, 10 (2): Article 3.

Stoll, C. (1989) *The Cuckoo's Egg*. Doubleday: New York.

Stoyanova, M., Nikoloudakis, Y., Panagiotakis, S., Pallis, E. and Markakis, E.K. (2020) 'A survey on the Internet of Things (IoT) forensics: challenges, approaches and open issues', *IEEE Communications Surveys & Tutorials*, 22 (2): 1191–1221.

Tully, G., Cohen, N., Compton, D., Davies, G., Isbell, R. and Watson, T. (2020) 'Quality standards for digital forensics: Learning from experience in England & Wales', *Forensic Science International: Digital Investigation*, 32: 200905.

van Baar, R.B., Van Beek, H.M.A. and Van Eijk, E.J. (2014) 'Digital Forensics as a Service: a game changer', *Digital Investigation*, 11: S54–S62.

van Beek, H.M.A., Van den Bos, J., Boztas, A., Van Eijk, E.J., Schramp, R. and Ugen, M. (2020) 'Digital Forensics as a Service: stepping up the game', *Forensic Science International: Digital Investigation*, 35: 1–13.

Volti, R. (2011) *An Introduction to the Sociology of Work and Other Occupations*. London and Los Angeles: Sage.

Wall, D. (2007) *Cybercrime: The Transformation of Crime in the Information Age*. London: Polity.

Wilson-Kovacs, D. (2020) 'Effective resource management in digital forensics: An exploratory analysis of triage practices in four English constabularies', *Policing: An International Journal*, 43 (1): 77–90.

Wilson-Kovacs, D., Rappert, B. and Redfern, L. (2021) 'Dirty work? Policing online indecency in digital forensics', *British Journal of Criminology*. First published online 21 June 2021. doi:10.1093/bjc/azab055.

# 10 Conclusion

Imagining and re-imagining forensic and biometric technologies

## Introduction and re-cap

This revised volume has sought to consider how we can anticipate and conceptualize forensic and biometric innovations and has situated them within sociological debates relating to discrimination and inequality, identity, epistemology and professions. In doing so it has pursued three aims. Firstly, it has sought to examine how the scientific and professional character of forensic practice continues to be shaped in different ways via a variety of standpoints, including those of the media, scientific organizations, government, individual practitioners and the law. These standpoints may themselves be fluid and variable. Second, this edition has addressed some key scientific and technological developments in the form of emerging DNA methods, facial recognition and digital forensics. A critical, sociologically informed approach revealed a slippery and problematic interdependence between the underlying scientific and technical basis of these methods and social orderings. Forensic genealogy, DNA phenotyping and facial recognition present significant social-ethical concerns, particularly regarding their perceived potential to unduly discriminate and challenge legal norms. Efforts to re-organize digital forensics platforms raise questions of how individuals' data will be protected in the midst of potentially complex sociotechnical arrangements and information flows, vulnerable to possibly flawed interpretation from either human or automated reasoners.

Third, this volume has sought to compare expectations and experiences of forensic and biometric systems. This final chapter develops this theme further in order to consider the prospects for governing and managing these technologies. Will societies inevitably have to bend, accept and adapt to the seemingly unstoppable march of technology, or can they reclaim control? Can and should we re-imagine this technology?

In order to look ahead, it is important to first take stock. Chapter 1 described the emergence and key earlier findings of forensic studies. Sociological studies of forensic science developed by initially focusing on epistemological questions concerning the production of scientific knowledge and legal decision making. Social research has challenged the status of forensic science as providing immutable claims to knowledge and has contrasted expectations with actuality. These studies illuminated the complexities involved in producing forensic evidence. They presented alternative views of forensic practices and demonstrated how scientific evidence is produced via interactions between different stakeholders with varying standpoints and understandings. Chapter 1 also introduced the concepts of science–society co-production and sociotechnical imaginaries. Other conceptual elements were introduced in Chapter 2. Through a focus on media representations of forensic science, this chapter introduced the concepts of the 'deficit' and 'surfeit' models of the public understanding of science.

DOI: 10.4324/9781003126379-10

Chapters 3 through to 5 sought to detail how the scientific and professional character of forensics has been shaped in different ways. Chapter 3 discussed the professional and organizational development of forensics, while chapter 4 focused on matters of policy and regulation across UK jurisdictions. Together these chapters highlighted the heterogeneity of actors, rules, regulations, laws, organizations and institutions which underpin forensic science and biometric systems. Chapter 5 explored the theme of expectations versus experiences by comparing formalized renditions of forensic reasoning with the practicalities of applying them to casework. This chapter demonstrated how the interplay between formalized protocols and intersubjective experience reflected a mode of reconstructing professional identity through the practice of reconstructing events.

Chapter 6 demonstrated how the status of emerging forensic technologies may be moulded by both the scientific and legal gaze. Contentions over low template DNA profiling revealed different framings of science–society relations. Chapter 6 built on the concepts of the deficit and surfeit models of scientific engagement introduced in Chapter 2 and identified a third variant, the social-realist model. This three-way typology is advanced further in later sections of this chapter by building on the observations of Chapters 7 to 9. Chapter 7 focused on DNA methods which have attracted law enforcement interest but have also raised ethical concerns. Chapter 8 focused on facial recognition, another ethically contentious technology. Chapter 9 focused on digital forensics and compared efforts to professionalize this practice with the experiences of casework and looked ahead to possible future developments.

This volume has explored how forensic and biometric technology continues to evolve and proliferate. DNA technology continues to develop in the forms of phenotyping and genealogical analysis, which present new and potentially problematic impacts upon identity and social justice. Facial recognition raises similar issues. Data has become many things to many people, a commodity but also a resource that forensic practice seeks to harness in a multitude of forms but which threatens to overwhelm law enforcement. Yet who gains access to our data, how it might be used and who gains from that use continue to raise concerns.

Forensic and biometric technology and attendant advances in automation and artificial intelligence are often framed, particularly in policy discourses, as developing rapidly. At times, this technology is portrayed as being beyond the control of society, something which is evolving under its own pace and direction. Elsewhere, however, other voices continue to justify investment in biometric systems in terms of the supposed rationalization and efficiency they may bring to law enforcement and to other functions such as border control and welfare entitlement. Either way, technology is often presented in a deterministic fashion, as an autonomous force which is shaping society, to which society can only accept and conform.

Addressing forensic and biometric systems with a critical and sociologically informed focus enables us to view this technology in a different light. Forensic science has received concerted social scientific attention which has questioned how it projects authority and objectivity. Forensic science may be imbued with a powerful aura of epistemic authority, but a closer look reveals it entangled in social settings which render it susceptible to being moulded by a variety of influences, including the media, politics and, of course, the law. More recently, researchers have gone further in questioning some more problematic aspects of biometric systems. These include forms of categorization based on questionable ontological foundations and technologies which may reflect and thus reinforce structural inequalities. Technological evolution may complicate matters further, raising the question of who or what is making decisions. With more automation, however, comes the possible risk that technology may be taken for granted, begetting more black boxes perceived to be unquestionable and immutable (Office of the Biometrics Commissioner [OBC] 2018).

This final chapter explores possible ways to keep these black boxes open. It considers to what extent it is possible to anticipate, regulate and govern forensic technology in the light of what seem to be rapid and potentially overwhelming advances but which raise issues of social justice. Forensic science and technology is embedded within a series of inter-linked spaces which include within them a variety of actors who have different relations to claims to forensic knowledge. The proliferation of data and devices has served to complicate that landscape further by shaping new networks of people, data and things. Biometric technology potentially creates new relations between technology, subjectivity and identity and between policy domains such as law enforcement, biomedicine and border control. Contemplating how society can govern forensics and biometrics, given this evolving sociotechnical landscape, requires us to think again about the role of social science. This final chapter sketches a renewed role for social science in re-thinking forensic and biometric technology.

In what follows, the framework of deficit, surfeit and social-realist discourses introduced earlier in this volume is developed further. It is suggested that these discourses inform and invoke a series of contending normative interpretations which project technology within differing orderings of science and society.

## A framework for science–society relations: three normative interpretations

This section develops themes which have emerged in previous chapters by considering how technology may be framed in different ways by different actors. These perceptions can be regarded as normative interpretations of technology (Williams 2008). They reflect distinct sets of expectations and concerns on the part of stakeholders but, more significant, they represent various projected configurations of relations between science and society at large. This section outlines how forensic science and biometric technology may be framed in different, competing ways: either discursively positioned dominantly and hegemonically over society, or as a narrower field of sceptical inquiry, or configured in an interdependent but more complex and problematic relationship with wider social factors.

A first series of normative interpretations are redolent of the so-called deficit model of public understanding of science introduced in Chapter 2, which assumes that lay audiences can be readily educated to accept the inevitable transformative, rationalizing momentum of science and technology (Bodmer 1985; Miller 2001). These framings are largely supportive of emerging technologies and perceive *social benefits*. They portray technology deterministically, as unproblematically beneficent and socially transformative. While some scientific voices have promoted technologies in this way, this technologically determinist interpretation is notably reflected in public, media, political and police support for biometric systems. Here, technology is portrayed as improving and updating law enforcement. Science and technology is framed as unquestionably reliable, which supports assertions that these technologies should be used widely. Ethical concerns are underplayed in favour of narratives of rationalization, other than to emphasize the moral hazards of not employing such technology to solve crime and the consequent risk to public safety.

A second series of normative interpretations relate to the 'surfeit' model, also introduced in Chapter 2 and developed further in Chapter 6. Surfeit discourses reflect concerns on the part of some that lay audiences assume too much knowledge of forensic science from media and overlook the complexities inherent in the actual application of science to law enforcement (Lynch 2009; Cole 2015). This is compatible with a norm of *epistemic caution* on the part of scientific authority. This sceptical mode interprets emerging forensic technologies as vulnerable to epistemic risk. This framing emphasizes the need for careful scientific scrutiny and the importance of rigorous standards, validation processes and expert oversight, seen as necessary to uphold scientific propriety. Such discourses may situate scientists as the primary arbiters of forensic and biometric technology, regardless of wider support or concern. Hence, they may construct boundaries around who is considered qualified to assess these technologies.

Chapter 6 introduced a third variant of interpretations which I term 'social-realist' to describe how they valorize extra-scientific concerns in sociotechnical engagements. These framings emphasize the assumed interplay of what Emile Durkheim regarded as *social facts* – the wide array of shared understandings and institutionalized constraints which order society, of which science is but one (Durkheim [1892] 1982). This normative interpretation reflects a more balanced and interdependent ordering of science and other social imperatives commensurate with Jasanoff's (2004) notion of 'co-production', which suggests a mutual interdependency, rather than a hierarchical or deterministic relationship. Technologies are framed in terms of social impact but are also perceived to be shaped in turn by extra-scientific domains such as law, jurisdictionality, commerce, culture, social justice, etc. Extra-scientific interventions in the form of, for example, legislation or legal decisions may be framed as necessary to protect against perceived harms.

These three types of framings can be discerned in claims made about the technologies featured in Chapters 7 to 9. Taking first the example of forensic genealogy, the deficit model or technological determinist discourses might emphasize public acceptance. They manifest themselves in claims that public users of genealogical services are educated about the status of submitted genetic material and that they support the use of data in criminal investigations. Voices justifying surreptitious sampling to verify genealogical analysis to solve violent crime could also be said to endorse a determinist narrative. They reflect a desire to see the potential of such methods to be fully realized. Surfeit-type discourses of epistemic caution, on the other hand, temper positive public attitudes towards forensic genealogy with concerns about over-expectations. Issues around accreditation and police perceptions of competency also reflect this perspective. Surfeit-type discourses may also emphasize the time-consuming nature of investigations, which might limit the utility of forensic genealogy (Wickenheiser 2019). Other such concerns include the potential for forensic genealogy and familial searching in general to perpetuate erroneous notions about criminality being a heritable trait. Social-realist/co-productionist narratives are reflected in ethical concerns. These include the possible function creep of using data for purposes which were not originally intended, ethical and legal concerns over surreptitious sampling, questions of exceptionality and what kinds of crimes justify the use of genealogy and whether this method should be combined with other forms of data such as public records. An emphasis on geographic differences could also be reflect a co-productionist framing, as in differences in legal protections on data privacy between jurisdictions such as the United States and European Union which limit the spatial reach of genealogical analysis.

DNA phenotyping also lends itself to being framed in a similar series of ways. Technological determinist standpoints are reflected in claims that the method is superior to eyewitness testimony. Positive media coverage of the technique and demands for laws to be changed to allow its use, as in Germany, can also be included among this type of normative interpretation. More epistemically cautious framings, on the other hand, challenge the underlying scientific reliability of phenotyping, questioning whether scientific complexities are overlooked and whether the method might withstand courtroom scrutiny (fieldwork 2015). Alternatively, co-productionist framings emphasize concerns about how phenotyping may reverse the principle of the presumption of innocence and whether it targets and discriminates against certain populations. Other concerns include the possibility that phenotyping for certain medical conditions might override the principle of the right to know or data protection rights. Co-productionist framings also invoke issues concerning how ethical boundaries and scientific categories are co-produced. This is particularly notable in social scientific observations which have critically examined assumptions which underpin the construction of phenotypic data and draws attention to the slippery relations between the scientific use of racial/ethnic categories, the latter arguably socio-cultural labels.

In relation to facial recognition, deficit or technological determinist framings may emphasize the capacity to guarantee safety in public places. FR might also be framed in benign terms, as something publics merely need to educate themselves about to assure themselves. Narratives of the supposed efficiency it brings to policing (Davies et al. 2018) or the claimed rationalization of identity processing (Home Office 2018) also reflect this kind of framing. On the other hand, surfeit-type discourses, or framings of epistemic caution, emphasize concerns about the accuracy and reliability of FR. Such framings also raise questions of what constitutes a valid trial of the technology and who should design and conduct these tests (OBC 2018). Further related questions concern the need to consider other aspects of the human–technology interface in terms of how decisions are made on the basis of FR (Fussey and Murray 2019). Social facts or co-productionist framings may emphasize the role of court interventions, such as the *Bridges* case, in reflecting how its use and acceptability can and should be determined through legal means. Questions about the adequacy of legislation represent a related emphasis. The way in which commercial interests influence the use of FR is another. Concerns about the tendency of FR to discriminate against certain groups reflect a perception of inter-related social imperatives. Questions over the level of diversity within the tech industry emphasize another interdependence between technology and society. Concerns over how FR is used in certain jurisdictions, particularly authoritarian regimes, reflect a further framing which foregrounds human rights and freedoms (Strittmatter 2019).

Finally, digital forensics also lends itself to this framework. Deficit-type or technological determinist narratives might emphasize the threat of crime assisted, enhanced or created through technological evolution (Wall 2007). They may emphasize the need for technology to help law enforcement keep up with criminal activity which is itself being transformed through the same rationalizing force. The promotion of digital forensics as a service (DFaaS) also reflects a certain rationalizing tendency commensurate which such framings. Surfeit-type or epistemically cautious framings might emphasize concerns of over-expectations of DF evidence on the part of the police. Other cautious discourses might emphasize the possibility of issues such as spoof images, problems in identifying deleted data or struggles to itemize data as technical complications which hinder the production of meaningful digital evidence (Biometrics and Forensics Ethics Group 2020). They are also reflected in wider concerns over quality standards. Demands placed by courts on DF practitioners to retrieve large amounts of data in short time frames may reflect a lack of understanding of the practicalities of casework. Co-productive discourses may highlight the lack of commercial motivation to assist DF or barriers such as digital rights management put in place by those firms. Ethical debates and legislation regarding data protection, privacy and informed consent also project a form of co-production between ethico-legal and technical factors.

These three normative interpretations promulgate different assumptions of how science and technology relate to society at large. By exploring how these interpretations situate forensic and biometric technologies, this volume has shown how they represent contested anticipations and interpretive flexibility on the part of various stakeholders. The varied science–society orderings which underpin these interpretations represent distinct positionings of forensic and biometric systems. They reflect differing competing expectations of how science and wider audiences should engage: *social benefits* emphasizes narratives of rationalization, *epistemic caution* prioritizes a narrower cohort of scientific actors, while *social facts* frames science and a host of other social orderings in a more balanced and interdependent way.

This latter notion of co-production is therefore only one possible way of framing technology, which may not be shared by all stakeholders and may be largely reflective of the purview of social science. Co-production co-exists and engages with the technological determinism of social benefits and the sceptical scientific hegemony of epistemic caution. This opens up further questions concerning precisely how these framings co-exist and engage. How might co-productionist thinking be promoted to a wider audience, and what possibilities exist to shape forensic and biometric technology in more socially just ways, given the co-existence of these three framings? How might it be possible to re-imagine this technology? The next section addresses sociotechnical imaginaries literature in more depth and looks further afield to consider the possibilities.

## Co-embedding imaginaries and stakeholders

There has been a tendency in much literature to regard sociotechnical imaginaries as largely cohesive and instrumental entities, which serve to unite groups through shared visions and assumptions of technology and social goods or risks. Here, the very nature of imagining suggests a process which closes off some questions or alternative scenarios and instead projects and thus determines a particular assumed relation between technology and society. Donovan's (2015) and Markó's (2016) studies of biometric imaginaries in South Africa and South Sudan respectively portray policy visions in a notably different light. Donovan's study focused on the development of biometric technology to identify welfare claimants, while Markó's explored the rollout of biometric infrastructure used to bestow citizenship in the newly-independent state. These authors contrasted elite projections of technological instrumentalism with empirical findings which included operational shortcomings and allegations of corrupt bids for technological contracts in South Africa. In South Sudan, the military exerted enduring influence in state bureaucracies whereby citizenship was actually bestowed via markedly non-biometric means despite investment in a state-of-the-art biometric system for this purpose. These studies identified significant divergences between visions for delivering social goods through technology and realities on the ground. They highlighted how these disparities manifested themselves in hitherto unanticipated responses on the part of those who found themselves caught up in these imaginaries.

The literature has also often tended to frame sociotechnical imaginaries as entities which actors either fully accept or resist by attempting to shape opposing imaginaries. Literature has focused on how sociotechnical imaginaries are mobilized to gain support and acceptance, but Donovan's (2015) and Markó's (2016) works indicate a need to consider how actors may become embedded within them in ways not fully of their choosing or which they perceive differently due to their role and location. Addressing this aspect draws attention to the significance of standpoint and interpretive flexibility of those embedded within sociotechnical imaginaries (Pinch and Bijker 1984). Some actors' perceptions may not align with others. Actors may differ over the precise ways to pursue a specific sociotechnical vision. They may contest the precise form of imaginaries based on their standpoint and interests, giving rise to what could be termed imaginative politics (Lawless 2020).

UK biometric policymaking is marked by efforts to promote imaginaries across a fragmented and heterogeneous landscape (Lawless 2021). The UK *Biometrics Strategy* presented a specific vision for the use of such data by the Home Office. It named a series of bodies, including the Forensic Science Regulator, the now-merged UK Biometrics Commissioner and Surveillance Camera Commissioner, the Information Commissioner and the Biometrics and Forensics Ethics Group as playing key roles in realizing the strategy. Postholders have, however, problematized the UK Government's imaginary by raising perceived technical, operational and legal shortcomings; matters of scientific detail; and ethical issues. They have done so via channels such as parliamentary inquiries or UK Government–hosted websites.

Sociotechnical imaginaries studies have tended to focus on how they embed themselves across existing economic orders and in collective memories such as national histories and traditions embodied by political institutions (Jasanoff 2015). The preceding discussion suggests, however, that the process of embedding imaginaries is dependent on the responses of those who find themselves embedded within them. It may therefore be more appropriate to talk in terms of *co*-embedding actors and imaginaries. Actors embedded within an imaginary may possess agency to challenge aspects of it. In the case of Home Office biometric policy, regulators, Commissioners and other parties have used established governmental and parliamentary mechanisms to do so. This has included a previous Forensic Science Regulator drawing attention to shortcomings in the accreditation of laboratories and their then lack of statutory powers and previous surveillance camera and UK Biometrics Commissioners criticizing government policy on facial recognition. In challenging aspects of an imaginary from within, these actors have served to re-translate it and the way in which it might embed itself. By drawing attention to matters of detail and ethical concerns, they have had the agency to challenge preconceived notions of this imaginary. At times their interventions have challenged assumptions about their roles by questioning their own status or by criticizing government.

This instance of co-embedding has been driven by the interplay of the various normative interpretations outlined earlier. The UK *Biometrics Strategy* frames its vision as a transformational, rationalizing one, repeatedly talking of facilitating greater efficiency among governmental functions through the technologically mediated re-platforming of data access (Home Office 2018), The technological determinism of the strategy is also reflected in the unproblematic framing of biometric data. The strategy is commensurate with what Melanie Smallman (2020: 589) described as a 'science to the rescue' imaginary found in elite policymaking circles which frames science as a problem-solver while decoupling social and ethical issues. The issues raised by regulators and Commissioners, however, reflect different framings. Recourse to operational and technical complexities such as matters of accreditation and technical standards is consistent with a surfeit mode framing. Ethical concerns, such as those raised in parliamentary inquiries or by the Biometrics and Forensics Ethics Group, reflect social-realist framings in that they invoke wider social impacts. Hence, a prevailing technologically determinist UK Government imaginary is challenged from within by contending interpretations which frame biometric systems in markedly different ways. These differing framings draw attention to potential disparities between the vision and the reality of implementation and may urge a re-think in terms of the way an imaginary may be embedded.

The phenomenon of co-embedding raises the question of what conditions might facilitate even more radical possibilities, in which actors embed themselves into new relationships with both science and state structures. Here, examples from Central and South America may provide some lessons. This region has seen public participation in the use of forensic science and biometric data, aided by non-governmental organisations. In

Argentina, a movement known as the Grandmothers of the Plaza de Mayo (the *abuelas*) campaigned to establish what happened to their children who disappeared under the military dictatorship or *junta*, which ruled the country between 1976–1983. In many cases, the *abuelas*' children themselves gave birth in captivity, with the *abuelas*' grandchildren (*nietas*) forcibly adopted by members of the regime (Adams Smith 2016). Following a transition to democracy, the *abuelas* campaigned for the use of DNA testing and encouraged people who may have been forcibly adopted to come forward to determine their true identity through scientific means.[1] In some cases, adopted persons were compulsorily obliged to submit to DNA testing via judicial investigations into crimes committed by their adopted parents.

More recently in Mexico there has been further public and non-governmental organization activity in response to the war against organized crime groups, which has claimed the lives of at least 150,000 people and in which over 26,000 people have allegedly disappeared (Schwartz-Marin and Cruz-Santiago 2016a; Cruz-Santiago 2020). Citizen-led forensics projects established a forensic DNA database created, managed and designed by relatives of the disappeared in Mexico (Schwartz-Marin and Cruz-Santiago 2016b). The first of its kind in the world, this database seeks to assist families to try and identify loved ones.

Citizen-led participation in forensics in Central and South America represents forms of imagining in which technology, justice and citizenship are co-produced in ways which extend beyond the state.[2] While still engaging with state structures, they represent responses to state shortcomings, in terms of either government-sanctioned human rights violations or weak state structures as in Mexico. While clearly a very different sociopolitical context to the UK, what is significant is that these imaginaries took hold at liminal moments where state governments were either weakened, emergent or in transition. The lesson here for co-embedding biometric imaginaries (Donovan 2015; Markó 2016; Lawless 2021) is that such liminal moments, where official policy is unclear or open-ended, may present opportunities for imaginaries to be re-shaped and which open up spaces for different kinds of agency and participation.

Thus, while a very different context, UK biometric policymaking is itself, at time of writing, also at something of a liminal moment. Legislation in the form of the Forensic Science Regulator Act in England and Wales, and elsewhere the Scottish Biometrics Commissioner Act, has recently been passed. These regulatory regimes have, however, yet to take shape and will be subject to review and revision as technology evolves. Important elements such as the mandated codes of practice have yet to be detailed. Both pieces of legislation allow considerable flexibility in terms of the form of these codes and with whom they allow the Regulator and Scottish Commissioner to consult when drafting them. Intervening in the preparation, review and revision of these codes provides examples of the ways in which science and technology studies (STS), and other social sciences, may be able to participate in the (re)-imagining of forensic and biometric systems. But how may STS, and social science in general, embed itself constructively into forensic and biometric policymaking?

STS is particularly well placed to intervene by raising a series of questions which could inform the development of these codes. One such issue concerns the interdependency between scientific and technical matters and social and ethical impact. We have seen how the science of DNA phenotyping has been critiqued for possibly falsely essentializing relations between genetic and social categorization. These links could nonetheless lead phenotyping to discriminate and construct 'suspect' populations and reverse the presumption of innocence. Facial recognition presents similar and more pressing concerns over accuracy and reliability and has been linked to the increased likelihood of misidentifying individuals who identify as BAME, women or transgender through faulty or poorly tested algorithms. These examples demonstrate how biometric technology, if insufficiently tested or validated, can unduly discriminate. Other technologies present similar risks. Voice and linguistic analysis has been used to verify identity in government settings and in asylum cases to establish a claimant's place of origin. Such analysis requires population-level data to establish the probability that a linguistic or phonetic feature may match with an individual (Parliamentary Office of Science & Technology 2015). Language may not, however, map directly onto geographic boundaries (Eades 2010). This example suggests the need for regulators and Commissioners to critically address the interdependence of scientific and social factors. Future technologies may well present other social impacts. The way in which biometric research and development takes into account physical and mental impairment is currently under-explored. STS researchers could find opportunities to embed themselves in policy and inform regulatory approaches by maintaining critical vigilance to new technological claims. Doing so may enable STS to identify problematic scientific or technical assumptions in a timely manner, which may help inform apposite responses.

Predicting future technologies is risky, and this volume has adopted a cautious stance toward making any bold assertions. If STS is to maintain a constructive vigilance, then it needs to engage at least in some horizon scanning. Even a brief consideration provides a glimpse of near-future possibilities. Work continues in developing biometric technology in areas such as voice, gait and vein pattern analysis. Behavioural biometrics could extend to the analysis of keystrokes or touchscreen gestures. Fingerprint data could be combined with chemical analysis to detect traces of sunscreen or insect repellent to indicate aspects of a person's lifestyle and where they have travelled. Advances in biochemical analysis may allow the aging of bodies or fluids to be measured. It is becoming less inconceivable that fake DNA sequences could be readily synthesized. Increasing numbers of people are fitted with devices, often for medical purposes, which collect data about them and their surroundings (Quigley and Ayihongbe 2018). Such data could be of forensic interest, but it could also possibly raise social and ethical issues around matters of consent. Such examples reflect the continuing heightened expectations of technology, but how may their affordances and risks be comprehended?

Interdisciplinary social science perspectives could also intervene by comparing how the letter of codes of practice are interpreted and enacted in *actual* practice. Purely technical standards may not fully account for human–technology interactions. Studies of the operational use of FR point to inconsistencies around decision making in the field and a paucity of adequate training. This raises the question of the extent to which codes of practice can and should address operational contexts and matters of accreditation. Qualitative social science has a role to play in comparing the hypothetical utility of technology with operational realities in which limitations may become exposed, such as in the work of Rappert and Wilson-Kovacs et al. on digital forensics tools (Wilson-Kovacs 2020; Rappert et al. 2021; Wilson-Kovacs et al. 2021). These findings suggest a need to compel technology producers and users to think more rigorously about what it means for a technology to be validated and to consider how organizational constraints might affect its application. Casework simulations, or 'war-gaming' of technology, may go some way to overcome the recognized problems in mixing testing with operational deployment. Social science would be well placed to play a role in the design and evaluation of such exercises.

Testing and trialling technology raises the question of what constitutes its 'effective' application in law enforcement and other operational contexts. A critical eye may assist in shaping codes which benefit all. The term 'proportionality' is often used in debates around forensics and biometrics to describe the balance between individual privacy and public safety. But how well do we know that biometric systems deliver the latter? What is meant by 'effectiveness' in delivering public safety and security? How is it measured? Does 'effectiveness' mean different things to different stakeholders? And might notions of 'effectiveness' be relative to different emerging technologies, whose limitations and risks may only become apparent over time in certain use-contexts? Terms such as 'effective' or 'proportional' warrant rigorous unpacking, particularly through empirical scrutiny. Social science may be key to ensuring that the meaning of such terms can be fully understood and fleshed out in codes of practice and avoid them being mere platitudes.

Through such possible interventions, STS could help to shape imaginaries, and attitudes, by heightening awareness of the limitations, realities and consequences of applying biometrics and to shape regulatory regimes which incorporate these observations. This could also help to challenge more fatalistic narratives which view technology as evolving rapidly and beyond control. Instead, STS could help to co-embed an imaginary which frames technology as partner, rather than master, of society. Such interventions should be as inclusive as possible, making the impact of biometrics fully visible, particularly in relation to those subjected to it who may otherwise be overlooked and rendered invisible.

As reflected in this volume, and elsewhere, the term 'co-production' is now arguably a familiar concept within STS. Researchers have readily observed claimed instances of co-production in various sites, but there are matters of reflexivity which should be addressed. If STS merely observes co-production from an elevated, distanced position, it risks missing opportunities to embed itself in such a way as to meaningfully challenge imaginaries and instead remains limited to describing them. STS should reflect more on how it could engage in co-production. One way could be to look for ways of networking with other stakeholders, such as civil society groups. It is also apparent that at least some within the tech community are promoting a more socially aware agenda (Buolamwini and Gebru 2018; Gebru 2020; Jo and Gebru 2020). Pursuing links and sharing perspectives and methods with these parts of the tech industry could help form coalitions which could influence regulators and Commissioners.

This in turn invites reflection on how STS communicates to the outside world. The uninitiated could be forgiven for finding the language of STS – perhaps including that sometimes used here – admittedly somewhat arcane and abstract. While STS has often addressed issues concerning public engagement with science, the field may need to face up further to how it engages with publics and other audiences. Communicating the value of STS insights, in appropriately accessible language, and with the requisite commitment to diversity, remains an area that necessitates much further exploration.

This volume has provided an updated overview of the way in which forensic science is constructed in a variety of contexts and interactions. It has also aimed to reflect the ongoing evolution and proliferation of biometric data, which encompasses law enforcement but is increasingly finding use elsewhere. It is hoped that this book has contributed some new ways of conceptualizing and understanding forensic and biometric technology. In particular, it is hoped that it illuminates the complex links between technical, ethical and social matters. From the viewpoint of policy, this volume has sought to constructively problematize the relationship between policy and outcomes and to suggest other ways of thinking about societal relations with biometric data. This is imperative given the rapid advances in technology and increasing social concerns in an interdependent world in which social justice matters more and more.

## Notes

1 Lindsay Adams Smith undertook a number of interviews with *nietas* and encountered a range of attitudes and feelings (Adams Smith 2016). Some who agreed to DNA testing proudly

embraced their new identities. They met their birth families and changed their names. Others, however, refused. Adams Smith also found that some interviewees, while willing to accept the DNA results and affirm their new identity, still supported the actions of the dictatorships and condemned their birth parents as terrorists. Some *nietas* changed their position over time and through engagement with the *abuelas*.

2 This story extends to other countries such as Guatemala and Colombia. The Argentine Forensic Anthropology Team (EAAF), a non-governmental organization founded in 1984 by US forensic anthropologist Clyde Snow, assisted with investigations into violations conducted by the *junta*. The EAAF subsequently travelled to Guatemala to assist in investigation of human rights abuses during the 30-year civil war and trained members of the Guatemalan Forensic Anthropology Foundation (FAFG). The FAFG subsequently assisted with investigations in Spain concerning civil war graves and with citizen-led forensic projects elsewhere (Moon 2016). In Colombia, the family of Luis Fernando Lalinde, who disappeared during a period of intra-state violence in 1984, trained themselves in forensic techniques and enlisted the help of foreign specialists. The claim that a body found in a clandestine grave was Luis Lalinde's was rejected by Colombia's leading geneticist at the time. Unconvinced by this conclusion, Luis Lalinde's family sent the samples for analysis abroad. Twelve years following Luis Fernando's disappearance, two independent identification reports stated that the remains corresponded to an offspring of Mrs Lalinde (Schwartz-Marin and Cruz-Santiago 2016a).

## Bibliography

Ada Lovelace Institute. (2019) *Beyond Face Value: Public Attitudes to Facial Recognition Technology*. London: Nuffield Foundation.

Adams Smith, L. (2016) 'Identifying democracy: citizenship, DNA and identity in post-dictatorship Argentina', *Science, Technology and Human Values*, 41 (6): 1037–1062.

Amelung, N., Granja, R. and Machado, H. (2021) *Modes of Bio-bordering: The Hidden (Dis)integration of Europe*. Singapore: Palgrave Macmillan.

Biometrics and Forensics Ethics Group. (2020) *Notes of 14th Meeting*, 3 December 2020; online at: https://assets.publishing.service.gov.uk/government/uploads/system/uploads/attachment_data/file/966986/BFEG_dec_2020_minutes_-_final.pdf (3 August 2021).

Biometrics and Forensics Ethics Group. (2021) *Briefing Note on the Ethical Issues Arising from the Public-Private Collaboration in the Use of Live Facial Recognition Technology*. London: Home Office.

Bodmer, W. (1985) *The Public Understanding of Science*. London: Royal Society.

Buolamwini, J. and Gebru, T. (2018) 'Gender shades: intersectional accuracy disparities in commercial gender classification', *Proceedings of Machine Learning Research*, 81: 1–15.

Bouzarovski, S., Bradshaw, M. and Wochnik, A. (2015) 'Making territory through infrastructure: The governance of natural gas transit in Europe', *Geoforum*, 64 (1): 217–228.

Cole, S.A. (2015) 'A surfeit of science: the "CSI effect" and the media appropriation of the public understanding of science', *Public Understanding of Science*, 24 (2): 130–146.

Cruz-Santiago, A. (2020) 'Lists, maps and bones: the untold journeys of citizen-led forensics in Mexico', *Victims & Offenders*, 15 (3): 350–369.

Davies, B., Innes, M. and Dawson, A. (2018) *An Evaluation of South Wales Police's Use of Automated Facial Recognition*. Universities' Police Science Institute & Crime & Security Research Institute, University of Cardiff.

Donovan, K. (2015) 'The biometric imaginary: bureaucratic technopolitics in post-apartheid welfare', *Journal of Southern African Studies*, 41 (4): 815–833.

Durkheim, E. [1892] (1982) *The Rules of Sociological Method, and Selected Texts on Sociology and Its Method*. London: Macmillan.

Eades, D. (2010) 'Nationality claims: language analysis and asylum cases', in M. Coulthard and A. Johnson (eds), *The Routledge Handbook of Forensic Linguistics*. London: Routledge, pp. 411–422.

Fussey, P. and Murray, D. (2019) *Independent Report on the London Metropolitan Police Service's Trial of Live Facial Recognition Technology*. Human Rights Centre, University of Essex.

Gebru, T. (2020) 'Race and gender', in M.D. Dubber, F. Pasquale and S. Das (eds), *The Oxford Handbook of Ethics of AI*. New York: Oxford University Press, pp. 253–270.

Home Office. (2018) *Biometrics Strategy: Better Public Services Maintaining Public Trust*. London: Home Office.

Jasanoff, S. (ed.). (2004) *States of Knowledge: The Co-Production of Science and Social Order*. London: Routledge.

Jasanoff, S. (2015) 'Imagined and invented worlds', in S. Jasanoff and S.-H. Kim (eds), *Dreamscapes of Modernity: Sociotechnical Imaginaries and the Fabrication of Power*. Chicago: Chicago University Press, pp. 321–342.

Jo, E.S. and Gebru, T. (2020) 'Lessons from archives: strategies for collecting sociocultural data in machine learning', in *Conference on Fairness, Accountability, and Transparency (FAT\* '20), January 27–30, 2020, Barcelona, Spain*. New York: ACM, pp. 306–316. doi:10.1145/3351095.3372829.

Kennet, D. (2019) 'Using genetic genealogy databases in missing persons cases and to develop suspect leads in violent crimes', *Forensic Science International* 301: 107–117.

Lawless, C.J. (2020) 'Assembling airspace: the Single European Sky and contested transnationalities of European air traffic management', *Social Studies of Science*, 50 (4): 680–704.

Lawless, C.J. (2021) 'The evolution, devolution and distribution of UK biometric imaginaries', *BioSocieties*. First published 5 May 2021. doi:10.1057/s41292–41021–00231-x.

Lynch, M. (2009) 'Science as a vacation: deficits, surfeits, PUSS, and doing your own job', *Organization*, 16 (1): 101–119.

Markó, F.D. (2016) '"We are not a failed State, we make the best passports": South Sudan and biometric modernity', *African Studies Review*, 59 (2): 113–132.

Miller, S. (2001) 'Public understanding of science at the crossroads', *Public Understanding of Science*, 10: 115–120.

Moon, C. (2016) 'Human rights, human remains: forensic humanitarianism and the human rights of the dead', *International Social Science Journal*, 65 (215–216):49–63.

Office of the Biometrics Commissioner. (2018) *Commissioner for the Retention and Use of Biometric Material: Annual Report 2017*. London: Her Majesty's Stationery Office.

Parliamentary Office of Science & Technology. (2015) *Forensic Language Analysis*. POSTNote No. 509.

Pinch, T.J. and Bijker, W.E. (1984) 'The social construction of facts and artefacts: or how the sociology of science and the sociology of technology might benefit each other', *Social Studies of Science*, 14 (3): 399–441.

Quigley, M. and Ayihongbe, S. (2018) 'Everyday cyborgs: on integrated persons and integrated goods', *Medical Law Review*, 26 (2): 276–308.

Rappert, B., Wheat, H. and Wilson-Kovacs, D. (2021) 'Rationing bytes: managing demand for forensic digital examinations', *Policing and Society*, 31 (1): 52–65.

Schwartz-Marin, E. and Cruz-Santiago, A. (2016a) 'Forensic civism: articulating science, DNA and kinship in contemporary Mexico and Colombia', *Human Remains and Violence*, 2 (1): 58–74.

Schwartz-Marin, E. and Cruz-Santiago, A. (2016b) 'Pure corpses, dangerous citizens: Transgressing the boundaries between experts and mourners in the search for the disappeared in Mexico', *Social Research*, 83 (2): 483–510.

Smallman, M. (2020) '"Nothing to do with the science": how an elite sociotechnical imaginary cements policy resistance to public perspectives on science and technology through the machinery of government', *Social Studies of Science*, 50 (4): 589–608.

Smith, J.M. and Tidwell, A.S.D. (2016) 'The everyday lives of energy transitions: contested sociotechnical imaginaries in the American West', *Social Studies of Science*, 43 (6): 327–350.

Strittmatter, K. (2019) *We Have Been Harmonized*. London: Old Street Publishing.

Wall, D. (2007) *Cybercrime: The Transformation of Crime in the Information Age*. London: Polity.

Wickenheiser, R.A. (2019) 'Forensic genealogy, bioethics and the Golden State Killer case', *Forensic Science International Synergy*, 1: 114–125.

Williams, R. (2008) 'Policing and forensic science', in T. Newburn (ed.), *Handbook of Policing*. Cullompton, UK: Willan, pp. 760–793.

Wilson-Kovacs, D. (2020) 'Effective resource management in digital forensics: An exploratory analysis of triage practices in four English constabularies', *Policing: An International Journal*, 43 (1): 77–90.

Wilson-Kovacs, D., Rappert, B. and Redfern, L. (2021) 'Dirty work? Policing online indecency in digital forensics', *British Journal of Criminology*. First published online 21 June 2021. doi:10.1093/bjc/azab055.

# Index

[NB Page numbers in **bold** refer to tables.]

AAFS *see* American Academy of Forensic Sciences
abandonment principle 101–2
abduction 62–3; *see also* Bayes' theorem
*abuelas see* Grandmothers of the Plaza de Mayo
acceptance of evaluative opinion 88–9
accountability 41–2, 74, 79–80
accreditation 41–4
accuracy of FR 81–2, 116–19
actionable leads 101
active criminal population 95
Ada Lovelace Institute 120–1
Adidas 23
adultery 99
AFR Locate 114–15
agency 75–6
AGR *see* automated gender recognition
AI *see* artificial intelligence
Alexa 135
alleles 68
Alston, Candra 104–5
alternative views 9–12
ambiguity 69–73
American Academy of Forensic Sciences 38–9, 41, 45
anthropometry 34
anti-CSI effect 22–3
anticipatory practices 106
antisocial behaviour 111
argot 132
arson 68–9
articulate collectives 1–2, 133
artificial intelligence 112, 121–2
Assimakopoulos, D. 4
Aston, V. 115–16
attrition models 2
automated gender recognition 117; *see also* facial recognition
autonomy 79, 127
Avery, Steven 26–8

BAFS *see* British Academy of Forensic Sciences
Bal, R. 7

BAME individuals *see* Black, Asian and minority individuals
Bayes' theorem 63–9, 73–5
Bayesian reasoning 63–7, 73–6
Bayesianization 72–3, 75
Bentham, Jeremy 115
behavioural biometrics 147
Berman, Susan 27–8
BFEG *see* Biometrics and Forensics Ethics Group
bias 88–9
Big Brother Watch 111–12, 117–18
'big data' 53
biometric data 9–10, 52–4
biometric policy (UK) 48–61; marketizing forensics 48–52; ongoing inquiries 55–7; oversight 59–60; Scottish Biometrics Commissioner 58–9; scrutiny 48; Transforming Forensics 54–5; widening scrutiny 52–4
Biometrics and Forensics Ethics Group 56, 99–102, 114–19, 128–30, 143, 145
*Biometrics Strategy* (UK) 55–6, 60, 111, 145
Birmingham Six 22, 41
Black, Asian and minority individuals 116–17, 119–21, 147; *see also* facial recognition
black box of evidence 6–7, 140–1
bloodstain patterning 35, 38, 70
bomb attacks 33, 80–1
*Bones* 18
Bridges, Edward 114
*Bridges v South Wales Police* 112–15, 143
British Academy of Forensic Sciences 40, 44
Bruzzi, S. 26–8
Buckskin Girl case 99–100
Budowle, B. 83, 85–6
Buolamwini, J. 116
Buoziz, M. 27

Caddy report 80–3
*Cagney and Lacey* 19
CAI *see* Case Assessment and Interpretation framework
Caldwell, Harry 38

Camps, Francis 40
Canal Killer case 99–100
Capote, Truman 26
Case Assessment and Interpretation framework 5, 64–9, 73–4
CCTV 125
Cellmark 50
challenges for DF 135–6
Chartered Society of Forensic Sciences 9, 36, 38, 40
cherry-picking 128
chilling effect 115–16
Chowdhury, A. 120–1
Christie, Agatha 18
CJA *see* Criminal Justice Act 2003
CJPA *see* Criminal Justice and Police Act 2001
Clark, Sally 22
Clarke, A. 5
cloud computing 119, 134–5
co-embedding imaginaries 144–8
co-producing forensic DNA phenotyping 105–6
codecs 127
codependency 75
cold cases 5, 23
Cole, S.A. 6, 20–1, 25–6, 38
collective identity 34
Collins, H. 32
Collins, Wilkie 17
competency 79
Conan Doyle, Arthur 17–18
conceptualizing innovations 139–51; re-cap 139–41; science–society relations 141–4
contact 69–70
controversy 11
Cooley, C.M. 20
Council for the Registration of Forensic Practitioners 43–4
counter-terrorism 132
courtroom scrutiny 6–8
COVID-19 53
'credible' evidence 6, 79
CRFP *see* Council for the Registration of Forensic Practitioners
crime displacement 111
crime features 22–8
crime scene examiners 3
crime scene to court 1–16; alternative views of FS 9–12; courtroom 6–8; crime scene 2–3; custody 8; laboratory 3–4; plurality of actors and spaces 1–2; policing and science 4–6; Prüm regime 8–9
Criminal Justice Act 2003 95
Criminal Justice and Police Act 2001 95
*Criminal Reconstruction* 34
criminalistics 34
criticisms of TV fiction 19–22
Crofts, Marion 80
cross-examination 37
CSEs *see* crime scene examiners

CSFS *see* Chartered Society of Forensic Sciences
*CSI* 8, 18–20, 22, 24; CSI effect 19–22
*CSI Britain* 23–4
CSI effect 19–22, 24–6, 29; in the news 25–6
*The Cuckoo's Egg* 125
*Current and Future Uses of Biometric Data and Technologies* 53
custody 8
cyber kiosks 129
cyber-attacks 56, 125
cynical perspectives 32–3

Dando, Jill 70
Data Protection Act 2018 102, 112–13
data protection impact assessment 113
*Daubert* requirement 85
Davies, B. 118
DDoS *see* direct denial of service
De Forest, P.R. 42
DeAngelo, Joseph James 100
death penalty 34
debates within *Forensic Science International: Genetics* 85–8
deduction 62–3
'defendant effect' 20
deficit model of public scientific understanding 26, 29, 89–90
defining forensic science 1–16
deleting custody images 57
dematerialization 106
detection 21, 111
deterrence 111
DF *see* digital forensics
DFaaS *see* digital forensics as a service
Dickens, Charles 17
*Digital Forensic Science Strategy* 133
digital forensics 125–37; challenges 135–6; professionalization vs practice 127–30; scientific standards 130–3; as a service 133–5; short history of 125–7
digital forensics as a service 133–6
digital forensics triage 128–9
digital profiles 126
Dioso-Villa, R. 20–1
direct denial of service 126
'disappeared' children 146
*Discipline and Punish* 115
discrimination 105, 117, 120–2
disruption 111
Dixon, Arthur 35–6
DNA phenotyping 102–6, 121; co-producing 105–6
DNA profiling 1–2, 5, 79, 87
DNABoost 23–4, 29
Doak, S. 4
domestic violence 71
Donovan, K. 144
*Double Indemnity* 18
DPIA *see* data protection impact assessment

## Index

Dr Crippen murder trial (1910) 35
*Dragnet* 18
dragnets 103
dramatic uncertainty 18–19
drug testing 55
Durkheim, É. 142
Durst, Robert 27–8
Duster, T. 96

Echo 135
economic exclusion 27
ECtHR *see* European Court of Human Rights
effectiveness 48
empowerment 21
enacting Bayes' theorem 67–9
ENFSI *see* European Network of Forensic Science Institutes
epistemic caution 141–2, 144
epistemological identity of FS 62–4
Erlich, Y. 99
error rates 20
ethical guidance on FR 114, 119–21
ethical issues with DNA technology 5–6, 24, 94–109
ethnicity 104
ethnographic models 2–4
ethnomethodology 75
eugenics 105
Eurofins 56
European Convention on Human Rights 96, 102, 114
European Court of Human Rights 96–8, 116
European Network of Forensic Science Institutes 40, 64
evaluative opinion 88–90
EVCs *see* external visible characteristics
Evett, I. 63
evidence 4, 6–8, 34–5, 65–7, 70–1, 75, 79–84
evidential contamination 3
evolution of FS 9–12
exchange of forensic data 8–9; *see also* Prüm regime
exchange principle 35, 62; *see also* Locard, Edmond
*The Executioner's Song* 26
exhumation 98
expert collaboration 5
expert witnesses 6–7, 41, 63, 79, 83–5, 91
expertise 33, 44–5
external visible characteristics 102–5

facial recognition 10–11, 52, 111–24, 140; accuracy of 121–2; *Bridges v South Wales Police* 114–15; fit for purpose 116–19; proportionality and chilling effect 115–16; public–private collaborations 119–21; rationale and use 111–14
Falconio, Peter 80
false positives 116, 118

familial searching 98–106; co-producing forensic DNA phenotyping 105–6; forensic DNA profiling 102–5; forensic genealogy 99–102
Familytree 100
FBI *see* Federal Bureau of Investigation
FDP *see* forensic DNA phenotyping
Federal Bureau of Investigation 100–1
fingerprinting 3, 6–7, 34–5, 37–8, 45, 52, 54–5, 96, 147
firearm discharge 70
food adulteration 33
Ford 23
Forensic Alliance 49
forensic DNA phenotyping 102–6
forensic DNA technology 94–109; familial searching 98–106; National DNA Database 94–6; probative force 106–7; *S & Marper* 96–8
'forensic dustmen' 3
forensic fiction 17–22; CSI effect 19–22; police procedurals 18–19
forensic genealogy 99–102
Forensic Institute 42
forensic medicine 33–4, 40
forensic policy *see* biometric policy (UK)
forensic practitioners 43–5, 50
forensic reasoning 62–4
*Forensic Science International: Genetics* 40, 85–8
forensic science providers 49, 54, 57
Forensic Science Regulation Act 2021 57, 59–60, 146
Forensic Science Regulators 49–50
Forensic Science Regulator's Code of Conduct 114
Forensic Science Service 12, 23–4, 33, 36–45, 49–50, 63–4, 79–80, 86; *see also* Chartered Society of Forensic Sciences
*Forensic Science Strategy* 53–4
forensic scientific reasoning 62
forensic scientific societies 38–41
forensic/biometric technology development 139–51
*Forensics: The Real CSI* 28
forensics as reconstruction 62–78
Foucault, Michel 115
FR *see* facial recognition
fraud 125
Freedom of Information Act 2000 112
*Fry* standard of evidential assessment 84–5
*FSI:G see Forensic Science International: Genetics*
FSPs *see* forensic science providers
FSRs *see* Forensic Science Regulators
FSS *see* Forensic Science Service
function creep 101
functionalism 44
further legal developments 88–9
Fussey, P. 118

Game, Philip 35
gatekeeping role 85

Gebru, T. 116
GEDMatch 100–1
genetic informant 98–9
genetic suspects 5
Georg, Barry 70
Ghoshray, S. 21
glamour 25
'Golden Age of Detective Fiction' 18
Golden State Killer case 100–2
Govco status 49
Grandmothers of the Plaza de Mayo 146
Granja, R. 106
Greytak, E.M. 100
Gross, Hans 32, 34–5
Guerrini, C.J. 100
guessing 63; *see also* abduction

Hackett, Paul 23
Haimes, E. 98
Halbach, Teresa 26
Hamidi, F. 117
handwriting analysis 35
Hansken 134
harmonized European approach 9; *see also* Prüm regime
heightened expectations 21
Herschel, William 34
Hoare, Samuel 36
Hoe, Peter 82
Hoey, Sean Gerard 80–1
holism 42, 60
Holmes, Sherlock 17–18, 29, 32, 34–5
Home Office 35–7, 40–1, 44, 48–50, 53, 55–6, 60, 113, 119, 145
homicide 101
Hopman, R. 105–6
HSBC 23
Huey, L. 21–2
human rights 112
Human Rights Act 1998 102, 112
Hurd, Nick 112
hypotheticodeductive method 62

IAI *see* International Association for Identification
ICO *see* Information Commissioner's Office
identifying human remains 96
imaginative politics 145
imagining technologies 139–51
*In Cold Blood* 26
incest 99
incrimination 115–16
indecent images of children 129
indexicality 75
induction 62–3
Information Commissioner's Office 113
Innes, M. 5
inter-propositional ambiguity 69–70, 72
International Academy of Criminalistics 35
International Association for Identification 38

International Society for Forensic Genetics 40
Internet of Things 127, 135
intimidation 104
intra-propositional ambiguity 69–70
IoT *see* Internet of Things
ISFG *see* International Society for Forensic Genetics
Ito, Judge Lance 6

Jamieson, Allan 42–3, 45, 62, 83–4
Jarecki, Andrew 28
Jasanoff, S. 10–11, 142
Jasinskyj, Tony 80
Jeffreys, Alec 80
*The Jinx* 27–8
Jo, E.S. 116
*Journal of Forensic Identification* 38
*Journal of Forensic Sciences* 39
Julie Valentine case 101
jurisprudential interventions 80–8
jury service 17

Kane, Dan 81
Kappen, Joseph 98
Kappen, Paul 98
Kayser, M. 103
Key Forensic Services 55
KGB 125
Kind, Stuart 36–41, 44
kinship 98
Kirby, D. 18–19
Kirk, P. 62
Kitzberger, M. 8, 21
Kosinski, M. 117
Krane, D. 19
Kruse, C. 4, 74

laboratory studies 3–4
Lacassagne, Alexandre 34–5
Lausanne School of Forensic Science 35
law enforcement 56, 100–1, 111–13
law–science interactions 79–93; accountability 79–80; deficit/surfeit models 89–91; further legal developments 88–9; LT-DNA 80–8
LCN *see* low copy number DNA analysis
Ley, B.L. 19–20
LGBTQ individuals 116–17
LGC 49–52
Liberty 114, 119
life sentences 80
likelihood approach 63–4, 66, 68–9, 71–2, 87
Lindh, Anna 80
Lipphardt, V. 103
Live FR 119
Locard, Edmond 32, 34–5, 62
London Policing Ethics Panel 119–20
looping *see* media looping
Losavio, M. 127–8
low copy number DNA analysis 80, 87

## Index

low-template DNA 80–90, 140; *Forensic Science International: Genetics* 85–8; *R v Hoey* 80–2; *R v Reed and Reed* 82–5
LT-DNA *see* low-template DNA
Ludwig, A. 3
Lynch, M. 6–8, 26

McCann, Madeline 22
McFarland Review 49
Machado, H. 22
machine learning 132
McNally, R. 7
Maguire Seven 41
mailer, Norman 26
*Making a Murderer* 26–8
managing ambiguity 69–73
Manlove Forensics 52
marketizing forensics 48–52, 59–60
Markó, F.D. 144
Marsh, Ngaio 18
May, John 41
M'charek, A. 3–4, 105–6
media depictions 17–31; forensic fiction 17–22; media looping 29; news media 22–8
media looping 25, 29
Medialink 23–4
medical jurisprudence 33–4
*Medicine, Science and the Law* 40
memory 5
Metropolitan Police Act 1829 33
Metropolitan Police Laboratory 35–6
Metropolitan Police Service 33, 35, 104, 111, 117–19, 125
Miller, Bryan Patrick 99
miscarriages of justice 22–3, 41
misidentification 118
missing persons 100
monitoring public spaces 111, 115, 117; *see also* facial recognition
Mopas, M. 24
Moran, Layla 121
MPL *see* Metropolitan Police Laboratory
MPS *see* Metropolitan Police Service
'mugshots' 111
murder 80–5, 98, 100–4, 125
'Murders in the Rue Morgue' 17
Murdoch, Bradley 80
Murray, D. 118

National Crime Agency 126
National DNA Database 5, 11–12, 24, 94–6
National Forensic Framework Agreement 50–1
National Police Chief's Council 133
NCA *see* National Crime Agency
NDNAD *see* National DNA Database
neo-Weberian perspectives 32–3, 44–5
Netfox 134
networking forensic data 133–5
new public management 59–60

new technology 79–93
news media 22–8; CFI effect in the news 25–6; DNABoost 23–4; true crime documentaries 26–8
NFFA *see* National Forensic Framework Agreement
noir genre 18
Nokia 23
non-DNA sampling 98
non-DNA testimony 88
nonqualifying offences 96
normative interpretations 141–4
NPCC *see* National Police Chief's Council
nuisance behaviour 119

offending database 97
O.J. Simpson trial 6
ongoing inquiries 55–7
'Ontogeny of Criminalistics' 62
Operation Minstead 104
ostracism 98–9
over-victimization 19
oversight 59–60

PACE *see* Police and Criminal Evidence Act 1983
panopticons 115
Parabon Nanolabs 100–1, 104
parent–child relationships 98
parliamentary inquiries 11
Parry, J. 32
Parry, N. 32
PCRs *see* polymerase chain reaction machines
Peel, Robert 33
Peirce, Charles Sanders 62–3
*People v Megnath* 84–5, 90
Pereira, Barbara 36
performativity 28, 62–78
Peritus 134
Peterson, Michael 27
philosophical pragmatism 62
plurality of FS actors 1–2
PND *see* Police National Database
Poe, Edgar Allen 17
PoFA *see* Protection of Freedom Act 2012
Police and Criminal Evidence Act 1983 94
police databases 2, 5
police harassment 96
Police National Database 111–12
police powers to retain DNA 5–6, 26, 94–5, **94, 97**
police procedurals 18–19
Police Scotland 37, 112, 129
policing and science 4–6
polymerase chain reaction machines 8
posterior probability 66
postmortems 33
*The Postman Always Rings Twice* 18
practice of DF 127–30
Prainsack, B. 8, 21

pre-emptive action 20
primary transfer 82
*Prime Suspect* 19
prior probability 66
prisoner perceptions 8, 21
privacy rights 115, 121–2
probability 62–78, 82; posterior 66; prior 66
probative force 106–7
procedural integration 5
procurement 50, 54
'producer effect' 20
professionalism 32–47
professionalization of DF 127–30
'professor version' 21
proportionality 115–16, 147–8
Protection of Freedom Act 2012 96–7, **97**, 112
Prüm regime 2, 8–10
public safety vs individual privacy 115–16, 130
public understanding of science 25–6
public–private collaborations 119–21
PUS *see* public understanding of science
putative familial matches 98

qualitative sociological research 3
'quotidian tools' 7–8, 75

*R v Adams* 7
*R v Dlugosz* 88–9
*R v Hoey* 80–4
*R v MDS* 88–9
*R v Pickering* 88–9
*R v Reed and Reed* 82–5, 90
*R v T* 63, 88, 90
*R v Weller* 88
racism 116
Rae-Venter, Barbara 100
random match probability 82
Randox 55
ransomware 126, 135
rape 80, 98, 100, 102–3, 125
Rappert, B. 128, 147
rationale for facial recognition 111–14
re-imagining technologies 139–51
reality of science 24, 26
reasonable doubt doctrine 21
recidivism 34
reconstructive science 62–78; Bayesian reasoning 65–7; enacting Bayes' theorem 67–9; epistemological identity of forensic reasoning 62–4; establishing FS identity 73–6; managing ambiguity 69–73
reflexivity 8, 75
Regulation of Investigatory Powers Act 2012 112
regulatory interventions 80–8
Reiss, Rudolphe 34
Rekognition (Amazon) 119
reliability of FR 116–19
retrospective facial recognition 111
role confusion 25

Royal Commission on Criminal Justice 41, 49
Runciman Commission 14

*S & Marper* 96–8
saliva 2
Santos, F. 22
Sayers, Dorothy 18
SCC *see* Surveillance Camera Commissioner
scene of the crime 2–3
Schneider, P.M. 103
*Science & Justice* 40, 42–3
'science to the rescue' 145
science vs medicine in law 33–8
science–society relations 10, 141–4
scientific method 62
scientific standards 130–3
Scientifics Ltd 49
Scottish Biometrics Commissioner 58–60, 146
Scottish Biometrics Commissioner Act 2020 58
scrutiny 6–8, 41, 48, 52–4, 98–9; biometric 48; courtroom 6–8; widening 52–4
Scudder, N. 101
Second World War 35, 37
secondary transfer 82
Seigfried-Spellar, K.C. 129
self-defence 28
self-denying prophecy 21
sensationalism 18
*Serial* 27
sexual offences 23, 26, 101
sexual orientation 117
shaping FS as discipline 32–47; 'expertise' 44; forensic scientific societies 38–41; science vs medicine 33–8; standardization/accreditation 41–4
short history of DF 125–7
silent witnessing 1–2
simulation 7
single-nucleotide polymorphisms 99
Sioux Falls Baby case 101
skewed rhetoric 6
skin pigmentation 106
Skinner, D. 104
Sloane, M. 121–2
Smallman, M. 145
Snapshot 104–5
SNPs *see* single-nucleotide polymorphisms
social commentary 27
social control 5
social exclusion 27
social issues with DNA technology 94–109
social progress 32
social realism 142, 144
*Social Studies of Science* 6
soft data 68, 74
SOPs *see* standard operating procedures
South Wales Police 114–15; *see also Bridges v South Wales Police*
spatial anonymity 102

Spilsbury, Bernard 35
*The Staircase* 27–8
stakeholders 2, 144–8
standard operating procedures 4, 41–2
standardization 41–4
statistical ambiguity 69–72
stereotyping 19
stigma 95, 105
stochastic interpretation effect 87
Stoll, C. 125
stop and search 120–1
Stratton brothers trial (1905) 34
striking a balance 2, 65
strong accusation rhetoric 22
'strong prosecution effect' 20
structural integration 4–5
substance abuse 71
surfeit model of public scientific understanding 25–6
Surveillance Camera Code 113
Surveillance Camera Commissioner 52, 113–14, 117
surveillance society 22
suspect population 104, 146
suspect watchlist 111, 118–20

tampering with evidence 81
technical assistance 4
television crime portrayals 8; *see also* media depictions
terrorism 33, 96
Tomlinson, Valerie 82–4
Toom, V. 9
Touch Ross 48
Tox 1335
trace forensics 130–2
transfer evidence 66
Transforming Forensics 54–5

transparency of reasoning 63, 106
true crime documentaries 26–8
*Truth Machine* 7
truth-making 27
Twain, Mark 17
23AndMe 100

UK Biometrics Commissioner 52–3, 57, 96–7, 113–14, 117
UKBC *see* UK Biometrics Commissioner
US Constitution 101–2
use of biometric data 9–10, 52–4

Vaatstra, Marianne 102–3
value of evidence 4
van Beek, H.M.A. 134
vandalism 19
variability 85
verisimilitude 105
Verogen 101
vigour 11
vulnerability 9, 79

*Waking the Dead* 18
Walton, D. 63
'war-gaming' of technology 147
Ward, J. 33–4
weak association rhetoric 22
'weak prosecution effect' 20
wet forensics 130–2
whodunits 18
widening scrutiny 52–4
Wienroth, M. 106
Williams, R. 2–4
Wilson-Kovacs, D. 128, 147
*The Wire* 19

YouGov 120